AAT

TECHNICIAN

NVQ AND LEVEL 4 DIPLOMA FOR ACCOUNTING TECHNICIANS (QCF)

COURSE **COMPANION** Unit 11

Drafting Financial Statements (Accounting Practice, Industry and Commerce)

For exams from June 2010

Revised and reprinted

BPP LEARNING MEDIA

Ninth edition February 2010
First edition 2002

ISBN 9780 7517 8514 2 (previous ISBN 9780 7517 6705 6)

British Library Cataloguing-in-Publication Data
A catalogue record for this book is available from the British Library

Published by

BPP Learning Media Ltd
BPP House,
Aldine Place,
London, W12 8AA

www.bpp.com/learningmedia

Printed in the United Kingdom

Your learning materials, published by BPP Learning Media Ltd, are printed on paper sourced from sustainable, managed forests.

CONTENTS

INTRODUCTION

BPP Learning Media's highly popular Companions range of AAT materials is ideal for students who like to get to grips with the essentials and study on the move.

The range comprises:

- **Course Companions**, covering all the knowledge and understanding and performance criteria specified by the Standards of Competence and needed by students, with numerous illustrations, practical examples and activities for students to use to consolidate their learning.

- **Revision Companions**, ideal for classroom courses, which contain an additional range of graded activities for each chapter of the Course Companion, plus specially written practice assessments and answers for the Unit, and a selection of AAT assessments set up to December 2008. Full answers to all activities and assessments, prepared by BPP Learning Media Ltd, are included.

- **Tutor Companions**, providing a further bank of questions, answers and practice assessments for classroom use, available separately only to lecturers whose colleges adopt the Companions for the relevant Unit.

This Course Companion for Technician Unit 11, Drafting Financial Statements (Accounting Practice, Industry and Commerce) has been written specifically to ensure comprehensive yet concise coverage of the Standards of Competence and performance criteria. It is fully up to date as at January 2010 and reflects both the Standards of Competence and the assessments set to date.

Each chapter contains:

- clear, step by step explanation of the topic
- logical progression and linking from one chapter to the next
- numerous illustrations and practical examples
- interactive activities within the text of the chapter itself, with answers at the back of the book
- a bank of questions of varying complexity, again with answers supplied at the back of the book

The emphasis in all activities and questions is on the practical application of the skills acquired.

If you have any comments about this book, please e-mail helendarch@bpp.com or write to Helen Darch, AAT Range manager, BPP Learning Media Ltd, BPP House, Aldine Place, London W12 8AA.

Diploma Pathway

This Course Companion is the ideal learning aid for Unit 11, directly relevant to both the NVQ and the AAT Diploma Pathway.

UNIT 11 STANDARDS OF COMPETENCE

Each Unit commences with a statement of the **knowledge and understanding** which underpin competence in the Unit's elements.

The Unit of Competence is then divided into **elements of competence** describing activities which the student should be able to perform.

Each element includes:

a) A set of **performance criteria** which define what constitutes competent performance.

b) A **range statement** which defines the situations, contexts, methods etc in which competence should be displayed.

The elements of competence for Unit 11 *Drafting Financial Statements* are set out below. Knowledge and understanding required for the unit as a whole are listed first, followed by the performance criteria and range statements for each element. Performance criteria are cross-referenced below to chapters in this Unit 11 Course Companion.

Unit 11: Drafting financial statements (accounting practice, industry and commerce)

Unit commentary

This unit is about drafting and interpreting financial statements of limited companies. The first element in this unit is about drafting limited company year-end financial statements from a trial balance. You are responsible for ensuring that the financial statements comply with any relevant domestic legislation and *either* the relevant UK standards (Statements of Standard Accounting Practice, Financial Reporting Standards and other relevant pronouncements) *or* the International Accounting Standards. You also need to show that you ensure that confidentiality procedures are followed. The second element requires you to interpret the financial statements of companies and the relationships between the elements using ratio analysis.

Elements contained within this unit are:

Element 11.1	Draft limited company financial statements
Element 11.2	Interpret limited company financial statements

Knowledge and understanding

To perform this unit effectively you will need to know and understand:

The business environment	**Chapter**
■ The elements and purposes of financial statements of limited companies as set out in the conceptual framework for financial reporting (Element 11.2)	1
■ The general legal framework of limited companies and the obligations of Directors in respect of the financial statements (Element 11.1)	2,3
■ The statutory form of accounting statements and disclosure requirements (Element 11.1)	3
■ The UK regulatory framework for financial reporting and the main requirements of relevant financial reporting standards or the relevant requirements of international accounting standards (Element 11.1)	1, 2, 4-8, 10-11
■ The forms of equity and loan capital (Element 11.1)	2
■ The presentation of Corporation Tax in financial statements (Element 11.1)	7
Accounting techniques	
■ Preparing financial statements in proper form (Element 11.1)	2-5, 10, 11
■ Analysing and interpreting the information contained in financial statements (Element 11.2)	9
■ Computing and interpreting accounting ratios (Element 11.2)	9

Accounting principles and theory	**Chapter**
■ Generally accepted accounting principles and concepts (Element 11.1)	1
■ The general principles of consolidation (Element 11.1)	10, 11
The organisation	
■ How the accounting systems of an organisation are affected by its roles, organisational structure, its administrative systems and procedures and the nature of its business transactions (Elements 11.1 and 11.2)	Throughout

Element 11.1: Draft limited company financial statements

Performance criteria

In order to perform this element successfully you need to:

A	Draft limited company financial statements from the appropriate information	2-8, 10-11
B	Correctly identify and implement subsequent adjustments and ensure that discrepancies, unusual features and queries are identified and either resolved or referred to the appropriate person	Throughout
C	Ensure that limited company financial statements comply with relevant accounting standards and domestic legislation and with the organisation's policies, regulations and procedures	2-5, 6-8, 10-11
D	Prepare and interpret a limited company cash flow statement	5
E	Ensure that confidentiality procedures are followed at all times	Throughout

Range statement

Performance in this element relates to the following contexts:

Limited company financial statements:

- Income statement
- Balance sheet (statement of financial position)
- Cash flow statement (not consolidated) (statement of cash flows)
- Statement of total recognised gains and losses (statement of comprehensive income)
- The supplementary notes required by statute
- Unitary
- Consolidated

Domestic legislation:

- Companies Act

Relevant accounting standards:

- International Accounting Standards or International Financial Reporting Standards

Element 11.2: Interpret limited company financial statements

Performance criteria		**Chapter**
In order to perform this element successfully you need to:		
A	Identify the general purpose of financial statements used in limited companies	9
B	Identify the elements of financial statements used in limited companies	1, 9
C	Identify the relationships between the elements within financial statements of limited companies	1, 9
D	Interpret the relationship between elements of limited company financial statements using ratio analysis	9
E	Identify unusual features or significant issues within financial statements of limited companies	9
F	Draw valid conclusions from the information contained within financial statements of limited companies	9
G	Present issues, interpretations and conclusions clearly to the appropriate people	9

Range statement

Performance in this element relates to the following contexts:

Financial statements:

- Balance sheet (statement of financial position)
- Income statement

Elements:

- Assets
- Liabilities
- Ownership interest
- Gains
- Losses
- Contributions from owners
- Distributions to owners

Relationship between elements:

- Profitability
- Liquidity
- Efficient use of resources
- Financial position

chapter 1: INTRODUCTION TO FINANCIAL STATEMENTS

chapter coverage 📖

In this chapter we will put the drafting of limited company financial statements in context by considering why we prepare financial statements, who uses them, and what makes them useful. We also look at several important ideas that underpin the preparation of financial statements. Some of this material should already be familiar to you from your earlier studies for Unit 5 of the AAT Intermediate Stage. The topics that we shall cover are:

- the objective of financial statements
- users of financial statements and their needs
- the different types of organisation
- the qualities that make financial information useful
- the regulatory framework
- accounting standards and the standard-setting process
- accounting concepts
- the elements of financial statements

KNOWLEDGE AND UNDERSTANDING AND PERFORMANCE CRITERIA COVERAGE

knowledge and understanding

- the elements and purposes of financial statements of limited companies as set out in the conceptual framework for financial reporting
- the UK regulatory framework for financial reporting
- generally accepted accounting principles and concepts

Performance criteria – element 11.2

- identify the elements of financial statements used in limited companies
- identify the relationships between the elements of limited company financial statements

THE OBJECTIVE OF FINANCIAL STATEMENTS

student notes

The objective of financial statements is to provide useful information about an organisation's financial position, financial performance and changes in financial position to a wide range of users. Users need information for two reasons:

- To make economic decisions. For example, information in the financial statements may help a user to decide whether or not to invest in a company.
- To assess the stewardship of the organisation's management. This is relevant where an organisation is managed by people other than its owners. For example, the shareholders of a company may appoint directors and managers to run the company on their behalf. Management is accountable to the owners of the organisation. It must safeguard the organisation's resources and use them properly in order to generate profits or other benefits.

USERS OF FINANCIAL STATEMENTS

Several different groups of people may be interested in the information provided by financial statements.

- **Investors and potential investors** need information that helps them to assess the performance (stewardship) of management and information that helps them to make decisions about their investment (eg, whether to buy or sell shares).
- **Employees** need information that helps them to assess their employer's ability to provide wages, salaries and other benefits and employment opportunities. Therefore they need information about their employer's stability and profitability (particularly in relation to the part of the organisation in which they work).
- **Lenders** are interested in information that helps them to assess whether their loans will be repaid and interest will be paid. They are also interested in information that helps them to decide whether to lend to an organisation and on what terms.
- **Suppliers and other trade creditors** need information that helps them to decide whether to sell to the entity and to assess the likelihood that amounts owing to them will be paid when due.
- **Customers** need information about the organisation's continued existence, particularly if they are dependent on the organisation's products (for example, because they may need specialised replacement parts).

student notes

- **Governments and their agencies** need information that helps them to allocate resources, assess taxation and regulate the activities of businesses and other organisations.

- **The public** is interested in information that is useful in assessing the trends and recent developments in an organisation's prosperity and the range of its activities. This is because businesses and other organisations all affect the community in some way, for example, by providing employment or by using local suppliers.

In addition, the **management** of an organisation need financial information about its past performance and current position in order to manage its activities and to develop strategies for the future. Managers generally require far more detailed information than the other groups of users, but at least in theory they are able to obtain whatever they need in whatever form they need it. The other groups of users are normally dependent on the information that an organisation provides to the outside world in the form of its financial statements.

It follows that the form and content of financial statements should generate information that meets the needs of their users. In practice some users are viewed as more important than others. In the UK and in many other countries, investors and potential investors are held to be the most important users of financial statements. The regulations that set out the form and content of the financial statements and generally accepted accounting practice have developed in order to protect their interests. Some of the implications of this will be discussed in later chapters.

Activity 1

Which groups of users would be most likely to be interested in the accounts of a small, family-owned company?

THE DIFFERENT TYPES OF ORGANISATION

There are several broad types of organisation. These can be classified into **profit-making** organisations and **not-for-profit** organisations. You will already have met some of these in your studies for Unit 5, *Maintaining financial records and preparing accounts*.

Profit making organisations

student notes

These consist of:

- **Sole traders:** businesses owned and managed by one person.
- **Partnerships:** businesses owned and managed by two or more people together, sharing profits and losses.
- **Companies:** businesses that are a **separate legal entity** from their owners. Unlike a sole trader or a partnership, a company can enter into contracts, purchase assets and incur liabilities in its own name. Companies are owned by their **shareholders**, who each contribute capital in the form of **shares**.

  Most companies are **limited companies**. This means that if the company ceases trading or is unable to pay its debts, the shareholders only lose the capital that they have invested. Unlike sole traders and partners, shareholders are not personally liable for a limited company's unpaid debts and cannot be required to meet its liabilities from their private resources.

In the next chapter, we will look more closely at the nature of limited companies and the reasons why they are different from sole traders and partnerships.

Not-for-profit organisations

These consist of:

- **Charities, clubs and societies:** owned by their members or trustees and created for a specific non-commercial purpose (eg, to give grants to the homeless, to enable members to enjoy a particular sport).
- **Public sector organisations:** these are owned by the general public and include central government; local government; the National Health Service; and public corporations.

Financial statements are always prepared for a business or other organisation as a **separate entity** from its owners. This applies regardless of whether the organisation is legally separate from its owners or not. Accounting regulations often use the term **entity** to refer to an organisation that prepares financial statements as a separate entity from its owners. An entity may be a sole trader, a partnership, a limited company, or a not-for-profit organisation.

For Unit 11, it is useful to have a broad awareness of the different types of entity. However, this Unit deals specifically with one important type of business organisation: the limited company.

student notes

WHAT MAKES FINANCIAL INFORMATION USEFUL?

If information in the financial statements is to be useful, it must possess certain qualities. It must be:

- understandable
- relevant
- reliable
- comparable with other information

Information that is **material** needs to be given in the financial statements. Giving information that is not material may impair the usefulness of the other information given.

Information is material if its misstatement or omission could influence the economic decisions of users taken on the basis of the financial statements.

Relevance

Information is relevant if it has the ability to influence the economic decisions of users.

Relevant information helps users to:

- evaluate the past, present or future performance of an entity and to draw conclusions, or
- helps users to confirm their past conclusions.

Reliability

Information is reliable if:

- it can be depended on to represent faithfully what it purports to represent or could reasonably be expected to represent;
- it is free from deliberate or systematic bias or material error;
- it is complete; and
- if it has been prepared under conditions of uncertainty, a degree of caution (prudence) has been applied when exercising judgement.

In practice, this means that:

- the financial statements should reflect the substance of transactions and other events, rather than their legal form, where these are different (faithful representation);

student notes

- items are not included in the financial statements if it is difficult or impossible to measure them accurately; instead they may be disclosed;
- information is not selected or presented in such a way as to deliberately influence the users to make a particular decision or to achieve a particular result (neutrality or freedom from bias);
- assets and income are not overstated and liabilities and expenses are not understated (prudence).

Substance over form and prudence are important concepts which are discussed in more detail later in this chapter.

Comparability

Users need to be able to identify and evaluate similarities and differences between the nature and effects of transactions and other events:

- over time
- between different entities.

This means that:

- similar items must be treated in the same way;
- items must normally be treated in the same way from one accounting period to the next;
- entities must disclose the accounting policies adopted in the financial statements.

Understandability

Information is understandable if its users can appreciate its significance. Users are assumed to have a reasonable knowledge of business and economic activities and accounting and a willingness to study the information with reasonable diligence.

However, information should not be excluded from the financial statements simply because some users might not understand it.

Conflicts between the different characteristics

Occasionally there are conflicts between the characteristics. For example:

- An entity can include a non-current (fixed) asset in the accounts either at its historic cost or at its market value. Market value is likely to be more relevant to users of the financial statements, but this is

student notes

subjective and less reliable than historic cost, which is a matter of fact.

- At the year end, a company makes a general provision or allowance for doubtful debts. This means that the trade receivables (debtors) figure in the financial statements is an estimate. It would be possible to delay publishing the financial statements until it was known for certain which amounts would be recovered. The financial statements would be more reliable, but less relevant, because the information would be out-of-date.

In these circumstances there must be a compromise that maximises the usefulness of the information in the financial statements.

Activity 2

Could there be a conflict between any other useful characteristics of information?

A 'true and fair view'

The accounts of limited companies are required by law to show 'a true and fair view' of their profit or loss (financial performance) during the accounting period and their state of affairs (financial position) at the period end. Sometimes this is known as a 'fair presentation' or 'presenting fairly' the information.

Financial information cannot be useful to users unless it represents a true and fair view. But what does 'true and fair' mean?

There is no definition of 'true and fair', but the following points are relevant:

- 'True and fair' is a legal concept and in extreme cases, its meaning may be decided by the courts.
- Financial statements prepared in accordance with all applicable regulations will normally give a true and fair view/fair presentation.
- 'True and fair' is a dynamic concept. Its meaning evolves over time and in accordance with changes in the business environment and in generally accepted accounting practice.

THE REGULATORY FRAMEWORK

student notes

Most entities, particularly limited companies, are required to observe various rules and regulations when preparing financial statements. These regulations cover the accounting treatment of items and the way in which information is presented. They ensure that financial statements actually do provide useful information.

If preparers of financial statements were able to adopt whatever accounting practices they chose it would be impossible to compare the financial statements of different entities and financial statements of the same entity over time. Information might be deliberately presented in such a way as to mislead users.

The most important sources of regulation for limited companies are:

- Companies legislation
- Accounting standards

These will be covered in detail in later chapters.

ACCOUNTING STANDARDS

What are accounting standards?

Accounting standards are authoritative statements of how particular types of transactions and other events should be reflected in financial statements. Compliance with accounting standards is normally necessary in order to produce financial statements which give a true and fair view or a fair presentation. In very exceptional circumstances, it may be necessary to depart from the requirements of an accounting standard in order to give a true and fair view or a fair presentation.

Although accounting standards state how particular items should be dealt with, many recent accounting standards are based on principles, rather than detailed rules. Preparers of financial statements should be guided by the spirit and reasoning behind accounting standards and not simply regard them as a set of rules to circumvent.

Sole traders and partnerships often adopt accounting standards, even though they may not be legally obliged to do so. Because accounting standards apply to all financial statements that are intended to give a true and fair view, or a fair presentation, limited companies must normally comply with all relevant accounting standards.

student notes

Two sets of accounting standards operate in the UK:

- UK accounting standards issued by the UK Accounting Standards Board (ASB). These are known as Financial Reporting Standards (FRSs) or Statements of Standard Accounting Practice (SSAPs).

- International accounting standards (IASs) or International Financial Reporting Standards (IFRSs) issued by the International Accounting Standards Board (IASB).

International Accounting Standards

Businesses increasingly operate across national boundaries and users need to be able to make comparisons between the financial statements of entities located in different countries. It follows that there is a need for a 'common language' of accounting practice, so that all companies throughout the world follow the same accounting regulations.

Although the IASB has no power to enforce its standards, most major industrialised nations, including the UK, ensure that their domestic standards reflect the requirements of international standards as far as possible.

Since January 2005, all listed companies operating within the European Union (EU) have been required to use international accounting standards. For the time being, other companies in the UK can choose whether to change to international standards or to continue to apply UK accounting standards.

You will be required to use international standards in the Exam-based Assessment.

The IASB's objectives

The objectives of the IASB are to:

- develop, in the public interest, a single set of high quality, understandable and enforceable global accounting standards that require high quality, transparent and comparable information in financial statements and other financial reporting to help participants in the world's capital markets and other users to make economic decisions;

- promote the use and rigorous application of those standards;

- work actively with national standard setters to bring about convergence of national accounting standards and International Accounting Standards.

The standard setting structure

student notes

International accounting standards are of two types:

- International Financial Reporting Standards (IFRSs): issued by the International Accounting Standards Board (IASB) since 2001.
- International Accounting Standards (IASs): issued before 2001 by the IASB's predecessor, the International Accounting Standards Committee (IASC).

When the IASB succeeded the IASC it adopted all the extant IASs so that they remained in force. The IASB has since improved many of them.

The IASB is part of a standard setting structure which consists of several bodies and is shown below:

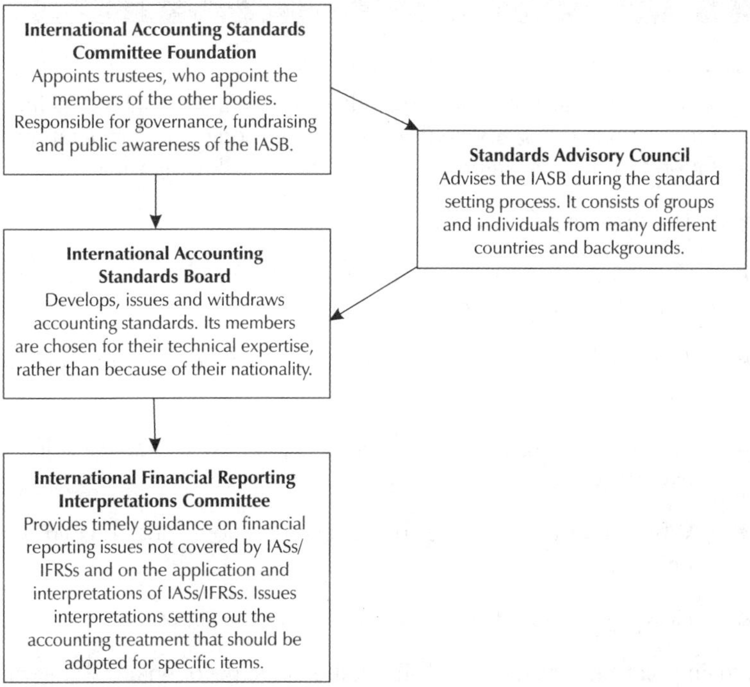

The standard setting process

International Financial Reporting Standards normally pass through several stages as they are developed:

- A topic is identified; then
- The IASB may set up an Advisory Committee to give advice on issues arising in the project. Throughout the project the IASB consults with the Advisory Committee and the Standards Advisory Council; then

student notes

- A Discussion Paper may be issued. This is circulated to interested parties, who comment on the issues discussed and any proposals made; then
- An Exposure Draft (ED) is published. An Exposure Draft is a draft version of the proposed standard. This is circulated to accountancy bodies, governments, regulatory bodies and other interested parties. All interested parties have an opportunity to comment. The IASB then examines the comments and suggestions received and may revise the proposals; then
- The International Financial Reporting Standard (IFRS) is issued.

The Framework for the Preparation and Presentation of Financial Statements

The *Framework for the Preparation and Presentation of Financial Statements* is the IASB's conceptual framework. In other words, it sets out the principles and concepts that the IASB believes should underlie the preparation and presentation of financial statements. It covers the following topics:

- The objective of financial statements
- Key assumptions made when preparing financial statements (underlying assumptions)
- The qualities that make financial information useful (qualitative characteristics)
- The elements of financial statements (e.g. assets, liabilities, income, expenses)
- When transactions and other events should be recognised in financial statements
- How items should be measured in financial statements

The main points in the *Framework* about the objective of financial statements and the qualities that make financial information useful were covered earlier in this chapter. We will be covering the main points of the remaining parts of the *Framework* later.

The *Framework* is not an accounting standard and entities are not required to comply with it. It has been developed by the IASB in order to:

- assist it in its development of future international accounting standards and in its review of existing standards;
- assist preparers of financial statements in applying international accounting standards and in dealing with topics that do not form the subject of an accounting standard; and

- assist users of financial statements in interpreting the information contained in financial statements prepared in conformity with international accounting standards.

Many of the IASB's standards have been strongly influenced by the ideas set out in the *Framework*.

student notes

ACCOUNTING CONCEPTS

The IASB believes that two accounting concepts are fundamental to the preparation of accounts. These concepts are so generally accepted that users can assume that they have been followed unless the accounts state otherwise. In the *Framework* they are known as the underlying assumptions:

- accruals or matching; and
- going concern.

Accruals

Revenue and costs are recognised in the financial statements for the accounting period in which they are earned or incurred, rather than in the period in which the cash is received or paid.

Financial statements prepared on this basis are useful because they inform users of both past transactions involving the payment and receipt of cash and of future transactions. Future transactions are shown as liabilities to pay cash and assets representing cash to be received in future.

Activity 3

Give two examples of the use of the accruals concept in accounts.

Going concern

It is assumed that the entity will continue to operate for the foreseeable future and this assumption is reflected in the way that the income statement (profit and loss account) and balance sheet are drawn up.

This is important because it affects the information that users need about the entity's assets and liabilities:

- If the entity is a going concern, users will be more interested in its ability to use its assets to generate cash and profits than in the amount that the assets would be worth on the open market. Therefore non-current (fixed) assets are stated at cost (or current value) less depreciation.

student notes

- If the entity is not a going concern, the information that is relevant to users is the amount that can be realised from selling off its assets. Therefore non-current assets are stated at the amount that they are worth if they are sold separately on the open market immediately ('break-up values').

Traditionally, two further accounting concepts have been held to be extremely important:

- Consistency; and
- Prudence.

The *Framework* does not discuss these. The IASB does not regard consistency and prudence as concepts, but as qualities that make financial information useful. Consistency is an aspect of comparability and prudence is an aspect of reliability.

Consistency

Similar items are treated in the same way within each accounting period. Items are treated in the same way from one period to the next.

For example:

- The same method of depreciation is used for all non-current (fixed) assets of a similar type

- The same method of depreciation is used from one period to the next

Prudence

When exercising judgement under conditions of uncertainty, a cautious approach should be taken, so that gains and assets are not overstated and losses and liabilities are not understated. For example:

- Revenue and profits are not normally included in the income statement or profit and loss account until they are reasonably certain to be realised (ie, either cash has been received or there is a reasonable certainty that it will be received).

- All known liabilities are normally recognised immediately, whether the amount of these is known with certainty or is a best estimate in the light of the information available.

Activity 4

Give two examples of the use of the prudence concept in accounts.

student notes

Other important concepts

Materiality

Information is **material** to the financial statements if its misstatement or omission might reasonably be expected to influence the economic decisions of users.

Materiality is sometimes known as a **threshold concept**. It provides a cut-off point. Immaterial information is not useful and may obscure the overall picture or distract users from information that is genuinely significant.

In practice, materiality is often judged in relation to a cut-off point (eg, 1% of sales revenue). However, whether an item is material depends not only on its size, but its nature and the context in which it is reported. For example, limited companies are required by law to disclose certain information about directors' earnings. This information must be exact, even though the amounts involved might not be material in relation to the accounts as a whole.

Accounting standards need not be applied to immaterial items.

Activity 5

A company has sales revenue of £1 million, net profit of £20,000 and net assets of £500,000. Which of these errors is material?

a) Revenue is overstated by £1,000
b) Plant and equipment are understated by £30,000

Separate entity

For the purpose of preparing accounts, a business is treated as a separate entity from its owners. This applies whether or not the business is a separate entity in law (eg, a company) or not (eg, a sole trader or a partnership).

For example, the accounts of a sole trader do not include his or her personal transactions or assets, only those relating to the business. If a sole trader pays private expenses from the business bank account, these are treated as drawings rather than expenses of the business.

Duality

Every transaction has two effects: a debit and a credit. This is the principle that underpins double entry bookkeeping.

Historic cost

Assets and liabilities are recorded in the accounts at their historic (original) cost rather than at their current value.

student notes

As we saw earlier in the chapter, this produces information that is reliable but not always relevant, particularly under conditions of rising prices. For this reason, some entities prepare accounts using a 'modified historic cost' basis, where certain assets, normally land and buildings, are stated at current value.

Money measurement

Only items that can be measured at a monetary amount are included in the accounts.

This means that items such as the experience and skill of the workforce are not included in the accounts. This may be vital to the success of the business, yet it cannot be measured in money terms.

Substance over form

The accounts must report the commercial and economic substance of a transaction, rather than its strict legal form, if these are different.

We will be looking at the effect of this important concept in more detail in a later chapter.

THE ELEMENTS OF FINANCIAL STATEMENTS

In your earlier studies you will have learned that financial statements are made up of a number of different items, for example: income; expenses; assets; liabilities; capital.

The *Framework for the Preparation and Presentation of Financial Statements* defines five elements of financial statements. These are:

- assets
- liabilities
- equity
- income
- expenses

Assets

In simple terms, an **asset** is a resource that a business owns or is able to use.

Assets are classified as either **non-current assets** or **current assets**. Non-current assets are sometimes called **fixed assets**.

- A **non-current asset** is an asset that a business intends to hold for some time (usually more than one year) in order to use it to generate income.

- A **current asset** is an asset that a business holds for the short term, for conversion into cash in the course of trading.

student notes

Activity 6

Give three examples of each of the following:

a) non-current assets

b) current assets

The *Framework* gives a more formal definition:

An **asset** is a resource controlled by the entity as a result of past events and from which future economic benefits are expected to flow to the entity.

This definition is very wide and there are two important things to note:

- An entity often owns its assets, but this need not be the case as long as it controls them. For example, a business may lease a motor vehicle under an agreement which gives it the right to use the vehicle throughout its useful life, even though it will never legally own it. The motor vehicle is an asset of the business because the business controls the motor vehicle.
- An asset is something that provides future economic benefit. This means that it should eventually result in an inflow of cash. For example, a factory is used to produce goods that will be sold for cash.

Liabilities

In simple terms, a liability is something which a business owes to somebody else.

Examples of liabilities:

- amounts owing to suppliers
- accruals for services
- advance payments received from customers
- bank overdraft
- loans

Like assets, liabilities are classified into current liabilities and long-term (non-current) liabilities.

- **Current liabilities** are payable within one year.
- **Long-term liabilities** are payable after more than one year.

The definition in the *Framework* is as follows:

A **liability** is a present obligation of the entity arising from past events, the settlement of which is expected to result in an outflow of resources embodying economic benefits from the entity.

student notes

There are three important things to note:

- There must be an obligation, in other words, an entity only has a liability if it cannot avoid an outflow of economic benefit.
- An outflow of economic benefits normally means incurring expenditure or paying cash to somebody, but this is not always the case. An entity might have a liability to provide goods or services in return for cash or another benefit.
- If an entity recognises a liability in its balance sheet, the transaction or event giving rise to the liability must have happened before the year-end.

Equity

Equity is the owners' residual interest in the assets of the entity after deducting all its liabilities.

Equity is sometimes known as **ownership interest**. In other words, equity is what the entity 'owes' to its owners. This is reported in the entity's balance sheet and in the accounts of a sole trader or a partnership, it is called **capital**.

Income and expenses

An entity's **income** normally comes from sales of goods or services, but can come from fees, interest received, dividends received or rent. This kind of income is known as **revenue** and it arises as a result of the ordinary activities of an entity. Income can also come from **gains**, for example, profits on the disposal of non-current assets.

Expenses include items which arise in the normal course of business, such as cost of sales, wages and depreciation. They also include **losses**, for example, the destruction of assets in a fire or flood, or a loss on disposal of a non-current asset.

Profit is the amount by which a business's income exceeds its expenditure. A business makes a loss if its expenditure exceeds its income.

The *Framework* defines income and expenses as follows:

Income is increases in economic benefits during the accounting period in the form of inflows or enhancement of assets or decreases of liabilities that result in increases in equity, other than those relating to contributions from owners.

Expenses are decreases in economic benefits during the accounting period in the form of outflows or depletions of assets or incurrences of liabilities that result in decreases in equity, other than those relating to distributions to owners.

student notes

Income increases assets or decreases liabilities. For example, a sale increases cash or amounts receivable (debtors).

Expenses decrease assets or increase liabilities. For example, the payment of wages decreases cash.

Contributions from owners are increases in equity (ownership interest) resulting from transfers from owners in their capacity as owners.

Distributions from owners are decreases in equity (ownership interest) resulting from transfers to owners in their capacity as owners.

Activity 7

In the accounts of a sole trader, how do owners contribute to ownership interest? Capital.

What is the term for distributions to owners? Drawings

The elements and the accounting equation

The relationship between the elements is shown below:

- ASSETS – LIABILITIES = EQUITY
- EQUITY = CONTRIBUTIONS FROM OWNERS + INCOME – EXPENSES – DISTRIBUTIONS TO OWNERS

This is simply a restatement of the accounting equation:

- ASSETS – LIABILITIES = CAPITAL
- CAPITAL = OPENING NET ASSETS + PROFIT – DRAWINGS

You may have noticed that income and expenses (and therefore profits and losses) are defined only in relation to changes in assets and liabilities. In other words:

- an increase in net assets results in income or a gain (a profit)
- a decrease in net assets results in an expense or a loss.

CHAPTER OVERVIEW

- The objective of financial statements is to provide information about an entity's financial performance and financial position that is useful to a wide range of users for assessing the stewardship of the entity's management and for making economic decisions
- Several different groups of people may be interested in the information provided by financial statements:
  - investors and potential investors (normally regarded as the most important)
  - employees
  - lenders
  - suppliers and other trade creditors
  - customers
  - governments and their agencies
  - the public
- There are several broad types of organisation:

  Profit making
  - sole traders
  - partnerships
  - companies

  'Not-for-profit'
  - charities, clubs and societies
  - public sector organisations
- Useful information must be:
  - understandable
  - relevant
  - reliable
  - comparable with other information
- Financial information must show a 'true and fair' view or be presented fairly if it is to be useful. This normally means that it must comply with all applicable regulations

KEY WORDS

Stewardship the accountability of management for the resources entrusted to it by the owners of an entity

Sole trader a business owned and managed by one person

Partnership a business jointly owned and managed by two or more people

Company a business that is a separate legal entity from its owners

Entity any organisation (whether profit making or not for profit) that prepares accounts as a separate entity from its owners

Accounting Standards authoritative statements of how particular types of transactions and other events should be reflected in financial statements

Accruals revenue and expenses are recognised in the profit and loss account or income statement in the period in which they were earned or incurred rather than the period in which the cash was received or paid

Going concern financial statements are prepared on the basis that an entity will continue in operational existence for the foreseeable future

Consistency similar items are treated in the same way in the financial statements; items are treated in the same way from period to period

Prudence caution is exercised when making judgements under conditions of uncertainty, so that assets and gains are not overstated and liabilities and losses are not understated

CHAPTER OVERVIEW cont.

- The most important sources of regulation in the UK are:
  - companies legislation
  - accounting standards (applicable to limited companies and best practice for other types of entity)
- International accounting standards are issued by the International Accounting Standards Board (IASB)
- The *Framework for the Preparation and Presentation of Financial Statements* sets out the principles and concepts that the IASB believes should underlie the preparation and presentation of financial statements
- The following are regarded as fundamental accounting concepts/underlying assumptions:
  - accruals
  - going concern
- Other important concepts:
  - consistency
  - prudence
  - materiality
  - separate entity
  - duality
  - historic cost
  - money measurement
  - substance over form
- The elements of financial statements are:
  - assets
  - liabilities
  - equity
  - revenue
  - expenses

KEY WORDS

Materiality an item is material if its misstatement or omission might reasonably be expected to influence the economic decisions of users

Separate entity concept for the purpose of preparing accounts, a business is treated as a separate entity from its owners

Duality every transaction has two effects: a debit and a credit

Historic cost concept assets and liabilities are recorded in the accounts at their historic (original) cost rather than at their current value

Money measurement concept only items that can be measured at a monetary amount are included in the accounts

Substance over form the financial statements must report the commercial and economic substance of a transaction, rather than its strict legal form, if these are different

Asset resource controlled by an entity as a result of a past event from which future economic benefits are expected to flow to the entity

Non-current assets assets that a business intends to hold for some time (usually more than one year)

Current assets assets that a business holds for the short term, for conversion into cash in the course of trading

Liability a present obligation of an entity arising from past events, the settlement of which is expected to result in an outflow of economic benefits

CHAPTER OVERVIEW cont.

- The elements restate the accounting equation:
  - Assets – Liabilities = Equity
  - Equity = Contributions from owners + Income – Expenses – Distributions to owners

KEY WORDS

Income increases in economic benefits in the form of increases of assets or decreases of liabilities that result in increases in equity other than contribution from owners

Expenses decreases in economic benefits during the accounting period in the form of decreases of assets or increases of liabilities that result in decreases in equity other than distributions to owners

Current liabilities liabilities that are payable within one year

Long-term liabilities liabilities that are payable after more than one year

Equity the residual amount found by deducting all of an entity's liabilities from all of an entity's assets

Contributions from owners increases in ownership interest resulting from transfers from owners in their capacity as owners

Distributions to owners decreases in ownership interest resulting from transfers to owners in their capacity as owners

HOW MUCH HAVE YOU LEARNED?

1 What is the objective of financial statements?

2 Who are the most important users of financial statements?

3 What makes financial information reliable?

4 Which four bodies form part of the standard setting structure?

5 What is the *Framework for the Preparation and Presentation of Financial Statements*?

6 What are the two most important accounting concepts (the assumptions underlying financial statements)?

7 What are the elements of financial statements?

8 A business has signed a contract to pay its managing director £200,000 per year for the next five years. He has agreed to work full time for the business over that period.

Does the business have a liability in respect of the contract?

chapter 2: INTRODUCTION TO LIMITED COMPANIES

chapter coverage

This is the first of two chapters that cover drafting financial statements for limited companies. In this chapter we look at the reasons why a limited company is different from a sole trader or a partnership, before moving on to explain some of the items which appear in limited company accounts. Limited companies have to publish their financial statements, and, unlike sole traders and partnerships, are obliged to follow accounting standards when preparing them. The format of the income statement (profit and loss account) and statement of financial position (balance sheet) for a limited company are introduced in this chapter and will be covered in more detail in the next chapter. The topics that we shall cover are:

- the nature of limited companies
- how the accounts of limited companies differ from those of sole traders and partnerships
- share capital
- reserves
- debentures
- drafting limited company accounts
- accounting for share issues
- capital instruments

KNOWLEDGE AND UNDERSTANDING AND PERFORMANCE CRITERIA COVERAGE

knowledge and understanding

- the general legal framework of limited companies and the obligations of directors in respect of the financial statements
- the **UK** regulatory framework for financial reporting and the main requirements of relevant financial reporting standards
- the forms of equity and loan capital
- preparing financial statements in proper form

Performance criteria – element 11.1

- draft limited company financial statements from the appropriate information
- ensure that limited company financial statements comply with relevant accounting standards and domestic legislation and with the organisation's policies, regulations and procedures

THE NATURE OF LIMITED COMPANIES

student notes

There are several ways in which a limited company differs from a sole trader or a partnership, the two types of entity that you dealt with in Unit 5.

Separate legal personality

- A company has a **separate legal personality** from those of its owners. It can enter into contracts, acquire assets and incur liabilities in its own name.
- This contrasts with the situation of sole traders and partnerships. For accounting purposes the **business** is treated as a separate entity (the separate entity concept), but the legal position is that it is the owners themselves who enter into contracts and who are personally liable for any debts incurred.

Limited liability

- A limited company gives its owners **limited liability**. Limited liability means that the owners' liability is limited to the amount that they have paid for their shares. If the company becomes insolvent, the maximum amount that the owners lose is the amount of capital that they have invested in the company.
- Sole traders and partners have **unlimited liability**. If the business does not have the resources to repay its liabilities as they fall due, the owners must sell their personal property in order to satisfy creditors and to meet claims against the business.

Size

- Most sole traders and partnerships are small businesses. (There are exceptions, such as large law and accountancy firms.)
- Although many limited companies are small businesses, a limited company may be a very large concern. Large public companies may have several hundred individual shareholders, most of whom have invested in them in order to obtain a share of their profits and possibly to realise a gain on the eventual sale of the shares. They are not involved in the day-to-day running of the companies in which they have invested.

student notes

Owners and managers

- Sole traders and partners normally own and manage their business themselves.
- Limited companies (particularly large ones) are often managed by persons other than their owners (see above):
  - Limited companies are owned by **shareholders**.
  - The shareholders appoint **directors** to manage the company on their behalf.

  One of the objectives of financial statements is to enable the shareholders to assess the way in which management are safeguarding the assets of the company and using them to generate profit (the **stewardship** of management).

  In practice, the directors and the shareholders may be the same people, particularly if the company is small. Even in large public companies directors and key management often have at least a small number of shares.

Types of limited company

There are two types of limited company:

- **Public companies** can invite members of the general public to invest in their shares. The shares of a public company may be (and usually are) traded on the Stock Exchange. Public companies have 'plc', which stands for 'public limited company' at the end of their name. They are generally very large businesses.
- **Private companies** cannot invite members of the general public to invest in their shares. They have the word 'limited' at the end of their name. Most UK companies are private companies.

Advantages of trading as a limited company

The main advantage is limited liability (see above). There are other potential advantages:

- It is easier to raise finance:
  - there may be any number of shareholders
  - investing in a listed company is less risky and therefore more attractive than investing in a partnership or a sole trader (limited liability)

student notes

- (In practice, shareholders in small companies are often asked to give personal guarantees to lenders, so that the advantage of limited liability no longer applies.)
- A limited company continues to operate regardless of the identity of the owners (unlike a partnership, where the old partnership ceases and a new one is formed whenever a partner is admitted or retires).
- Limited companies are taxed as separate entities (tax is treated as an appropriation of profits). Partners and sole traders are personally liable for tax on their share of the business profits.
- It is reasonably easy to transfer shares from one owner to another.

Disadvantages of trading as a limited company

- Limited companies must publish their annual accounts. This means that in theory they can be seen by anybody, including competitors. Sole traders and partnerships do not have to publish their accounts.
- Limited companies must comply with a great many legal and administrative formalities (although some of the rules do not apply to small companies). In particular, they must prepare accounts in accordance with the Companies Act 2006. The accounts must comply with the requirements of accounting standards. Sole traders and partnerships may comply with accounting standards, but are not obliged to do so.
- The accounts of larger companies must be **audited** (subjected to independent examination to ensure that they present a true and fair view or fair presentation of the company's affairs). This can be inconvenient, time consuming and expensive.
- Companies must comply with the requirements of the Companies Act when they issue shares. It can be difficult to reduce capital (for example, there are restrictions on buying back shares). Although the rules have recently been simplified, this can cause problems where shareholders wish to be 'bought out'. Sole traders and partnerships can increase or withdraw capital whenever the owners wish.

student notes

HOW THE ACCOUNTS OF LIMITED COMPANIES DIFFER FROM THOSE OF SOLE TRADERS AND PARTNERSHIPS

The income statement (profit and loss account) of a sole trader or a partnership

The income statement provides information about the financial performance of a business. It shows the income generated and the expenditure incurred during an accounting period.

The exact format of the income statement varies according to the type of business, but the basic structure is always the same:

Sales	X
Less: cost of sales	(X)
Gross profit	X
Less: other expenses	(X)
Net profit	X

There are two parts.

- The first part is sometimes known as the trading account. This shows the gross profit generated by the business, in other words, sales less expenses directly incurred in producing or purchasing goods or services for sale.

- The second part shows the other items of income and expenditure earned and incurred by the business. These are deducted from gross profit to arrive at net profit.

student notes

Example

Income statement for the year ended 31 December 20X0

	£	£
Sales		774,000
Less: cost of sales		
Opening stock	156,000	
Purchases	612,000	
	768,000	
Closing stock	(180,000)	
		(588,000)
Gross profit		186,000
Less: other expenses		
Wages and salaries	109,200	
Office expenses	9,000	
Rates	7,200	
Electricity	8,000	
Depreciation	4,350	
Bad and doubtful debts	3,600	
		(141,350)
Net profit		44,650

The statement of financial position (balance sheet) of a sole trader or a partnership

The statement of financial position provides information about the financial position of a business. It shows the assets, liabilities and ownership interest of a business at the end of an accounting period.

The statement of financial position reflects the accounting equation:

ASSETS – LIABILITIES = CAPITAL; or

ASSETS = LIABILITIES + CAPITAL.

The statement of financial position of a sole trader or a partnership is normally structured as follows:

- The first part shows assets and liabilities. Assets and liabilities are always shown in the same order: fixed (non-current) assets, assets and current assets; current liabilities; long-term liabilities.
- The second part shows equity. For a sole trader, this is normally capital, plus profits, less drawings (income less expenses plus contributions from owners less distributions to owners).

student notes

Example

Statement of financial position at 31 December 20X0

	£	£
Fixed assets:		
Leasehold premises		67,500
Fixtures and fittings		10,800
		78,300
Current assets:		
Stocks	180,000	
Debtors	311,640	
Prepayments	1,800	
Cash at bank	24,300	
Cash in hand	300	
	518,040	
Current liabilities:		
Creditors	390,000	
Accruals	2,000	
	392,000	
Net current assets		126,040
		204,340
Represented by:		
Capital at 1 January 20X0		174,090
Net profit for the year ended 31 December 20X0		44,650
		218,740
Less: drawings		(14,400)
		204,340

student notes

Activity 1

The following trial balance has been extracted from the accounts of Amelia, a sole trader.

Trial balance as at 30 June 20X1

	Dr	Cr
	£	£
Sales		350,000
Purchases	219,000	
Carriage inwards	1,000	
Carriage outwards	1,200	
Wages and salaries	55,000	
Rent and rates	9,600	
Heat and light	4,500	
Stock at 1 July 20X0	12,700	
Drawings	15,600	
Equipment at cost	91,000	
Motor vehicles at cost	39,000	
Accumulated depreciation:		
Equipment		20,500
Motor vehicles		8,000
Debtors	48,000	
Creditors		33,000
Bank	4,800	
Sundry expenses	7,300	
Cash	500	
Capital		97,700
	509,200	509,200

The following information as at 30 June 20X1 is also available.

a) £700 is owing for heat and light.

b) £900 has been prepaid for rent and rates.

c) Depreciation is to be charged for the year as follows:

Equipment – 10% on cost
Motor vehicles – 20% on cost.

d) Stock at the close of business was valued at £14,900.

Task

Prepare Amelia's income statement (profit and loss account) for the year ended 30 June 20X1 and her statement of financial position (balance sheet) at that date.

student notes

The income statement of a limited company

This is prepared in exactly the same way as that of a sole trader or partnership, down to net profit.

Net profit is then appropriated:

- The tax payable on the profits, known as **corporation tax**, is deducted. This is because a company is taxed as a separate entity from its owners. Tax does not appear in the accounts of sole traders and partnerships, because the owners are taxed, rather than the business itself.
- The profit remaining after tax is available for distribution to the shareholders, in the form of **dividends**. Dividends can be viewed as the equivalent of drawings in a sole trader or a partnership.
- Any profit not distributed as dividends is retained by the company.

Activity 2

At a company's annual general meeting one of the shareholders complained that the dividend of £50,000 seemed small compared with profit after tax of £250,000.

Why is it unlikely that the company could distribute the full amount of profit after tax as a dividend?

The statement of financial position of a limited company

The sections of the statement of financial position which list the assets and liabilities of the business are prepared in exactly the same way as for a sole trader or a partnership.

The section of the statement of financial position which shows ownership interest consists of:

- share capital
- reserves.

The ownership interest in a limited company is normally referred to as its **equity**.

SHARE CAPITAL

student notes

Share capital is the capital invested in a company by its owners. The capital of a company is divided into a number of identifiable units, called shares. When a company is formed, it issues shares, which are purchased by investors.

Nominal value and market value

Shares have a nominal value and a market value.

- The nominal value of a share (sometimes known as par value) is its 'face value'. The nominal value of shares is decided when the shares are issued and always remains the same from then onwards. Shares are stated in the statement of financial position at their nominal value.
- The market value of a share is the value at which it is traded on the Stock Exchange. This changes over time and bears no relation to the nominal value. The market value of a company's shares is irrelevant to the accounts.

HOW IT WORKS

On 1 January 20X0 X plc issues 200,000 50p ordinary shares. At 31 December 20X0 A, who purchased 200 shares, sells her shares to B for £2.25 each.

- The nominal value of the shares is 50p. (To have the same amount of share capital, X plc could have issued 100,000 £1 ordinary shares or 400,000 25p ordinary shares.) The double entry to record the issue is:

DEBIT	Bank (200,000 x 50p)	£100,000	
CREDIT	Share capital		£100,000

- The shares are stated in the statement of financial position at £100,000.
- At 31 December 20X0, the market value of the shares is £2.25 each.
- When A sells her shares to B, the transaction is between A and B and X plc does not receive any further cash as a result. The shares continue to be stated in the statement of financial position at £100,000.

student notes

Issued share capital

Issued share capital is the nominal amount of share capital that has actually been issued to shareholders.

The term **allotted share capital** is sometimes used. Shares are allotted to shareholders when shares are issued. Allotted share capital is the same as issued share capital.

Types of shares

There are two main types of share:

- preference shares
- ordinary shares

Preference shares

Preference shares are shares which carry the right to a fixed rate of dividend.

- The preference dividend must be paid out of available profits before any ordinary dividend is paid.
- In the event of a liquidation, preference shareholders normally have the right to return of their capital before any capital is returned to ordinary shareholders.
- Preference shares **do not** carry the right to a vote.

Ordinary shares

student notes

Ordinary shares are shares which entitle the holders to share in profits after all prior claims (for example, those of creditors and preference shareholders) have been satisfied. They entitle the holder to **vote** in general meetings.

This means that:

- Ordinary shareholders cannot be certain of the amount of their dividend as it depends on the level of profit.
- If the company ceases trading, the ordinary shareholders are entitled to any capital remaining after creditors and preference shareholders (if any) have received the amounts due to them. They may lose their original investment or (in theory) they may receive more than their original investment.
- Because ordinary shareholders can vote, in theory they can determine the policies of the company. (Whether they can do this in practice depends on the percentage of shares that they hold and the percentage held by other ordinary shareholders. In a small company, an individual shareholder is likely to have at least some power; in a large public company, individual shareholders have very little power and the company's policies are generally determined by the directors.)

Ordinary shareholders are therefore the effective owners of the company and bear the risk associated with trading.

The majority of shares issued are ordinary shares.

Ordinary shares are often known as **equity shares. Equity** is the same as ownership interest. A company's equity is its ordinary share capital and its reserves.

The precise rights attaching to ordinary shares and preference shares vary from company to company. A company may have several different classes of ordinary shares or preference shares, all giving slightly different rights.

RESERVES

Reserves are the cumulative total of the company's retained profits.

A company has:

- **distributable reserves** (sometimes called **revenue reserves** or **non-statutory reserves**) which can be used for paying dividends to shareholders; and may have

student notes

- **non-distributable reserves** (sometimes called **capital reserves** or **statutory reserves**) which cannot be used for paying dividends to shareholders.

Reserves may consist of:

- retained profits (often called retained earnings or accumulated profits)
- share premium account
- revaluation reserve
- capital redemption reserve

} reserves which the company is legally obliged to set up in certain circumstances; these are not distributable

- general reserve (which may be set up by the directors)
- other reserves set up by the directors and designated for a specific purpose (for example, non-current asset replacement reserve).

General reserves and other designated reserves are theoretically available for the payment of dividends. However, the fact that the reserves have been set up suggests that the directors do not intend to use them for this purpose.

HOW IT WORKS

A company wants to transfer £20,000 to a general reserve. Retained profit for the year is £35,000.

The double entry is:

DEBIT	Retained earnings reserve	£20,000	
CREDIT	General reserve		£20,000

DEBENTURES

Debentures are another method by which a company can raise finance. They are long term loans made to a company, which carry a fixed rate of interest.

Debentures may also be known as debenture stock, loan capital or loan stock.

Like share capital, debentures are divided into a number of identifiable units and may be held by a large number of individuals. They have a nominal value (at which they are stated in the balance sheet) and a market value.

Debentures may be secured on particular assets of the company or they may be unsecured. If debentures are secured, debenture holders have the right to make the directors sell the asset(s) in order to meet the debt due to them.

student notes

However, they differ from share capital in a number of important ways:

- Debenture holders are creditors, while shareholders are members (owners) of the company.

- Debenture holders receive a fixed rate of interest regardless of the profits or losses made by the company. Interest is calculated on the nominal value of the debentures and usually paid half-yearly. The amount of dividend received by ordinary shareholders depends on the level of profit made by the company.

- Debenture interest is an expense and charged in the income statement, while dividends are an appropriation of profit.

- Debenture holders can take legal action against a company if their interest is not paid when it is due or repayment of the loan is not made on the due date. Ordinary shareholders are not automatically entitled to receive a dividend and therefore cannot take action against the company if no dividend is paid.

- Debentures normally have a fixed repayment date, whereas share capital is only repaid when the company is wo[illegible]

- Debentures do not carry a vote. Ordinary shar[illegible] general meetings and therefore (at least in [illegible] influence on the company's policies.

HOW IT WORKS

A company issues £100,000 8% debentures.

The double entry to record the issue is:

DEBIT	Bank	£100,[illegible]
CREDIT	Debentures	

Annual interest on the debentures is £8,000 (8% £100,[illegible]

Activity 3

A company has £200,000 12% debentures. The year-end is 31 December. Interest is payable half-yearly on 31 July and 31 January.

What is the total interest payable for the year? What accounting adjustment must be made at the year-end?

student notes

DRAFTING ACCOUNTS FOR LIMITED COMPANIES

The formats

Limited companies are required to publish their accounts. This means that their accounts must be presented in such a way that they provide useful information to users, in an acceptable format.

Limited company accounts for internal use only can, of course, be prepared in any format that the directors wish.

Pro-forma accounts based on the requirements of the Companies Acts and of IAS 1 *Presentation of financial statements* are shown below. They will be covered in more detail in the next chapter.

There are two things to notice:

- The statement of financial position is presented differently from the examples shown earlier. The first part shows total assets and the second part shows total equity and total liabilities:

  ASSETS = EQUITY + LIABILITIES

- The statements use some terms that are different from the ones that you will have learned in your earlier studies, when preparing accounts for sole traders and partnerships. The most obvious difference is that the profit and loss account is called the income statement and that the balance sheet is called the statement of financial position. We explain some of the other differences below.

student notes

Income statement for the year ended...

	£
Revenue	X
Cost of sales	(X)
Gross profit	X
Distribution costs	(X)
Administrative expenses	(X)
Profit/(loss) from operations	X
Finance costs	(X)
Profit before tax	X
Tax	(X)
Profit/(loss) for the period	X

Statement of financial position as at....

	£	£	£
Assets			
Non-current assets			
Property, plant and equipment		X	
			X
Current assets			
Inventories		X	
Trade and other receivables		X	
Cash and cash equivalents		X	
			X
Total assets			X
Equity and liabilities			
Equity			
Share capital		X	
Share premium		X	
Revaluation reserve		X	
Retained earnings		X	
			X
			X
Non-current liabilities			
Bank loans	X		
		X	
Current liabilities			
Trade and other payables	X		
Tax liabilities	X		
Bank overdraft	X		
		X	
Total equity and liabilities			X

student notes

Inventories = Stock

The income statement

In the income statement, items cannot be listed out, but must be analysed under the various headings.

Revenue is sales.

Distribution costs are the costs of selling and delivering items to customers. They may include:

- sales force's salaries and commissions
- depreciation of sales force's cars
- delivery costs
- advertising.

Administrative expenses are expenses other than direct costs of production and distribution costs. They may include:

- rent and rates
- light and heat
- office salaries
- postage and telephone
- directors' remuneration
- depreciation on office equipment, fixtures and fittings.

Finance costs are normally interest payable on bank loans and on other loans.

The statement of financial position

Inventories are stocks.

Trade and other receivables are trade debtors, prepayments and other debtors. (These items may be shown separately in the statement of financial position.)

Cash equivalents are short term investments that can be very easily converted into cash.

Trade and other payables normally consist of trade creditors and accruals.

HOW IT WORKS

student notes

Tycho Ltd is a private limited company. The trial balance for the year ended 31 March 20X1 is shown below:

	£	£
Ordinary shares of £1 each		50,000
Land and buildings: Cost	150,000	
Land and buildings: Accumulated depreciation		9,000
Motor vehicles: Cost	22,000	
Motor vehicles: Accumulated depreciation		6,800
Plant and machinery: Cost	34,000	
Plant and machinery: Accumulated depreciation		5,100
Inventory at 1 April 20X0	38,600	
Trade receivables	31,900	
Prepayments	4,200	
Bank current account		2,600
Petty cash	200	
Trade payables		28,300
Accruals		5,600
10% Loan stock		50,000
Sales		314,900
Purchases	221,500	
Administrative expenses	35,700	
Distribution costs	26,900	
Bank interest	300	
Loan stock interest	2,500	
Dividend paid	1,500	
Share premium		25,000
Retained earnings at 1 April 20X0		72,000
	569,300	569,300

The following information is also available:

a) Inventory at 31 March 20X1 was £42,100

b) Corporation tax for the year has been estimated at £12,500

c) The directors wish to declare a final ordinary dividend of 6p per share.

student notes

The adjustments

Inventory

DEBIT	Inventory (statement of financial position)	£42,100	
CREDIT	Inventory (income statement)		£42,100

Being the adjustments for closing inventories

Corporation tax

Tax charged on the profits made by a limited company is corporation tax and is an expense of the company as a separate legal entity. It is a charge against profits and a liability in the statement of financial position.

DEBIT	Corporation tax charge (income statement)	£12,500	
CREDIT	Corporation tax payable (statement of financial position)		£12,500

Being the corporation tax charge for the year ended 31 March 20X1

Loan stock interest

The charge in the income statement is £2,500, in other words only half the year's interest has been charged. Total loan stock interest for the year is £5,000 (10% × 50,000). A further £2,500 must be accrued.

DEBIT	Loan stock interest (income statement)	£2,500	
CREDIT	Accruals (statement of financial position)		£2,500

Being an accrual for loan stock interest

Dividends

As well as declaring an ordinary dividend at the year end, companies may pay an interim dividend part way through the year. In this case the company has already paid an interim dividend of £1,500 and is now declaring a final dividend of 6p per ordinary share.

Dividends are not shown in the income statement because they are not an expense, but a distribution to the shareholders. Instead, dividends that are paid during the year are deducted from the retained earnings reserve. This is similar to the way in which drawings (also a distribution to owners) are deducted from capital in accounts of a sole trader.

The final dividend has been proposed after the year end. It is not a liability because the company had no obligation to pay it at the reporting date (the year-end), (see the definition of a liability in Chapter 1). Therefore no adjustment is needed.

The accounts

student notes

We can now draw up the income statement and the statement of financial position.

Income statement for the year ended 31 March 20X1

	£
Revenue	314,900
Cost of sales (38,600 + 221,500 – 42,100)	(218,000)
Gross profit	96,900
Distribution costs	(26,900)
Administrative expenses	(35,700)
Profit from operations	34,300
Finance costs (300 + 2,500 + 2,500)	(5,300)
Profit before tax	29,000
Tax	(12,500)
Profit for the year	16,500

student notes

Statement of financial position at 31 March 20X1

	£	£
Property, plant and equipment:		
Land and buildings (150,000 – 9,000)		141,000
Plant and machinery (34,000 – 5,100)		28,900
Motor vehicles (22,000 – 6,800)		15,200
		185,100
Current assets:		
Inventories	42,100	
Trade and other receivables (31,900 + 4,200)	36,100	
Cash	200	
		78,400
Total assets		263,500
Equity:		
Share capital		50,000
Share premium		25,000
Retained earnings (72,000 + 16,500 – 1,500)		87,000
		162,000
Non-current liabilities		
Loan stock	50,000	
Current liabilities:		
Trade and other payables (28,300 + 5,600 + 2,500)	36,400	
Tax liabilities	12,500	
Bank overdraft	2,600	
	51,500	
Total liabilities		101,500
Total equity and liabilities		263,500

student notes

Activity 4

The following balances have been extracted from the trial balance of Triton Ltd, a wholesaler.

	£'000
Sales	3,534
Opening inventory	228
Purchases	2,623
Closing inventory	264
Directors' salaries	32
Wages and salaries:	
sales staff	131
office staff	197
Advertising and marketing costs	16
Office expenses	128
Light and heat	16
Depreciation:	
freehold buildings	2
fixtures and fittings	36
delivery vans	10
Audit fees	5
Debenture interest	24
Corporation tax	105

Draft the income statement, in a format suitable for publication.

ACCOUNTING FOR SHARE ISSUES

To issue shares, a company can make:

- a normal issue at par (nominal value);
- a normal issue at a premium (above nominal value);
- a bonus issue; or
- a rights issue.

Activity 5

Benton Ltd issues 250,000 50p ordinary shares at par. The shares are fully paid at the time of issue. What is the double entry to record the share issue?

student notes

Share premium

A company may issue shares at a premium, in other words, at above the nominal value of the shares. The premium is the difference between the nominal value of the shares and their market price.

When this happens, the Companies Act requires that a sum equal to the premium is transferred to a share premium account. The share premium account is a non-distributable reserve. In other words, it cannot be used to pay dividends to shareholders.

Setting up a share premium reserve protects the company's creditors. It ensures that the total amount invested by shareholders remains available to meet the company's liabilities should the need arise.

HOW IT WORKS

A company issues 150,000 50p ordinary shares at 75p each. The shares are fully paid in cash at the time of issue.

For each share purchased, the shareholders have paid the nominal value of 50p and a premium of 25p. The total amount received by the company is:

	£
Nominal value (150,000 x 50p)	75,000
Premium (150,000 x 25p)	37,500
	112,500

The double entry to record the share issue is:

DEBIT	Bank	£112,500	
CREDIT	Share capital		£75,000
CREDIT	Share premium		£37,500

In the statement of financial position, the shares will appear as follows:

Equity:

Ordinary share capital	75,000
Share premium	37,500

Bonus issues

student notes

A bonus issue is the issue of extra shares to existing shareholders at no cost. Bonus issues are made to shareholders in proportion to their existing shareholdings. A bonus issue is sometimes known as a scrip issue.

For example, suppose that A holds 1,000 ordinary shares in X plc. The directors of X plc declare a bonus issue of 1 for 5 new ordinary shares. A receives one bonus share for every five shares that she currently holds, so she receives 200 new shares in total. She does not have to pay anything for these shares.

A bonus issue does not raise any additional finance for the company. It is simply a means of reclassifying reserves as share capital. A company may wish to do this in order to increase the capital base of the company or to encourage investment by making shares appear cheaper (because the market price of the shares will fall).

Any reserve can be used to make a bonus issue, but the share premium account is the reserve most commonly used as it is non-distributable. This is one of the few legally permitted uses of the share premium account.

HOW IT WORKS

A company has the following equity:

	£
Share capital (£1 ordinary shares)	100,000
Share premium	50,000
Retained earnings	350,000
	500,000

It makes a 1 for 4 bonus issue, using the share premium account.

The total number of new shares issued is 25,000 (100,000 ÷ 4).

The double entry to record the bonus issue is:

DEBIT	Share premium	£25,000	
CREDIT	Share capital		£25,000

Equity now appears as follows:

	£
Share capital (£1 ordinary shares)	125,000
Share premium	25,000
Retained earnings	350,000
	500,000

student notes

Rights issues

A rights issue is an issue of shares to existing shareholders at below market value. The shares are offered to shareholders in proportion to their existing shareholdings. The shareholders can choose whether or not to take the shares offered to them.

A rights issue is a relatively cheap and convenient way of raising extra capital. It has the further advantage that existing shareholders retain control of the company.

HOW IT WORKS

A company has the following equity:

	£
Share capital (£1 ordinary shares)	50,000
Share premium	10,000
Retained earnings	90,000
	150,000

It makes a 1 for 5 rights issue at £1.10 per share. All the existing shareholders take up the new shares for cash.

The total number of new shares issued is 10,000 (50,000 ÷ 5).

The double entry to record the rights issue is:

DEBIT	Bank (10,000 x £1.10)	£11,000	
CREDIT	Share capital		£10,000
CREDIT	Share premium		£1,000

Equity now appears as follows:

	£
Share capital (£1 ordinary shares)	60,000
Share premium	11,000
Retained earnings	90,000
	161,000

student notes

Activity 6

Hemsell Ltd has the following share capital and reserves:

	£
Share capital (25p ordinary shares)	100,000
Share premium	30,000
Retained earnings	170,000
	300,000

It makes a rights issue of 1 new share for every 5 existing shares at a price of 40p per share. All the existing shareholders take up the rights issue for cash. It then makes a bonus issue of 1 new share for every 8 existing shares, using non-distributable reserves.

Show how equity appears after both these issues have been made.

CAPITAL INSTRUMENTS

Capital instruments are all instruments issued by reporting entities as a means of raising finance, including shares, debentures, loans and debt. They also include options and warrants, which give the holder the right to obtain capital instruments.

Shares, debentures and loans are the commonest types of capital instrument. For this Unit, you do not need to know how to deal with the more complex instruments, such as options and warrants.

All capital instruments should be accounted for in the statement of financial position either as:

- liabilities; or
- shareholders' funds (equity).

Capital instruments that carry an obligation to transfer economic benefits should be treated as liabilities. Debentures are a liability because debenture interest has to be paid, and eventually the debentures themselves must be repaid.

Capital instruments that do not carry an obligation to transfer economic benefits should be included in equity. Ordinary shares are not liabilities because the company does not have to pay a dividend, nor does it have to repay the capital until the company is wound up.

CHAPTER OVERVIEW

- A limited company:
  - has a separate legal personality from those of its owners
  - gives its shareholders (owners) limited liability
- Limited liability means that the owners' liability is limited to the amount that they have paid for their shares. This is the maximum amount that they can lose if the company is wound up
- Limited companies are owned by shareholders and managed by directors
- There are two types of limited company:
  - public companies
  - private companies
- Advantages of trading as a limited company:
  - limited liability
  - it is easier to raise finance
  - the company continues even if the owners change
  - there may be tax advantages
  - it is easy to transfer shares
- Disadvantages of trading as a limited company
  - publication of annual accounts
  - legal and administrative formalities (including compliance with accounting standards)
  - restrictions on issuing shares and reducing capital
- The net profit of a limited company is appropriated to:
  - corporation tax
  - dividends
  - transfers to reserves (if any)

KEY WORDS

Public companies companies that can invite members of the general public to invest in their shares

Private companies companies that cannot invite members of the general public to invest in their shares

Corporation tax the tax payable on the profits of a limited company

Dividends amounts paid to shareholders from profits or distributable reserves

Share capital the capital invested in a company by its owners, divided into a number of identifiable shares

Issued share capital the nominal amount of share capital that has been issued to shareholders (allotted share capital)

Preference shares shares which carry the right to a fixed rate of dividend

Ordinary shares shares which entitle the holders to share in profits after all prior claims have been satisfied

Equity ownership interest. A company's equity is its ordinary share capital and its reserves

Reserves the cumulative total of the company's retained profits

Distributable reserves (revenue reserves, non-statutory reserves) reserves which can be used for paying dividends to shareholders

CHAPTER OVERVIEW cont.

- The ownership interest of a limited company is called shareholders' funds or equity and consists of:
  - share capital
  - reserves
- Share capital is reported in the statement of financial position at their nominal ('face') value
- There are two main types of share:
  - preference shares
  - ordinary shares
- Reserves are either:
  - distributable (including retained profits); or
  - non-distributable (including share premium and revaluation reserve)
- Debentures are used to raise finance. Debenture holders are creditors. They receive a fixed rate of interest, which is an expense in the income statement

KEY WORDS

Non-distributable reserves (capital reserves, statutory reserves) reserves which cannot be used for paying dividends to shareholders

Debentures long term loans made to a company, which carry a fixed rate of interest

Share premium a non-distributable reserve consisting of the difference between consideration received for shares and the nominal value of the shares issued

Bonus issue (scrip issue) an issue of extra shares to existing shareholders at no cost, made to shareholders in proportion to their existing shareholdings

Rights issue an issue of shares to existing shareholders at below market value, offered to shareholders in proportion to their existing shareholdings

- The income statement and statement of financial position of a limited company must follow a specific format
- To adjust for corporation tax:

DEBIT	Corporation tax charge (income statement)	X
CREDIT	Corporation tax payable (statement of financial position)	X

- If a company issues shares at a premium (above their nominal value), a sum equal to the premium is transferred to a share premium account

HOW MUCH HAVE YOU LEARNED?

1 Which of the following items are included in the statement of financial position of a limited company but not in the balance sheet of a partnership or a sole trader?

a) debentures

b) drawings

c) share premium

d) taxation payable

2 Knave Ltd issues 200,000 50p ordinary shares at a market price of 80p. All shares are fully paid in cash as soon as they are issued.

What is the double entry to record the issue?

3 Complete the table:

Reserves	*Distributable*	*Non-distributable*
General reserve	....	....
Plant replacement reserve	....	....
Retained earnings	....	....
Revaluation reserve	....	....
Share premium	....	....

4 Diamond Ltd made a profit from operations of £140,000 for the year ended 31 December 20X5. Throughout the year the company has had 250,000 £1 ordinary shares and £150,000 9% debentures. Corporation tax has been estimated at £74,000 for the year.

What is the retained profit for the year ended 31 December 20X5?

5 The trial balance of Hearts Ltd at 31 December 20X2 is shown below:

	£'000	£'000
Administrative expenses	3,185	
Bank		420
Debentures		2,100
Debenture interest	105	
Distribution expenses	727	
Retained earnings reserve		3,955
Purchases	10,493	
Revaluation reserve		1,365
Sales		16,100
Share capital (£1 ordinary shares)		840
Inventory (at 1 January 20X2)	4,515	
Property, plant and equipment (net book value)	5,852	
Trade payables		3,675
Trade receivables	3,578	
	28,455	28,455

Inventories were £5,292,000 at 31 December 20X2.

Corporation tax on profits for the year is estimated to be £280,000.

Required

Prepare an income statement and statement of financial position for Hearts Ltd for the year ended 31 December 20X2.

chapter 3: PUBLISHED FINANCIAL STATEMENTS OF LIMITED COMPANIES

chapter coverage

The previous chapter explained the ways in which limited companies are different from sole traders and partnerships and introduced the format of the limited company income statement and statement of financial position. This chapter concentrates on the financial statements: the required formats and the information that must be disclosed. Although the formats and the disclosures should be learned, the best way to master the drafting of financial statements for limited companies is to practise on as many questions and past assessment tasks as possible. The topics that we shall cover are:

- responsibilities of the directors
- presentation of financial statements
- the income statement and the statement of financial position
- the directors' report

KNOWLEDGE AND UNDERSTANDING AND PERFORMANCE CRITERIA COVERAGE

knowledge and understanding

- the general legal framework of limited companies: obligations of directors in respect of the financial statements
- the statutory form of accounting statements and disclosure requirements
- preparing financial statements in proper form

Performance criteria – element 11.1

- draft limited company financial statements from the appropriate information
- ensure that limited company financial statements comply with relevant accounting standards and domestic legislation and with the organisation's policies, regulations and procedures.

student notes

RESPONSIBILITIES OF THE DIRECTORS

Publishing the accounts

The directors of a limited company are responsible for preparing its annual accounts, having them audited and presenting them to the shareholders in a general meeting. Every shareholder is entitled to receive a copy of the company's annual accounts.

The shareholders approve the accounts and the directors must then **file** (deposit) them with the Registrar of Companies. The Registrar of Companies keeps copies of the annual accounts of all limited companies and any member of the public may inspect them for a small charge.

In addition to filing accounts with the Registrar of Companies, most public limited companies publish a printed version, including a Chairman's Statement which comments on the activities of the company during the year and its future plans and prospects. This is circulated to shareholders (who may choose to receive 'summary financial statements' instead). Members of the public can obtain these accounts either by applying to the company directly or (in most cases) through a service offered by the Financial Times. For public limited companies, the published accounts are an important method of promoting the company to potential investors. Quoted companies (companies whose shares are listed on a recognised stock exchange) are now required to publish their annual report and accounts on their website.

Smaller companies do not normally 'publish' their accounts in this way. However, because of the potential 'publicity' that can follow from filing accounts with the Registrar, the financial statements of limited companies prepared for external use are known as **published accounts** or **published financial statements**.

Because they are required by statute (law), they may also be referred to as **statutory accounts**.

What must be published

Unless they are listed companies, UK companies have a choice when preparing accounts for publication:

- They can follow UK standards. This means that they must also follow certain rules set out in the Companies Act itself; these set out the format of the profit and loss account and the balance sheet, the accounting principles to be followed, and other disclosures that must be made. The Companies Act describes these accounts as **Companies Act accounts**.

- They can follow IASs and IFRSs. This means that they do not follow all the additional rules set out in the Companies Act. Instead, they

student notes

comply with IAS 1 *Presentation of financial statements*, which contains requirements that are very similar to those in the Companies Act. The Companies Act describes these accounts as **IAS accounts**.

Listed companies are required to prepare IAS accounts.

Companies Act accounts

The Companies Act 2006 states that the following items must be filed with the Registrar of Companies:

- A **profit and loss account** showing the profit or loss for the accounting period;
- A **balance sheet** showing the state of the company's affairs on the last day of the accounting period;
- A directors' report;
- An auditors' report;
- **Group accounts** (if the company has subsidiaries).

The profit and loss account and balance sheet are supported by notes, which analyse the figures in the main statements and may disclose additional information.

IAS accounts

IAS 1 states that a complete set of financial statements comprises:

- a **statement of financial position** at the end of the period;
- a **statement of comprehensive income** for the period;
- a **statement of changes in equity** for the period (see Chapter 4);
- a **statement of cash flows** for the period (see Chapter 5);
- **notes**, comprising a summary of significant accounting policies and other information.

IAS 1 also states that an entity should present all the financial statements with equal prominence.

The Companies Act also requires:

- A directors' report;
- An auditors' report;
- **Group accounts** (if the company has subsidiaries).

Whichever set of regulations the directors follow, they also have a legal duty to **keep proper accounting records**.

student notes

A true and fair view

The Companies Act states that published accounts must show a **true and fair view** of the company's results for the period and its assets and liabilities at the end of the period. This normally means that they must comply with the requirements of the Companies Acts and applicable accounting standards.

Where IAS accounts are prepared, this requirement is met if the accounts **present fairly** the financial position and financial performance of the entity (as required by IAS 1).

However, (in very exceptional circumstances), the directors may override any of these rules if following them would result in the financial statements not showing a true and fair view (the 'true and fair view override').

PRESENTATION OF FINANCIAL STATEMENTS

In the Exam based Assessment, you will be expected to prepare IAS accounts. IAS 1 *Presentation of financial statements* sets out overall requirements for the presentation of financial statements.

The purpose of financial statements

The objective of financial statements is to provide information about the financial position, financial performance and cash flows of an entity that is useful to a wide range of users in making economic decisions.

Financial statements also show the results of management's stewardship of the resources entrusted to it.

Note that this is the same as the objective of financial statements set out in the *Framework*.

Fair presentation

IAS 1 states that:

- Financial statements shall **present fairly** the financial position, financial performance and cash flows of an entity.

Like 'true and fair view', 'present fairly' is not defined, but the standard goes on to say that:

- Fair presentation requires the faithful representation of the effects of transactions, other events and conditions in accordance with the definitions and recognition criteria for assets, liabilities, income and expenses set out in the *Framework*.

student notes

- Fair presentation can normally be achieved if financial statements comply with IFRSs.
- IFRSs includes all standards and interpretations adopted by the IASB:
  - International Financial Reporting Standards (IFRSs)
  - International Accounting Standards (IASs)
  - Interpretations issued by IFRIC or by its predecessor, the Standing Interpretations Committee (SIC)

  (You do not need to know the content of any Interpretations for your exam.)

The recognition criteria

We have already looked at the definitions of assets, liabilities, income and expenses set out in the *Framework* (see Chapter 1).

IASs and IFRSs use the terms **recognition** and **derecognition**.

- When an item is included in the financial statements it is said to be **recognised**.
- When an item is removed from the financial statements it is **derecognised**.

The *Framework* sets out a basic principle:

An item that meets the definition of an element (eg, an asset or a liability) should be recognised if:

- it is **probable** that any **future economic benefit** associated with the item will flow to or from the entity; and
- the item has a cost or value that can be measured with **reliability**.

Suppose that an entity buys a machine. The machine exists in a physical sense; the entity intends to use it to make goods for resale, so it is probable that economic benefits (sales revenue) will flow to the entity (cash will eventually be received). The cost of the machine to the entity is a matter of fact and there is documentation to prove it (it can be measured with reliability).

Contrast this with internally generated goodwill. Most businesses generate some goodwill and this gives rise to future economic benefits (it meets the definition of an asset). However, it fails to meet both recognition criteria: it is very difficult to prove that it really exists; and it is impossible to value it objectively. This is why internally generated goodwill and similar intangible assets are not normally recognised in the financial statements.

student notes

Activity 1

A company spends £100,000 on an advertising campaign to promote its products. Should the company recognise an asset?

Complying with IFRSs

- Where financial statements comply with IFRSs this must be stated explicitly in the notes.
- Financial statements must not be described as complying with IFRSs unless they comply with **all** the requirements of IFRSs (an entity cannot comply with some standards and not others, or some requirements of a standard and not others).
- There is an exception to this last rule. In **extremely rare circumstances,** complying with a particular requirement in a standard may result in financial statements that are so misleading that they do not provide useful information. In this situation, an entity departs from that requirement and adopts a different accounting treatment which does present the information fairly. The notes to the financial statements then disclose:
  - that management has concluded that the financial statements present fairly the entity's financial position, financial performance and cash flows;
  - that it has complied with applicable standards, except that it has departed from a particular requirement to achieve a fair presentation;
  - the title of the relevant standard and information about the departure: the treatment that the standard would normally require; the reason why this treatment would be misleading in the circumstances; and the treatment actually adopted; and
  - the financial impact of the departure on each item affected, for each period presented.

Accounting principles

Going concern

Financial statements must be prepared on a going concern basis, unless the entity is not a going concern.

- Management must make an assessment of the entity's ability to continue as a going concern.

student notes

- Any material uncertainties about the entity's ability to continue as a going concern must be disclosed.
- If financial statements are not prepared on a going concern basis, this must be disclosed, together with the reason why the entity is not regarded as a going concern.

Accruals

Financial statements must be prepared on the accruals basis, except for cash flow information.

Consistency of presentation

An entity must present and classify items in the financial statements in the same way from one period to the next unless:

- there has been a significant change in the entity's operations which means that a different presentation is now more appropriate; or
- a new IFRS requires a different presentation.

Materiality and aggregation

Financial statements cannot report every single aspect of every relevant transaction and event, because this would obscure the overall picture. Individual items are aggregated (added together) so that significant totals are shown, rather than individual figures.

This has to be done in such a way that the information is helpful to users, rather than misleading. IAS 1 states that:

- each material class of similar items must be presented separately in the financial statements.
- items that are dissimilar must be presented separately. They cannot be aggregated unless they are individually immaterial.

For example, inventories, receivables and cash are all shown as separate classes of items in the statement of financial position, grouped together under the heading of current assets.

Offset

Assets and liabilities, and income and expenses, should not be offset (netted off against each other) unless this is required or permitted by a standard.

For example, a company may have two bank accounts, one of which is overdrawn. The bank account which is not overdrawn is shown in current assets; the bank overdraft is shown in current liabilities. The two accounts cannot be netted off against each other.

student notes

Comparative information

Comparative figures must be disclosed for the previous period for all amounts reported in the financial statements, unless another standard requires otherwise.

You will almost certainly not be asked to provide comparative figures in the Exam.

Identification of the financial statements

An entity should clearly identify the financial statements and should distinguish them from other information published in the same document.

In many cases a company annual report contains material (such as the Chairman's Statement) that is mainly there to present the company's activities in a favourable light. IFRSs only apply to the financial statements and the notes, not to any other material presented with them. Users need to be able to distinguish between these items.

In addition, the following information must be displayed prominently:

- the name of the reporting entity
- whether the financial statements are for a single entity or a group
- the date at the end of the reporting period, or the period covered
- the currency in which the financial statements are presented (eg, £)
- the level of rounding used (eg, £'000, or £million).

The reporting period

Financial statements should be prepared at least annually.

If the end of the reporting period (year-end) changes so that the financial statements are prepared for a different period, the entity should disclose:

- the reason for the change; and
- the fact that the comparative figures are not entirely comparable.

THE INCOME STATEMENT AND THE STATEMENT OF FINANCIAL POSITION

The formats for the income statement and statement of financial position are shown below. They are very similar to the ones that you met in the previous chapter.

IAS 1 does not actually require specific formats, but it *does* provide illustrations of formats that meet its requirements. The formats shown below

student notes

are adapted from these illustrations and are very similar to the ones that you met in the last chapter.

You will be expected to follow these formats in the Exam. The examiner will provide you with pro-forma statements to fill in.

The statement of comprehensive income

IAS 1 requires a **statement of comprehensive income**. An entity's comprehensive income consists of:

- its profit or loss; and
- other comprehensive income.

Profit or loss is income less expenses.

Other comprehensive income is items of income and expense that are not recognised in profit or loss. For example, when a non-current asset is revalued, the difference between its original cost less depreciation and its fair or market value is not included in profit or loss for the period. Instead, it is recognised as part of other comprehensive income.

We will look at other comprehensive income again in Chapter 4.

IAS 1 allows the statement of comprehensive income to be presented as either a single statement, or as two separate statements:

- an income statement (showing income less expenses to give the profit or loss for the period); and
- a statement of comprehensive income (showing profit or loss and items such as gains and losses where non-current assets are revalued).

In the Exam-based Assessment, you will be asked to draft two separate statements: an income statement; and/or a statement of comprehensive income.

Where an IAS or an IFRS states that an item should be recognised 'in profit or loss', this means that it is included in the income statement section of the statement of comprehensive income or in the separate income statement (if two statements are prepared).

In this chapter we will concentrate on the income statement.

student notes

Format of the income statement

Income statement for the year ended

	£'000
Continuing operations	
Revenue	X
Cost of sales	(X)
Gross profit	X
Distribution costs	(X)
Administrative expenses	(X)
Profit/(loss) from operations	X
Finance costs	(X)
Profit/(loss) before tax	X
Tax	(X)
Profit/(loss) for the period from continuing operations	X
Discontinued operations	
Profit/(loss) for the period from discontinued operations	(X)
Profit/(loss) for the period attributable to equity holders	X

Analysis of expenses

There are two ways of analysing expenses:

- based on the nature of the expenses; or
- based on their function within the entity.

The income statement above analyses expenses based on their function within the entity.

An income statement that analysed expenses based on their nature would show material costs, depreciation and staff costs rather than distribution costs and administrative expenses. You will not be asked to prepare this form of income statement in the Assessment.

Information to be presented in the income statement

- All items of income and expense recognised in a period must be included in profit and loss unless a standard requires or permits otherwise.

- The income statement must include line items that present the following amounts for the period:

  - revenue
  - finance costs
  - tax expense
  - profit or loss.

student notes

- An entity should present additional line items, headings and subtotals in the income statement when this is helpful to users in understanding its financial performance.

Unusual items

In theory, there are two types of unusual item that might need to be disclosed separately in the income statement:

- **Extraordinary items** are material items possessing a high degree of abnormality which arise from events or transactions that fall **outside the ordinary activities** of an entity and which are not expected to recur.

- **Other material items** which derive from events or transactions that fall within the **ordinary activities** of an entity. These need to be disclosed because of their size or incidence if the financial statements are to give a fair presentation of the entity's financial performance. These items are sometimes called **exceptional items**.

IAS 1 states that an entity must not present any item of income and expense as an extraordinary item.

Why IAS 1 prohibits extraordinary items

The bottom half of a pro-forma income statement is shown below. It illustrates the way in which extraordinary items and other material items used to be disclosed, before extraordinary items were prohibited.

Extract from the income statement for the year ended

	£m
Profit from operations	X
Material (exceptional) items	X
Finance costs	(X)
Profit on ordinary activities before tax	X
Tax on profit on ordinary activities	(X)
Profit on ordinary activities after tax	X
Extraordinary items	(X)
Profit for the year	X

Extraordinary items were **not** part of profit on ordinary activities. Therefore they were disclosed below profit on ordinary activities after tax.

Investors and their advisers normally took profit on ordinary activities after tax as the starting point for their analysis of an entity's performance for the year. Preparers of accounts could and often did manipulate the profit figure by treating unusual gains as ordinary material items ('above the line') and treating unusual losses as extraordinary items ('below the line'). This made the entity's performance appear much better than it actually was.

student notes✍

Material items

Material items of income and expense should be disclosed separately. If they are very material, they may need to be disclosed in the income statement, otherwise they are disclosed in the notes to the financial statements.

Examples of items that might need to be disclosed separately:

- losses where inventory or property, plant and equipment are written down
- expenses of restructuring the activities of an entity
- gains or losses on disposal of items of property, plant and equipment
- income from insurance claims or the settlement of legal proceedings.

Discontinued operations

A **discontinued operation** is a component of an entity that has either been disposed of or is held for sale and represents a separate major line of business or geographical area of operations.

If an operation or an asset is classified as held for sale, it should be available for immediate sale and the sale should be highly probable. Management should be committed to the sale (taking active steps to find a buyer) and the sale must be expected to take place within the next twelve months.

- A discontinued operation can be a department or division within a single company or a separate company within a group.
- To qualify as discontinued, the operation and its cash flows must be able to be clearly distinguished, operationally and for financial reporting purposes, from the rest of the entity.

Continuing operations are operations that are not discontinued.

Both IAS 1 and IFRS 5 *Non-current assets held for sale and discontinued operations* require the post tax profit or loss of discontinued operations to be disclosed in the income statement.

Information about discontinued operations enables users to forecast the future performance of an entity. Users are made aware that profits or losses relating to a discontinued operation will not occur in future periods.

Activity 2

The IASB has deliberately made the definition of a discontinued operation quite narrow. Why do you think this might be?

Format of the Statement of financial position

student notes

Statement of financial position at

	£'000
Assets	
Non-current assets	
Intangible assets	X
Property, plant and equipment	X
	X
Current assets	
Inventories	X
Trade and other receivables	X
Cash and cash equivalents	X
	X
Total assets	X
Equity and liabilities	
Equity	
Share capital	X
Share premium	X
Revaluation reserve	X
Retained earnings	X
	X
Non-current liabilities	
Bank loans	X
Long term provisions	X
	X
Current liabilities	
Trade and other payables	X
Tax liabilities	X
Bank overdrafts and loans	X
	X
Total liabilities	X
Total equity and liabilities	X

The statement of financial position only shows total amounts. The analysis of the totals is given in the notes.

Current and non-current assets

The statement of financial position must classify assets and liabilities as either current or non-current.

student notes

Current and non-current assets and liabilities

The statement of financial position must classify assets and liabilities as either current or non-current.

An asset is current if:

- It is expected to be received (as cash or another asset) within the entity's normal operating cycle (within the time that would normally pass between the purchase of inventories and the receipt of cash from their sale as finished goods)
- It is held primarily for trading
- It is expected to be received within twelve months after the reporting period
- It is cash or a cash equivalent (a short term investment or deposit that can be easily converted into cash)

A liability is current if:

- It is expected to be settled within the entity's normal operating cycle
- It is held primarily for trading
- It is due to be settled (paid) within twelve months after the reporting period
- The entity does not have the unconditional right to delay settling it for at least twelve months after the reporting period.

All other assets and liabilities are non-current.

Information to be presented in the statement of financial position

The statement of financial position must include line items that present the following amounts for the period:

- intangible assets
- property, plant and equipment
- investment property (see Chapter 6)
- non-current assets held for sale (see Chapter 6)
- inventories
- trade and other receivables
- cash and cash equivalents
- trade and other payables
- provisions (see Chapter 7)

- liabilities and assets for current tax (see Chapter 7)
- liabilities and assets for deferred tax (see Chapter 7)
- issued capital and reserves attributable to owners (equity shareholders) of the parent.

Further analysis of items in the statement of financial position

The line items shown in the statement of financial position should be analysed further, where this is necessary.

- The analysis can be shown either in the statement of financial position or in the notes.
- Line items should be subclassified in a manner appropriate to the entity's operations.

Examples:

- Property, plant and equipment is analysed into classes, for example: land and buildings, plant and machinery, motor vehicles;
- Receivables are analysed into trade receivables, other receivables and prepayments;
- Inventories are analysed between raw materials, work in progress and goods for resale.

Share capital and reserves

The following must be disclosed, either in the statement of financial position or in the statement of changes in equity (see Chapter 4) (normally) in the notes:

- the number of shares authorised
- the number of shares issued and fully paid
- the par (nominal) value per share
- a description of the nature and purpose of each reserve within equity.
- a reconciliation of the number of shares outstanding at the beginning and at the end of the period.

student notes

student notes

Activity 3

Limited companies have to disclose a great deal of specific information. Why is this?

Notes to the financial statements

Notes provide or disclose information that is not presented in the statement of financial position, the statement of comprehensive income, statement of changes in equity or statement of cash flows:

- where it is required by other IFRSs; or
- where additional information is relevant to an understanding of any of the financial statements.

They should also present information about the basis of presentation of the financial statements and the accounting policies used.

Notes should be presented in a systematic manner. Each item in the main statements should be cross-referenced to any related information in the notes.

Accounting policies

The notes should disclose a summary of significant accounting policies adopted by the entity:

- the measurement basis (or bases) used (for example, historic cost, fair value, net realisable value); and
- other accounting policies that are relevant to an understanding of the financial statements.

Dividends proposed

The notes should also disclose:

- the amount of any dividends proposed or declared before the financial statements were authorised for issue; and
- the amount of dividend per share.

This disclosure is necessary because dividends proposed after the end of the reporting period are not recognised in the financial statements.

Directors' emoluments

Directors' emoluments are directors' salaries and other benefits that they receive as a result of their services as directors, for example, amounts paid into pension schemes on their behalf.

Disclose:

- Total directors' emoluments, analysed between amounts relating to:
  - salaries, fees, bonuses, benefits in kind

- gains on the exercise of share options
- amounts receivable under long term incentive schemes
- company contributions paid to a pension scheme.

- Number of directors accruing benefits under pension schemes.
- Where total directors' emoluments (excluding contributions to pension schemes) are £200,000 or more, disclose the emoluments of the highest paid director, analysed between emoluments and company contributions paid to a pension scheme.

Auditors' remuneration

Disclose the total amount and also separate totals for:

- audit fees and expenses; and
- fees paid to auditors for non-audit work (analysed by type of service (eg tax advice, valuation))

HOW IT WORKS

It is extremely unlikely that you will have to draft financial statements with a full set of notes in your Exam based assessment. However, there is a very good chance that you will be asked to draft an income statement and a statement of financial position in the correct format from a trial balance or an extended trial balance.

The extended trial balance of Cottage Ltd as at 31 December 20X1 is set out on the next page.

You have been given the following further information:

a) The issued share capital of the business consists of ordinary shares with a nominal value of £1.

b) Depreciation has been calculated on all items of property, plant and equipment held by the business and has already been entered on a monthly basis into the distribution costs and administrative expenses ledger balances as shown on the extended trial balance.

c) The corporation tax charge for the year has been calculated as £581,000.

d) The company has paid an interim dividend during the year. It has also proposed a final dividend of 8p per share.

e) Interest on the 8% loan stock has been paid for the first six months of the year only.

Ignore any effect of these adjustments on the tax charge for the year as given above.

student notes

Description	Trial balance Debit £'000	Trial balance Credit £'000	Adjustments Debit £'000	Adjustments Credit £'000	Income statement Debit £'000	Income statement Credit £'000	Statement of financial position Debit £'000	Statement of financial position Credit £'000
Cash at bank	253						253	
8% loan stock		2,700						2,700
Trade receivables	2,709						2,709	
Allowance for doubtful debts		100		35				135
Sales		16,375				16,375		
Purchases	9,620				9,620			
Land and buildings: Cost	2,991						2,991	
Fixtures and fittings: Cost	1,119						1,119	
Motor vehicles: Cost	1,429						1,429	
Office equipment: Cost	322						322	
Returns inwards	122				122			
Inventory	3,602		4,195	4,195	3,602	4,195	4,195	
Accruals				95				95
Prepayments			45				45	
Returns outwards		87				87		
Land and buildings: Accumulated deprecation		330		172				502
Fixtures and fittings: Accumulated depreciation		323		280				603
Motor vehicles: Accumulated depreciation		389		333				722
Office equipment: Accumulated depreciation		36		54				90
Interim dividend	192						192	
Trade payables		1,628						1,628
Interest	108				108			
Distribution costs	2,571		434		3,005			
Administrative expenses	1,895		490		2,385			
Intangible assets	3,208						3,208	
Share capital		3,500						3,500
Retained earnings		3,273						3,273
Share premium		1,400						1,400
Profit					1,815			1,815
	30,141	30,141	5,164	5,164	20,657	20,657	16,463	16,463

The adjustments

student notes

You will probably be asked to set these out in the form of journals. Taking each of the items of further information in turn:

a) No adjustment required

b) No adjustment required

c) Corporation tax:

DEBIT	Corporation tax charge (income statement)	£581,000	
CREDIT	Corporation tax payable (statement of financial position)		£581,000

Being the tax charge for the year ended 31 December 20X1.

d) No adjustment required.

e) Loan stock interest:

DEBIT	Interest payable (income statement)	£108,000	
CREDIT	Accruals (statement of financial position)		£108,000

Being the loan stock interest for the second six months of the year ended 31 December 20X1 (2,700,000 x 8% x 6/12).

The income statement

The figures for distribution costs and administrative expenses are taken straight from the ETB. The others must be built up using workings.

1 Revenue

	£'000
Sales per ETB	16,375
Less returns inwards	(122)
	16,253

2 Cost of sales

	£'000
Opening inventory	3,602
Purchases	9,620
Less returns outwards	(87)
	13,135
Closing inventory	(4,195)
	8,940

student notes

3 Finance costs

This is the loan stock interest of £216,000 (2,700,000 x 8%) (adjustment e)).

4 Tax

This is the corporation tax charge of £581,000 (adjustment c))

We can now draw up the income statement.

Cottage Ltd: Income statement for the year ended 31 December 20X1

	£'000
Continuing operations	
Revenue (W1)	16,253
Cost of sales (W2)	(8,940)
Gross profit	7,313
Distribution costs	(3,005)
Administrative expenses	(2,385)
Profit from operations	1,923
Finance costs (W3)	(216)
Profit before tax	1,707
Tax (W4)	(581)
Profit for the year from continuing operations attributable to equity owners	1,126

The statement of financial position

Again, some of the figures can be taken directly from the ETB, but most of them must be built up from workings.

1 Property, plant and equipment

	Cost	*Acc depn*	
	£'000	£'000	£'000
Land and buildings	2,991	502	2,489
Fixtures and fittings	1,119	603	516
Motor vehicles	1,429	722	707
Office equipment	322	90	232
	5,861	1,917	3,944

2 Trade and other receivables

	£'000
Trade receivables	2,709
Less allowance for doubtful debts	(135)
	2,574
Prepayments	45
	2,619

student notes

3 Trade and other payables

		£'000	£'000
Trade payables			1,628
Accruals:	per ETB	95	
	interest (adjustment e))	108	
			203
			1,831

4 Retained earnings

	£'000
At 1 January 20X1	3,273
Profit for the year	1,126
Dividend paid (from ETB)	(192)
At 31 December 20X1	4,207

We can now draw up the statement of financial position.

Cottage Ltd: Statement of financial position as at 31 December 20X1

Assets	£'000
Non-current assets:	
Intangible assets	3,208
Property, plant and equipment (W1)	3,944
	7,152
Current assets:	
Inventories	4,195
Trade and other receivables (W2)	2,619
Cash and cash equivalents	253
	7,067
Total assets	14,219
Equity and liabilities	
Equity:	
Share capital	3,500
Share premium	1,400
Retained earnings (W4)	4,207
	9,107
Non-current liabilities	
8% loan stock	2,700
Current liabilities	
Trade and other payables (W3)	1,831
Tax liabilities	581
	2,412
Total liabilities	5,112
Total equity and liabilities	14,219

student notes

Further points

- You may find it helpful to tick off each figure in the ETB and the supporting information as you deal with it.

- The format of your workings does not matter as long as they are neat and cross referenced to the main answer. Simple workings, for example, the working for the revenue figure, can be done on the face of the income statement or statement of financial position.

THE DIRECTORS' REPORT

Limited companies must file a directors' report with their annual accounts.

The directors' report is intended to give users of the financial statements a more complete picture of the current position and future prospects of the company.

It should state:

- The names of persons who were directors at any time during the financial year.

- The principal activities of the company during the year.

- The amount (if any) that the directors recommend should be paid as dividends.

The business review

Unless the company is a small company, the directors' report must also contain a business review, which must include:

- a fair review of the company's business; and

- a description of the principal risks and uncertainties facing the company.

The business review must analyse the development and performance of the company's business during the financial year, and the position of the company's business at the end of that year. It must be balanced and must be appropriate to the size and complexity of the business. To achieve this, the directors may need to include information about factors likely to affect the future development of the company's business; the impact of the company's business on the environment; the company's employees; and social and community issues. The business review should also include additional explanations of amounts included in the financial statements, if this would be helpful to users.

Other information required

student notes

This includes:

- Estimates of any significant differences between the book value and the market value of land held as a non-current asset.
- Political and charitable donations made, if these exceeded more than £2,000 in the year.
- Particulars of any important events affecting the company which have occurred since the end of the year.
- An indication of the activities (if any) of the company in the field of research and development.

If the average number of the company's UK employees is more than 250, the company must disclose information about its policies for the employment of disabled persons and in relation to employee involvement.

Public companies and large private companies owned by a public limited company must give details of their policy and practice on payment of creditors.

CHAPTER OVERVIEW

- The Companies Act 2006 states that the directors of a limited company must file annual accounts with the Registrar of Companies
- These can be either 'Companies Act accounts' or 'IAS accounts'
- Every shareholder in a limited company is entitled to receive a copy of the company's annual accounts
- Published IAS accounts consist of:
  - a statement of financial position;
  - a statement of comprehensive income;
  - a statement of changes in equity;
  - a statement of cash flows;
  - notes;
  - a directors' report;
  - an auditors' report.
- Directors have a legal duty to keep proper accounting records
- The published accounts must show a true and fair view/fair presentation: they must comply with the requirements of the Companies Acts and applicable accounting standards
- An item that meets the definition of an element should be recognised if: it is probable that any future economic benefit associated with the item will flow to or from the entity; and the item has a cost or value that can be measured with reliability
- Financial statements must comply with all the requirements of IFRSs that apply
- Where complying with a particular requirement results in financial statements that are misleading, an entity departs from that requirement and discloses information about the departure (extremely rare)
- Financial statements must be prepared on a going concern basis and on the accruals basis
- An entity must present and classify items consistently from one period to the next

KEY WORDS

Published accounts/financial statements the financial statements of limited companies that are circulated to shareholders and filed with the Registrar of Companies (also referred to as statutory accounts)

Companies Act accounts published accounts that comply with the accounting rules in the Companies Act 2006 and with the requirements of UK accounting standards

IAS accounts published accounts that comply with the requirements of IASs/IFRSs

Recognition including an item in the financial statements

Profit or loss income less expenses

Derecognition removing an item from the financial statements

Extraordinary item material items possessing a high degree of abnormality which arise from events or transactions that fall outside the ordinary activities of an entity and which are not expected to recur

Discontinued operation a component of an entity that has either been disposed of or is held for sale and represents a separate major line of business or geographical area of operations

Directors' emoluments directors' salaries and other benefits that they receive as a result of their services as directors, for example, amounts paid into pension schemes on their behalf

Other comprehensive income items of income and expense that are not recognised in profit or loss

CHAPTER OVERVIEW cont.

- Each material class of similar items must be presented separately in the financial statements
- Assets and liabilities, and income and expenses, should not be offset
- Financial statements should be prepared at least annually
- IAS 1 sets out the line items which should be disclosed in the statement of financial position and the income statement
- All items of income and expense recognised in a period must be included in profit or loss (ie in the income statement) unless a standard requires otherwise
- The post tax profit or loss of discontinued operations should be disclosed in the income statement
- The statement of financial position classifies assets and liabilities as either current or non-current
- An asset or a liability is normally current if: it is held primarily for the purpose of being traded; or it is expected to be received or paid within twelve months after the end of the reporting period

HOW MUCH HAVE YOU LEARNED?

1 IAS 1 states that two important accounting principles must be applied when preparing the financial statements. What are they? Accruals and going concern

2 Fill in the gaps:

Income statement for the year ended

	£'000
Revenue	X
Less COGS Purchase + Closing Stock - opening stock	X
Gross profit	X
	X
Less expenses.	X
Profit from operations	X
Finance costs	X
Tax	X
Net Profit	X

3 List the items that appear in the statement of financial position under 'Current assets'.

CASH AND BANK.

4 You are provided with the following balances relating to a company:

	£'000	£'000
Trade receivables	4,294	
Bank overdraft		474
Retained earnings		4,503
Allowance for doubtful debts		171
Land: Cost	3,439	
Buildings: Cost	4,285	
Fixtures and fittings: Cost	1,867	
Motor vehicles: Cost	3,786	
Office equipment: Cost	1,308	
Inventory	3,061	
Trade payables		1,206
Corporation tax		1,458
Buildings: Accumulated depreciation		468
Fixtures and fittings: Accumulated depreciation		649
Motor vehicles: Accumulated depreciation		1,764
Office equipment: Accumulated depreciation		397
Prepayments	94	
Accruals		169
Loan		5,400
Ordinary share capital		3,000
Share premium		1,950
Revaluation reserve		525
	22,134	22,134

Draft a statement of financial position in accordance with the requirements of IAS 1.

chapter 4: REPORTING FINANCIAL PERFORMANCE

chapter coverage

In this chapter we look more closely at an entity's performance and the way in which it is presented in the financial statements. In particular, we look at the idea of other comprehensive income and at the statement that forms the 'bridge' between the statement of comprehensive income and the statement of financial position: the statement of changes in equity. We also explain the requirements of an important accounting standard: IAS 8 *Accounting policies, changes in accounting estimates and errors*.

We also look briefly at two other accounting standards: IAS 33 *Earnings per share* and IFRS 8 *Operating segments*. Earnings per share is an important measure of an entity's performance and it is widely used by investors and their advisors. IAS 33 sets out the way in which it should be calculated. IFRS 8 requires public companies which carry out several different activities to provide information about the performance of each business 'segment'.

The topics that are to be covered are:

- assessing financial performance
- accounting policies
- other comprehensive income
- changes in equity
- segment reporting

KNOWLEDGE AND UNDERSTANDING AND PERFORMANCE CRITERIA COVERAGE

knowledge and understanding

- the UK regulatory framework for financial reporting and the main requirements of relevant financial reporting standards
- preparing financial statements in proper form

Performance criteria – element 11.1

- draft limited company financial statements from the appropriate information
- ensure that limited company financial statements comply with relevant accounting standards and domestic legislation and with the organisation's policies, regulations and procedures

student notes

ASSESSING FINANCIAL PERFORMANCE

What is performance?

Shareholders and other users of the financial statements need information about the financial performance of an entity.

But what exactly is financial performance? The simple view is that it is the amount that is available for distribution to the shareholders, in other words, profit before dividends, or profit after tax.

An alternative view is that financial performance is wider than profit. It is the total return that an entity retains on the resources that it controls and encompasses all gains and losses, whether or not they have actually been realised in the form of cash or are likely to be realised in the near future. It can be expressed using the accounting equation:

PERFORMANCE (INCOME – EXPENSES) =
CLOSING EQUITY – OPENING EQUITY; or

NET GAINS/(LOSSES) =
CHANGE IN NET ASSETS IN THE ACCOUNTING PERIOD.

The IASB has adopted this second, wider view of performance.

The statement of comprehensive income required by IAS 1 shows **total comprehensive income**. IAS 1 defines this as

> The change in equity during a period resulting from transactions and other events, other than those changes resulting from transactions with owners in their capacity as owners.

An entity's total comprehensive income is:

- Its profit or loss for the period; plus
- Its other comprehensive income.

Activity 1

A company has revalued one of its buildings during the year, resulting in a significant gain.

Is the gain part of the company's performance?

Should the gain be included in profit or loss?

student notes

Earnings per share

Earnings per share is an important measure of financial performance. Investors and analysts use it to assess and compare the performance of different companies. It is also used to calculate other important ratios for assessing a company's performance.

IAS 33 *Earnings per share* states that:

- Earnings per share is calculated by dividing the profit or loss for the period attributable to ordinary equity holders (ie, ordinary shareholders) by the weighted average number of ordinary shares outstanding during the period.
- An **ordinary share** is an equity instrument that is subordinate to all other classes of equity instruments. Ordinary shareholders only share in the profit for the period after preference shareholders have received their dividends.
- Therefore the profit or loss for the period attributable to ordinary equity holders is the profit or loss after deducting dividends and other appropriations in respect of preference shares.
- All companies that publicly trade their shares must calculate and disclose earnings per share in the income statement. (In practice, this means that most public companies must disclose earnings per share.)
- Where a company has discontinued operations during the period, earnings per share must be calculated and disclosed in the income statement:
  - for the company as a whole; and
  - for continuing operations.

  Earnings (or loss) per share for discontinued operations is shown in the notes.
- The standard also applies to any other company that chooses to disclose earnings per share.

HOW IT WORKS

At 1 January 20X1 Ranby Ltd had 500,000 ordinary shares of 50p each. On 30 June 20X1 it issued 100,000 new ordinary shares of 50p each.

An extract from the income statement for the year ended 31 December 20X1 is shown below:

student notes

	£'000
Profit before tax	100
Tax	(40)
Profit for the year	60

Dividends of £20,000 were paid during the year, so retained profit for the year was £40,000.

Step 1 Calculate net profit attributable to ordinary equity holders

Net profit attributable to ordinary equity holders is profit after tax, which is £60,000.

Step 2 Calculate the weighted average number of ordinary shares outstanding during the year

There has been a share issue exactly half way through the year. The weighted average number of shares is calculated accordingly:

	£'000
1 January – 30 June (500,000 x 6/12)	250
1 July – 31 December (600,000 x 6/12)	300
	550

Step 3 Calculate earnings per share

Earnings per share is expressed in pence.

$$\frac{\text{Net profit}}{\text{Weighted average number of shares}} \quad \frac{60,000}{550,000} = 10.9\text{p}$$

Using earnings per share

Earnings per share provides a useful starting point for looking at a company's performance and comparing it with the performance of similar companies. However, some users of financial statements focus on earnings per share and do not go any further.

This can cause problems:

- If users only focus on one figure they may miss other important information in the income statement and elsewhere in the financial statements. This other information would give users a far better idea of how a company had performed **and was likely to perform in the future** than the earnings per share figure alone.

- If the performance of a company (and its directors) is judged almost entirely on earnings per share, the directors will be under pressure to make earnings per share as high as possible. This means that they

student notes

may employ 'creative accounting' to boost the figure for profit after tax.

Creative accounting is a term used to describe accounting treatments which are technically within the law and accounting standards but which give a biased impression of a company's performance.

ACCOUNTING POLICIES

Preparers of accounts need to decide how they will treat particular items in the financial statements. For example, they may need to decide how to value a particular item of property, plant and equipment. All preparers of financial statements must select and apply **accounting policies**.

Accounting policies are the specific principles, bases, conventions, rules and practices applied by an entity in preparing and presenting financial statements.

Examples of accounting policies:

- Property, plant and equipment is stated at fair value
- Inventories are valued using the first-in-first out method

As well as selecting accounting policies, preparers of accounts have to make accounting estimates to arrive at amounts for items such as bad debts and useful lives of assets. There are accepted techniques for making estimates, for example:

- Methods of depreciation (such as straight line and reducing balance)
- Methods of estimating allowances for doubtful debts

These methods and techniques are **not** accounting policies.

In basic terms, an accounting policy determines:

- how and when an item is recognised;
- how (the basis) on which an item is measured; or
- how an item is presented.

Selecting accounting policies

IAS 8 *Accounting policies, changes in accounting estimates and errors* describes the way in which accounting policies should be selected. It states that:

- Where a specific IAS or IFRS applies to a transaction or event, this should be followed.

student notes

- Where there is no standard that specifically applies, management must use judgement. The accounting policy selected must result in information that is:

  – relevant to the economic decision making needs of users; and
  – reliable.

  Relevant and reliable have the same meanings as in the IASB *Framework*.

- When judging what is the most appropriate accounting policy, management should refer to the following sources of guidance:

  – standards dealing with similar and related issues; then

  – the definitions, recognition criteria and measurement concepts for assets, liabilities, income and expenses in the *Framework*. (We will look briefly at this process in a later chapter.)

- Management may also consider recent pronouncements of other standard setting bodies (eg, the UK Accounting Standards Board) and accepted industry practices, if these do not conflict with international standards and the *Framework*.

Activity 2

What are the characteristics of reliable information?

Consistency

An entity should select and apply its accounting policies consistently for similar transactions, other events and conditions, unless a standard requires otherwise.

Changes in accounting policy

A company should only change an accounting policy if the change:

- is required by a standard; or

- results in the financial statements providing reliable and more relevant information.

The following are **not** changes in accounting policy:

- the introduction of an accounting policy where there are transactions or events that are clearly different in substance from those previously occurring;

- a change in an accounting estimate.

student notes

It can sometimes be difficult to tell the difference between a change in an accounting policy and a change in an accounting estimate. A change in accounting policy results in a change to:

- the way in which an item is recognised; or
- the way in which an item is presented; or
- the way in which an item is measured.

Activity 3

An entity has previously depreciated vehicles using the reducing balance method at 40% per year. It now uses the straight line method over a period of five years.

Is this a change in accounting policy or a change in accounting estimate?

Applying changes in accounting policies

An accounting policy may have to be changed because a new standard has been introduced. Most new standards contain transitional arrangements, which explain how the change should be dealt with. Any transitional arrangements must be followed.

There are two possible ways of dealing with a change in accounting policy:

- **retrospective application**: adjusting the financial statements so that they appear as if the new accounting policy has always been followed.

- **prospective application**: adjusting the financial statements so that the new policy is followed from the date of the change; the full effect of the change is included in the profit or loss for the current period.

IAS 8 states that where there are no transitional arrangements in a new standard, or where the entity has chosen to change an accounting policy, the change must be applied **retrospectively**.

This involves:

- restating the comparative figures for the preceding period in the income statement and statement of financial position and the notes; and

- adjusting the opening balance of retained earnings.

This process is often called making a **prior period adjustment** or making a prior year adjustment.

student notes

HOW IT WORKS

Changeable Ltd was incorporated on 1 January 20X1. In the first two years' accounts it did not charge depreciation on certain freehold properties. The directors then decided that starting with the year ended 31 December 20X3, it should depreciate all property, plant and equipment.

Depreciation that would have been charged if the new policy had been applied from incorporation:

Year	£'000
20X1	30
20X2	60

The accounts for the year ended 31 December 20X2 showed the following movements on retained earnings.

	£'000
Retained earnings at 1 January 20X2	1,470
Retained earnings for the year	910
Retained earnings at 31 December 20X2	2,380

Profit for the year ended 31 December 20X3 (applying the new policy) is £915,000.

The prior period adjustment is the difference between retained earnings as reported and opening retained earnings as they would have been if the new policy had always been applied. This is £90,000 (30,000 + 60,000).

Movements on the retained earnings reserve are as follows:

	20X3	*20X2*
	£'000	£'000
Retained earnings at the beginning of the year:	2,380	1,470
Change in accounting policy	(90)	(30)
Restated balance	2,290	1,440
Retained earnings for the year	915	850
Retained earnings at the end of the year	3,205	2,290

Changes in accounting estimates

Where there is a change in accounting estimate, the change must be recognised **prospectively**.

The effect is included in profit or loss only in the period of the change. There is no prior period adjustment.

student notes

Errors

Sometimes errors are made in preparing financial statements and these are not discovered until the following year, or even later. When they are discovered they must be corrected.

IAS 8 defines **prior period errors** as omissions from, and misstatements in, an entity's financial statements for one or more prior periods.

They arise from a failure to use reliable information that:

- was available when the financial statements were authorised for issue; and
- could reasonably be expected to have been obtained and taken into account.

They can include:

- mathematical mistakes;
- mistakes in applying accounting policies;
- oversights;
- misinterpretations of facts; and
- fraud.

Activity 4

In its financial statements for the year ended 31 December 20X3, a company makes an allowance of £30,000 for doubtful debts (based on a percentage of all trade receivables outstanding at the year-end date). After the financial statements have been published, it is discovered that the actual amount of debts not recovered is £50,000.

Is this a prior period error? If not, why not?

IAS 8 states that **material** prior period errors must be corrected **retrospectively**. The financial statements must be restated as if the error had never occurred.

The method is the same as for a change in accounting policy: restate the comparative figures for the preceding period and adjust the opening balance of retained earnings.

OTHER COMPREHENSIVE INCOME

IAS 1 states that all items of income and expense recognised in a period should be included in profit or loss (the income statement) for that period, unless another standard requires otherwise.

student notes

An entity may have items of income and expense that are not recognised in profit or loss. Examples are:

- gains and losses on revaluation of non-current assets (normally property, plant and equipment)
- some types of foreign currency translation differences.

Because these items are part of total comprehensive income, they are recognised as **other comprehensive income**. They are shown either in a single statement of comprehensive income, below profit or loss, or in a separate statement of comprehensive income, after the income statement.

The statement of comprehensive income provides users of the financial statements with useful information by bringing together all the income and expenses of an entity for an accounting period. It provides users with useful information about the different components of an entity's performance and highlights the effect of items such as revaluation gains.

You may have to deal with revaluation gains and losses in the Exam-based Assessment. It is unlikely that you will have to deal with any other items recognised in other comprehensive income.

Example of a statement of comprehensive income (a single statement including profit and loss)

Statement of comprehensive income for the year ended

	£'000
Continuing operations	
Revenue	X
Cost of sales	(X)
Gross profit	X
Distribution costs	(X)
Administrative expenses	(X)
Profit/(loss) from operations	X
Finance costs	(X)
Profit/(loss) before tax	X
Tax	(X)
Profit/(loss) for the period from continuing operations	X
Discontinued operations	
Profit/(loss) for the period from discontinued operations	(X)
Profit/(loss) for the period attributable to equity holders	X
Other comprehensive income for the period:	
Gains on property revaluation	X
Tax in respect of items in other comprehensive income	X
Other comprehensive income for the period, net of tax	X
Total comprehensive income for the year attributable to equity holders	X

student notes

Example of a statement of comprehensive income (where there is a separate income statement)

If an entity chooses to prepare two statements, the statement below would be presented immediately after the income statement.

Statement of comprehensive income for the year ended

	£'000
Profit/(loss) for the period	X
Other comprehensive income for the period:	
Gains on property revaluation	X
Tax in respect of items in other comprehensive income	X
Other comprehensive income for the period, net of tax	X
Total comprehensive income for the year	X

In the Exam-Based Assessment you will be asked to produce two statements: an income statement and (possibly) a separate statement of comprehensive income.

CHANGES IN EQUITY

We have seen that when there is a change in an accounting policy or where a material prior period error is discovered, IAS 8 requires the effect of the change or correction to be taken directly to equity (the retained earnings reserve). It is not included in the statement of comprehensive income (or income statement) unless it relates to the current year.

Therefore IAS 1 has introduced the statement of changes in equity. This can be thought of as a 'bridge' between the statement of comprehensive income and the statement of financial position.

What the statement shows

IAS 1 requires the following items to be shown in the statement of changes in equity:

- total comprehensive income for the period (from the statement of comprehensive income)
- the effects of changes in accounting policies (retrospective application) for each component of equity (ie, for share capital and each reserve)
- the effects of correcting prior period errors (retrospective restatement) for each component of equity
- the amounts of transactions with owners in their capacity as owners (share issues and the payment of dividends)
- a reconciliation between the amounts at the beginning and the end of the period for each component of equity. Each change must be separately disclosed.

student notes

IAS 1 also requires disclosure of the amount of dividends recognised as distributions to owners during the period and the amount per share. This can be presented either in the statement of changes in equity or in the notes.

Example of a statement of changes in equity

Statement of changes in equity for the year ended

	Share capital	Revaluation reserve	Retained earnings	Total equity
	£'000	£'000	£'000	£'000
Balance at beginning of year	X	X	X	X
Changes in accounting policy			(X)	(X)
Restated balance	X	X	X	X
Changes in equity for the year				
Total comprehensive income for the year		X	X	X
Dividends			(X)	(X)
Issue of share capital	X	X		X
Balance at end of year	X	X	X	X

Activity 5

Chickpea Ltd made a profit of £609,000 for the year ended 31 December 20X3.

During the year:

a) freehold properties were revalued, resulting in a gain of £125,000

b) the company issued £200,000 new £1 ordinary shares at a price of £1.50 each

c) a dividend of £100,000 was paid to equity shareholders.

Total equity at 1 January 20X3 was £2,020,000.

Draft a statement of comprehensive income and a statement of changes in equity (total column only) for the year ended 31 December 20X3.

student notes

SEGMENT REPORTING

Some companies carry out several different activities or operate in several different geographical locations. Users of the accounts need information that enables them to judge how profitable each of these operations is and how each of them contributes to the company's total sales revenue and profit.

Suppose that a company has three divisions, each operating in a different country. The following information is available:

	Revenue	*Net profit*
	£'000	£'000
UK	10,000	200
USA	25,000	(200)
Mexico	2,000	500
	37,000	500

The total amounts for revenue and net profit would tell the reader very little on their own. The figures for each geographical market give the reader much more information: the USA operation is the biggest but makes a loss, while the operation in Mexico is the smallest but is highly profitable. Comparative figures for the previous year would provide still more information: the reader would be able to see whether, for example, the company has been withdrawing its business from the USA and expanding its operations in Mexico.

Segmental information:

- helps users to understand an entity's past performance and therefore to assess its future prospects
- makes users aware of the impact that changes in significant components of a business have on the business as a whole.

IFRS 8 Operating segments

IFRS 8 applies to public companies (those whose equity or debt securities are publicly traded) and to companies in the process of becoming public companies. IFRS 8 also applies to other companies that choose to disclose segment information.

IFRS 8 states that an entity should disclose the following information for each of its operating segments:

- profit or loss
- total assets
- total liabilities (if management uses this information to make decisions about the entity).

student notes

IFRS 8 defines an operating segment as a component of an entity:

- that engages in business activities from which it earns revenues and incurs expenses;
- whose operating results are regularly reviewed by the entity's chief operating decision maker to make decisions about resources to be allocated to the segment and to assess its performance; and
- for which discrete financial information is available.

Management receives financial and other information at regular intervals to enable it to see how the company has performed and to make decisions about the future running of the business. Most companies analyse this information between different parts of the business. Usually this analysis is based on different products and services or on different geographical markets. Each of these different parts of the business is an operating segment.

Entities must also disclose:

- the factors used to identify the entity's reportable segments, including the basis of segmentation (for example, whether segments are based on products and services, geographical areas or a combination of these).
- the types of products and services from which each reportable segment derives its revenues.

Why the usefulness of segmental information is limited

There are a number of problems:

- The directors define segments. There is still some scope for 'hiding' loss making divisions.
- Because the identification of segments depends on judgement and the way in which the entity is organised, segment information is not normally comparable with that of other companies.
- It can be difficult to allocate common costs to segments and to deal with inter-segment transactions.

CHAPTER OVERVIEW

- Users of the financial statements need information about the financial performance of an entity
- Financial performance (income – expenses) = closing equity – opening equity (change in net assets in the accounting period)
- All companies that publicly trade their shares must calculate and disclose earnings per share in the income statement
- Earnings per share = $\frac{\text{net profit/loss after tax}}{\text{weighted average number of ordinary shares}}$
- Selecting an accounting policy:
  - follow any applicable IAS/IFRS
  - if none, management uses judgement
  - the policy selected must result in information that is relevant and reliable
- An entity should select and apply its accounting policies consistently for similar transactions, other events and conditions, unless a standard requires otherwise
- A company should only change an accounting policy if the change is required by a standard; or results in reliable and more relevant information
- Changes in accounting policy are normally applied retrospectively. This involves:
  - restating the comparative figures for the preceding period in the income statement and balance sheet and the notes; and
  - adjusting the opening balance of retained earnings
- Changes in accounting estimates are recognised prospectively; the effect is included in profit or loss only in the period of the change
- Material prior period errors must be corrected retrospectively; so that the financial statements appear as if the error had never occurred

KEY WORDS

Creative accounting accounting treatments which are technically within the law and accounting standards but which give a biased impression of a company's performance

Accounting policies the specific principles, bases, conventions, rules and practices applied by an entity in preparing and presenting financial statements

Prior period errors omissions from, and misstatements in, an entity's financial statements for one or more prior periods

Total comprehensive income The change in equity during a period resulting from transactions and other events, other than those changes resulting from transactions with owners in their capacity as owners

Operating segment a component of an entity that engages in business activities from which it earns revenue and incurs expenses and whose operating results are regularly reviewed by the entity's chief operating decision maker in order to make decisions about resources to be allocated to the segment and to assess its performance

CHAPTER OVERVIEW cont.

- The statement of comprehensive income shows the profit or loss for the year and items such as revaluation gains and losses which are not recognised in profit or loss.
- The statement of changes in equity shows the movements in share capital and in each reserve for the year:
  - changes in accounting policies;
  - correction of prior period errors;
  - total comprehensive income for the year;
  - issues of share capital;
  - dividends paid.

HOW MUCH HAVE YOU LEARNED?

1 A company has the following issued share capital:

	£
Ordinary shares of 50p each	250,000

Profit for the year is £17,500.

Calculate earnings per share.

2 Fill in the gaps

.... are the specific principles, bases, conventions, rules and practices applied by an entity in .... and ....

3 There are two acceptable reasons for changing an accounting policy. What are they?

4 Changes in accounting policy are always applied retrospectively. True or false?

5 Below are two statements about prior period errors.

1 All prior period errors must be corrected.

2 The correction of a prior period error affects the opening balance of retained earnings.

Which of the statements are correct?

A 1 only
B 2 only
C Both statements
D Neither statement

6 Extracts from the accounts of Light Ltd are shown below:

Income statement for the year ended 31 December 20X5 (extract):

	£'000
Profit before tax	500
Tax	(200)
Profit for the year	300

Equity at 1 January 20X5:

Share capital (£1 ordinary shares)	1,000
Share premium	300
Retained earnings	700
	2,000

The following transactions and events took place during the year:

On 31 December 20X5 a freehold property was revalued to £500,000 and this valuation was incorporated into the financial statements. The property had previously been carried at historic cost less depreciation and had a net book value of £350,000 immediately before the revaluation.

On 1 July 20X5 the company issued a further 100,000 £1 ordinary shares at a market price of £1.20.

On 31 December 20X5 the company paid a dividend of £50,000.

a) Draft a statement of comprehensive income for the year ended 31 December 20X5 (assuming that Light presents a separate income statement).

b) Draft a statement of changes in equity for the year ended 31 December 20X5.

Profit 300
Revaluation 150
450

Retained earnings 700
Share Capital (1000+100) 1100
Share Premium (300+20) 320
Retained earnings 450
Dividends (50)
2520

chapter 5: THE STATEMENT OF CASH FLOWS

chapter coverage

In this chapter we introduce the statement of cash flows (sometimes called the cash flow statement). The income statement and the statement of financial position provide information about an entity's performance and financial position. The statement of cash flows, as its name suggests, shows the way in which an entity has generated and spent cash. IAS 7 *Statement of cash flows* requires companies to include a statement of cash flows in their annual accounts and sets out the way in which the statement should be prepared and presented.

The topics that we shall cover are:

- the importance of cash
- IAS 7 *Statement of cash flows*
- classifying cash flows
- calculating cash generated from operations
- preparing the statement of cash flows
- how useful is the statement of cash flows?
- interpreting the statement of cash flows

KNOWLEDGE AND UNDERSTANDING AND PERFORMANCE CRITERIA COVERAGE

knowledge and understanding

- the UK regulatory framework for financial reporting and the main requirements of relevant financial reporting standards
- preparing financial statements in proper form

Performance criteria – element 11.1

- draft limited company financial statements from the appropriate information
- ensure that limited company financial statements comply with relevent accounting standards and domestic legislation and with the organisation's policies, regulations and procedures
- prepare and interpret a limited company cash flow statement

student notes

THE IMPORTANCE OF CASH

However profitable a business may appear to be, it will not survive without adequate cash. Businesses need cash to pay suppliers and employees, to pay dividends to shareholders, to repay debt to lenders and to purchase property, plant, equipment and inventories to enable them to go on producing goods or providing services.

The needs of users

Users of the financial statements can get information about an entity's performance from the statement of comprehensive income (or separate income statement). The statement of financial position shows the financial position (state of affairs) of the entity. Users also need information about the liquidity and solvency of an entity; the cash resources that it has and its ability to pay its debts as they fall due. They also need information about **financial adaptability**; an entity's ability to take effective action to alter the amount and timing of its cash flows in order to respond to unexpected needs or opportunities.

Why profit is not the same as cash flow

The income statement and statement of financial position are drawn up on an accruals basis. Income and expenditure are recognised in the period in which they are earned and incurred, rather than the period in which they are received or paid. These can be very different. The period in which an item is recognised in the income statement and statement of financial position may depend on:

- the accounting policies adopted and the estimates used by the entity
- the judgement of the directors (where estimates have to be made).

Cash flow is a matter of fact (it can be verified by looking at the entity's bank statement). It is difficult to manipulate and is less likely to be distorted by 'creative accounting'.

Activity 1

Why might a loan creditor be more interested in cash flow than in profit?

student notes

IAS 7 Statement of cash flows

IAS 7 requires all companies to include a statement of cash flows in their published accounts. A **statement of cash flows** summarises all movements of cash into and out of a business during the accounting period.

Basic format of the statement of cash flows

IAS 7 requires entities to classify their cash inflows and outflows under three standard headings. These are:

- operating activities
- investing activities
- financing activities

The total cash flows for each heading are totalled to give the net inflow or outflow of cash and cash equivalents for the period.

Cash and cash equivalents

Cash flows are inflows and outflows of cash and cash equivalents.

For most entities, 'cash' is made up of several different items: cash in hand, bank current accounts, deposits and loans. IAS 7 defines cash as:

- cash in hand (bank current accounts and petty cash); and
- demand deposits (ie, deposits repayable on demand).

In practice, cash also includes bank overdrafts if (as is usual) they are repayable on demand.

Cash equivalents are short-term, highly liquid investments that are readily convertible to known amounts of cash and which are subject to an insignificant risk of changes in value.

Many entities may use short term investments in order to manage their cash flow. Surplus cash is put into deposit accounts or used to buy investments in order to generate additional cash flow from interest or dividends. IAS 7 suggests that an investment is normally a cash equivalent if it matures within three months of the date of acquisition.

By basing the statement of cash flows on cash and cash equivalents, rather than simply on bank accounts and petty cash, IAS 7 enables users of the statement of cash flows to appreciate the way in which entities manage cash flow in practice. There is a potential problem because it can be difficult to decide whether or not a current asset investment is actually a cash equivalent; the classification can be subjective.

In the exam it will be made clear if a current asset investment is a cash equivalent.

CLASSIFYING CASH FLOWS

student notes

Operating activities

IAS 7 defines **operating activities** as the principal revenue producing activities of the entity and other activities that are not investing or financing activities.

Cash flows from operating activities consist of:

- cash received from customers (receipts from the sale of goods or the rendering of services)
- cash paid to suppliers for goods and services
- cash paid to and on behalf of employees.

In other words, the net cash flow from operating activities can be thought of as profit from operations adjusted for non-cash items.

Cash flows from operating activities also include payments and refunds of income tax unless they can be specifically identified with investing or financing activities. Corporation tax payments relate to profits from operations and so they are a cash flow from operating activities.

Investing activities

Investing activities are the acquisition and disposal of long-term assets and other investments not included in cash equivalents.

Cash flows from investing activities include:

- payments to acquire property, plant or equipment and other long-term assets
- receipts from sales of property, plant and equipment and other long term assets
- payments to acquire investments other than cash equivalents
- receipts from sales of investments other than cash equivalents
- cash advances and loans made to other parties and receipts from their repayment

Cash flows from investing activities also include cash flows from sales and purchases of investments in subsidiaries (other companies that the investor controls) and other businesses. These are unlikely to feature in your Assessment because you will not be asked to prepare a statement of cash flows for a group of companies.

student notes

Cash flows from acquisitions and disposals of subsidiaries and other businesses should be presented separately in the statement of cash flows.

Financing activities

Financing activities are activities that result in changes in the size and composition of the contributed equity (share capital) and borrowings of the entity.

The main cash flows included under this heading are:

- proceeds from issuing shares
- proceeds from issuing debentures and other loans
- repayment of amounts borrowed

Interest and dividends

IAS 7 does not assign cash flows relating to interest and dividends to a specific heading.

For example, interest paid is often shown under operating activities because it is deducted in arriving at the profit for the period. It could also be shown under financing activities, because it is a cost of obtaining finance.

Interest and dividends received are normally shown under investing activities because they are returns on investments, but in some cases it might be possible to justify a different treatment. For example, a financial institution such as a bank would probably classify them as operating cash flows.

Dividends paid can be shown either under cash flows from operating activities or (normally) under cash flows from financing activities.

IAS 7 states that from interest and dividends received and paid should be disclosed separately and that they must be classified in a consistent manner from period to period.

Activity 2

Which of the following items is always included in the statement of cash flows under the heading 'cash flows from financing activities'?

A Cash received from the sale of property, plant and equipment
B Equity dividends paid
C Interest received
D Repayment of loans

student notes

Net cash flows and gross cash flows

The total cash flow reported under each of the standard headings may be made up of several different items. For example, the net cash outflow for investing activities may be cash paid to purchase property, plant and equipment less cash received from the disposal of property, plant and equipment.

The total cash flows are the **net cash flows**. The individual cash flows are **gross cash flows**. Major classes of gross cash receipts and gross cash payments arising from investing and financing activities must be disclosed separately.

CALCULATING CASH GENERATED FROM OPERATIONS

There are two methods of arriving at this figure:

- List and total the actual cash flows: cash received from customers less cash paid to suppliers and cash paid to and on behalf of employees. This is known as the **direct method**.
- Adjust profit for non-cash items such as depreciation, movements in working capital (normally inventories, receivables and payables) and any items that relate to investing or financing activities. This is known as the **indirect method**.

IAS 7 allows either method.

The indirect method

Using this method, the first part of the statement of cash flows is a reconciliation of profit from operations or profit before tax to cash generated from operations:

Cash flows from operating activities

	£'000
Profit from operations	X
Depreciation	X
(Increase)/decrease in inventory	X
(Increase)/decrease in receivables	X
Increase/(decrease) in payables	X
Cash generated from operations	X

student notes

HOW IT WORKS

A company has a profit from operations of £20,500 for the year ended 31 December 20X2. The depreciation charge for the year is £4,000. Profit from operations also includes a loss on disposal of £500 on an item of plant.

Extracts from the statement of financial position are shown below:

	20X2	*20X1*
	£	£
Inventory	17,400	16,100
Receivables	21,500	20,500
Trade payables	18,400	17,600

The company's profit is adjusted for non-cash items in order to arrive at the cash inflow from operating activities.

Step 1 Add back depreciation

Depreciation has been charged in arriving at profit from operations, but it does not involve the movement of cash. Therefore it is added back to profit from operations.

Step 2 Adjust for any profits or losses on the disposal of assets

The cash received from the sale of an asset is not a cash flow from operating activities. The profit or loss on sale must be removed from profit from operations:

- a profit on disposal is deducted;
- a loss on disposal is added back.

Step 3 Adjust for changes in working capital (inventories, receivables and payables)

The movements in working capital represent the differences between sales and cash received and purchases and cash paid.

Suppose that sales for the year were £100,000. Opening receivables were £20,500 and closing receivables were £21,500. Therefore cash received was £99,000: £1,000 less than the sales figure. The difference between sales and cash inflow is the difference between opening receivables and closing receivables: £1,000.

Suppose that total operating expenses were £75,000:

- Opening inventories were £16,100 and closing inventories were £17,400. This means that total purchases were £76,300 (75,000 + 17,400 – 16,100).

student notes

- Opening payables were £17,600 and closing payables were £18,400. Therefore cash paid was £75,500 (76,300 + 17,600 – 18,400).
- The difference between operating expenses and cash inflow is £500, which is the difference between opening and closing inventories (£1,300 increase) less the difference between opening and closing payables (£800 increase).

In practice we simply adjust profit for the differences between the opening and closing amounts:

- Increase in inventories: deduct £1,300 (cash outflow)
- Increase in receivables: deduct £1,000 (cash outflow)
- Increase in trade payables: add £800 (cash inflow)

We can now draw up a reconciliation of profit from operations to cash generated from operations:

Profit from operations

	£'000
Profit from operations	20,500
Depreciation	4,000
Loss on disposal of property, plant & equipment	500
Increase in inventories	(1,300)
Increase in receivables	(1,000)
Decrease in payables	800
Cash generated from operations	23,500

This information helps users of the financial statements to understand the difference between profit and cash flow. It also shows the movements on the individual items within working capital. This enables users to see how successful or otherwise the entity has been in managing inventories, receivables and payables in order to generate cash.

The direct method

An entity may choose to show the net cash flow from operating activities using the direct method. This summarises the actual cash flows as follows:

	£'000	£'000
Cash received from customers	X	
Cash payments to suppliers	(X)	
Cash paid to and on behalf of employees	(X)	
Other payments of cash	(X)	
Cash generated from operations		X

The advantage of the direct method is that by showing the actual cash flows it enables users to see how the company generates and uses cash.

student notes

HOW IT WORKS

A company has profit from operations of £20,500 for the year ended 31 December 20X2. This was made up as follows:

	£
Revenue	100,000
Cost of sales	(59,700)
Gross profit	40,300
Other expenses (including depreciation of £4,000, loss on disposal of £500 and wages and salaries of £10,500)	(19,800)
Profit from operations	20,500

Extracts from the statement of financial position are shown below:

	20X2	*20X1*
	£	£
Inventories	17,400	16,100
Receivables	21,500	20,500
Trade payables	18,400	17,600

Step 1 Calculate cash received from customers

Receivables

	£		£
Balance b/f	20,500	Cash received (bal fig)	99,000
Sales	100,000	Balance c/f	21,500
	120,500		120,500

Step 2 Calculate cash paid to suppliers

Purchases:

	£
Cost of sales	59,700
Add: closing inventory	17,400
Less: opening inventory	(16,100)
	61,000
Operating expenses (19,800 – 4,500 – 10,500)	4,800
	65,800

Trade payables

	£		£
Cash paid (bal fig)	65,000	Balance b/f	17,600
Balance c/f	18,400	Purchases	65,800
	83,400		83,400

student notes

Step 3 Calculate cash generated from operations

	£	£
Cash received from customers	99,000	
Cash payments to suppliers	(65,000)	
Cash paid to and on behalf of employees	(10,500)	
Cash generated from operations		23,500

Activity 3

Extracts from the statement of financial position of Barking Ltd are shown below:

	20X6	*20X5*
	£	£
Inventory	5,100	5,800
Receivables and prepayments	7,500	7,000
Cash at bank	1,700	1,400
Trade payables	4,700	5,200
Accruals	1,000	800

Profit from operations and depreciation for the year ended 30 June 20X6 were £20,000 and £5,000 respectively.

What is the cash generated from operations for the year ended 30 June 20X6?

PREPARING THE STATEMENT OF CASH FLOWS

In the Exam-Based Assessment, the statement of cash flows is drafted in two parts:

- a reconciliation of profit from operations to net cash flow from operating activities; this shows the cash flows from operating activities using either the direct or the indirect method;
- a statement of cash flows showing cash flows from investing activities, cash flows from financing activities and the net movement in cash and cash equivalents for the period.

You may be asked to prepare either or both parts.

In practice, different formats are possible. For example, the illustration in IAS 7 *Statement of cash flows* shows a single statement starting with profit before tax and with the reconciliation section headed 'Cash flows from operating activities'. All the formats show the same information, presented slightly differently.

student notes

In the Assessment, you will be given a pro-forma to follow.

Reconciliation of profit from operations to net cash inflow from operating activities for the year ended 31 December 20X2

	£'000
Profit from operations	3,350
Adjustments for:	
Depreciation	490
Gain on disposal of property, plant and equipment	(100)
Operating cash flows before movements in working capital	3,740
Decrease in inventories	1,050
Increase in trade and other receivables	(500)
Decrease in trade payables	(1,740)
Cash generated from operations	2,550
Interest paid	(270)
Tax paid	(900)
Net cash from operating activities	1,380

Statement of cash flows for the year ended 31 December 20X2

	£'000	£'000
Net cash from investing activities		1,380
Investing activities		
Purchase of property, plant and equipment	(900)	
Proceeds on disposal of property, plant and equipment	20	
Interest received	200	
Dividends received	200	
Net cash used in investing activities		(480)
Financing activities		
Proceeds of share issue	250	
New bank loans raised	160	
Dividends paid	(1,200)	
Net cash used in financing activities		(790)
Net increase in cash and cash equivalents		110
Cash and cash equivalents at beginning of period (note)		120
Cash and cash equivalents at end of period (note)		230

student notes

Note: Cash and cash equivalents

	20X2	*20X1*
	£'000	£'000
Cash on hand and balances with banks	40	25
Short-term investments	190	95
	230	120

IAS 7 requires this note, which discloses the components of cash and cash equivalents and reconciles the amounts in the statement of cash flows with the equivalent items reported in the statement of financial position.

This note is not often required in the Exam-Based Assessment. The Assessor will ask you to draft the note, if it is required.

Activity 4

Draft the statement of cash flows from the information provided below:

Cash flows	£
Cash and cash equivalents at the beginning of the period	7,000
Cash generated from operations	56,000
Proceeds on disposal of property, plant and equipment	10,000
Dividends paid	8,000
Dividends received	4,000
Increase in cash and cash equivalents for the period	10,000
Interest paid	3,000
Proceeds of share issue	50,000
Purchase of property, plant and equipment	65,000
Repayment of long-term loan	20,000
Tax paid	14,000

student notes

HOW IT WORKS

The statement of financial position of Flow Ltd for the year ended 31 December 20X7 is shown below, together with comparative figures.

	20X7		20X6	
	£'000	£'000	£'000	£'000
Assets				
Property, plant and equipment:				
Cost		720		480
Less: depreciation		(240)		(150)
		480		330
Current assets:				
Inventory	130		110	
Trade and other receivables	180		110	
Cash and cash equivalents	–		30	
		310		250
Total assets		790		580
Equity and liabilities				
Equity:				
Share capital		70		60
Share premium		30		20
Retained earnings		320		250
		420		330
Non-current liabilities:				
Long term borrowings		210		150
Current liabilities				
Trade payables	80		50	
Tax liabilities	50		40	
Accruals	10		10	
Bank overdraft	20		–	
		160		100
Total liabilities		370		250
Total equity and liabilities		790		580

The summarised income statement for the year ended 31 December 20X7 is shown below:

	£'000
Profit from operations	170
Interest payable	(20)
Profit before tax	150
Tax	(40)
Profit for the year	110

student notes

During the year the company sold non-current assets which had originally cost £50,000 and which had a carrying amount (net book value) of £30,000. The loss on the sale of these assets was £10,000.

Step 1 Reconstruct the non-current asset accounts

This gives us:

- the depreciation charge (which is needed to calculate cash generated from operations)
- cash paid to acquire property, plant and equipment and cash received from asset disposals (reported under investing activities)

For many of the workings it is helpful to use 'T' accounts.

Property, plant and equipment: cost

	£'000		£'000
Balance b/f	480	Disposals	50
Additions: cash paid (balancing figure)	**290**	Balance c/f	720
	770		770

Property, plant and equipment: depreciation

	£'000		£'000
Disposals (50 – 30)	20	Balance b/f	150
Balance c/f	240	**Charge for year (balancing figure)**	**110**
	260		260

Cash received from disposals:

	£'000
Carrying amount (net book value)	30
Loss on disposal	(10)
	20

Step 2 Calculate cash generated from operations

Add back depreciation and loss on disposal of assets to profit from operations. Loss on disposal of assets is a non-cash item and also it relates to investing activities. Then adjust for movements in inventories, receivables, trade payables and accruals.

Inventories have increased, so cash has been used to pay for the extra goods. Receivables and payables have both increased, meaning that less cash has been collected from customers and less cash has been paid to suppliers than in previous periods.

student notes

The increase in inventories and receivables is deducted from profit (cash outflow) and the increase in payables is added to profit (cash inflow).

	£'000
Profit from operations	170
Adjustments for:	
Depreciation	110
Loss on sale of property, plant and equipment	10
Operating cash flows before movements in working capital	290
Increase in inventories (130 – 110)	(20)
Increase in receivables (180 – 110)	(70)
Increase in payables (90 – 60)	30
Cash generated from operations	230

Step 3 Interest and tax

There are no accruals for interest payable. Therefore the figure is taken directly from the income statement.

If there have been no over or underprovisions of tax:

- the figure in the income statement will be the same as the closing liability in the statement of financial position
- the cash paid in the period will be equal to the opening liability in the statement of financial position.

In this case, the income statement figure is different from the closing liability. We must reconstruct the ledger account in order to arrive at the cash outflow. Again, it is useful to draw up a 'T' account.

Tax

	£'000		£'000
Cash paid (bal fig)	**30**	Balance b/f	40
Balance c/f	50	Income statement	40
	80		80

We can now complete the reconciliation of profit from operations to net cash from operating activities.

	£'000
Cash generated from operations	230
Interest paid	(20)
Tax paid	(30)
Net cash from operating activities	180

student notes

Step 4 Investments and financing

In this case, all the cash flows are simply the differences between the opening and closing figures in the statement of financial position.

The cash inflow from the issue of shares is made up of an increase in share capital of £10,000 (70,000 – 60,000) plus an increase in share premium of £10,000 (30,000 – 20,000). This is reported under financing activities.

Long term borrowings have increased in the year and therefore there is a cash inflow of £60,000 (210,000 – 150,000) also reported under financing activities.

Step 5 Dividends

We have not been given any information about dividends paid in the year. However, we can calculate the amount by looking at the movement in the retained earnings reserve. If closing retained earnings is less than opening retained earnings plus profit after tax for the year, the difference is dividends paid.

The easiest way to do this is by drawing up a 'T' account.

Retained earnings

	£'000		£'000
Cash paid (bal fig)	**40**	Balance b/f	250
Balance c/f	320	Profit for the year	110
	360		360

Step 6 Cash and cash equivalents

We need figures for cash and cash equivalents at the beginning and end of the year. The difference between these figures is the net increase or decrease in cash for the year, which should be the same as the total of the individual cash flows from operating, investing and financing activities.

	At 1 Jan 20X7	*Cash flows*	*At 31 Dec 20X7*
	£'000	£'000	£'000
Cash	30	(30)	–
Bank overdraft	–	(20)	(20)
	30	(50)	(20)

We are now able to complete the statement of cash flows.

student notes

Step 7 Draft the completed statement of cash flows

Reconciliation of profit from operations to net cash from operating activities for the year ended 31 December 20X7

	£'000	£'000
Profit from operations		170
Adjustments for:		
Depreciation		110
Loss on sale of property, plant and equipment		10
Operating cash flows before movements in working capital		290
Increase in inventories (130 – 110)		(20)
Increase in receivables (180 – 110)		(70)
Increase in payables (90 – 60)		30
Cash generated from operations		230
Interest paid		(20)
Tax paid		(30)
Net cash from operating activities		180

Statement of cash flows for the year ended 31 December 20X7

Net cash from operating activities		180
Investing activities:		
Purchase of property, plant and equipment	(290)	
Proceeds on disposal of property, plant and equipment	20	
Net cash used in investing activities		(270)
Financing activities:		
Proceeds of share issue	20	
Proceeds from long term borrowings	60	
Dividends paid	(40)	
Net cash from financing activities		40
Net decrease in cash and cash equivalents		(50)
Cash and cash equivalents at 1 January 20X7		30
Cash and cash equivalents at 31 December 20X7		(20)

Note: Cash and cash equivalents

	At 1 Jan 20X7	*Cash flows*	*At 31 Dec 20X7*
	£'000	£'000	£'000
Cash	30	(30)	–
Bank overdraft	–	(20)	(20)
	30	(50)	(20)

student notes

HOW USEFUL IS THE STATEMENT OF CASH FLOWS?

Useful information provided by a statement of cash flows

Most people agree that the statement of cash flows provides useful information. It alerts users to possible liquidity problems by highlighting inflows and outflows of cash.

There are other advantages of presenting a statement of cash flows:

- It shows an entity's ability to turn profit into cash (by allowing users to compare profit with cash flows from operating activities).
- Cash flow is a matter of fact and is difficult to manipulate.
- Cash flow information is not affected by an entity's choice of accounting policies or by judgement.
- The statement may help users to predict future cash flows.
- Cash flow is easier to understand than profit.
- The standard format enables users to compare the cash flows of different entities.

Limitations of the statement of cash flows

There are some important limits to the usefulness of the statement of cash flows:

- Cash balances are measured at a point in time and therefore they can be manipulated. For example, customers may be offered prompt payment discounts or other incentives to make early payment, or an entity may delay paying suppliers until after the year end. These are legitimate ways of managing cash flow (which is part of stewardship), but users may not be aware that this is being done, and may believe that the entity's position is better than it actually is.
- A high bank balance is not necessarily a sign of good cash management. Entities sometimes have to sacrifice cash flow in the short term to generate profits in the longer term, for example, by purchasing new plant and equipment. A business must have cash if it is to survive in the short term, but if it is to survive in the longer term it must also make a profit. Focusing on cash may mean that an entity has a healthy bank balance and makes a loss.
- The statement of cash flows is based on historical information and therefore it is not necessarily a reliable indicator of future cash flows.

student notes

Neither the income statement nor the statement of cash flows provide a complete picture of an entity's performance or position by themselves.

INTERPRETING THE STATEMENT OF CASH FLOWS

You may be asked to interpret a statement of cash flows in the Exam-based Assessment. This can be done by simple observation.

Look at the net cash flow for the period and then at each category of cash flows in turn.

Net cash flow for the period

- Has cash increased or decreased in the period?
- How material is the increase/decrease in cash compared with the entity's cash balances?
- Does the entity have a positive cash balance or an overdraft?

A decrease in cash is not always a bad sign, particularly if the entity has used the cash to finance capital expenditure or has used surplus cash to purchase liquid resources.

Operating activities

Have inventories, receivables and payables increased or decreased?

A material increase in working capital is a worrying sign, particularly if the entity has a cash outflow from operating activities.

Interest, tax and dividends

Is there enough cash to cover:

- Interest payments?
- Taxation?
- Dividends?

As well as looking at the current period's cash outflows, look at the liabilities in the statement of financial position, if this information is available; these are the next period's cash outflows.

Remember that interest and corporation tax have to be paid when they are due, but the entity can delay payment of equity dividends until the cash is available.

student notes

Investing activities

A cash outflow to purchase assets is usually a good sign, because the assets will generate profits (and cash inflows) in future periods.

If there has been capital expenditure, where has the cash come from? Usually it will have come from several sources: operations; issuing shares or debentures; taking out a loan; and taking out an overdraft.

If the entity has taken out or increased an overdraft, this is usually a worrying sign. In theory, a bank overdraft is repayable on demand.

Financing activities

Ask the following questions:

- Is debt increasing or decreasing?
- Will the entity be able to pay its debt interest?
- Will the entity be able to repay the debt (if it falls due in the near future)?
- Is the entity likely to need additional long term finance? (This might be the case if the bank overdraft is rapidly increasing or nearing its limit, or if the entity has plans to expand in the near future.)

student notes

Activity 5

Look at the statement of cash flows below. Do you think that the company is having problems in managing its cash flow? Give your reasons.

Reconciliation of profit from operating activities to net cash from operating activities for the year ended 31 December 20X5

	£'000
Profit from operations	4,214
Adjustments for:	
Depreciation	1,400
	5,614
Operating cash flow before movements in working capital	
Decrease in inventories	280
Increase in receivables	(910)
Increase in trade payables	32
Cash generated from operations	5,016
Interest paid	(560)
Tax paid	(1,170)
Net cash from operating activities	3,286

Statement of cash flows for the year ended 31 December 20X5

Net cash from operating activities		3,286
Investing activities		
Purchase of property, plant and equipment	(2,830)	
Proceeds on disposal of property, plant and equipment	96	
		(2,734)
Net cash used in investing activities		
Financing activities		
Repayment of loan stock	(310)	
Dividends paid	(480)	
Net cash used in financing activities		(790)
Decrease in cash and cash equivalents for the period		(238)
Cash and cash equivalents at the beginning of the period		240
Cash and cash equivalents at the end of the period		2

CHAPTER OVERVIEW

- Businesses need cash in order to survive
- Users of the financial statements need information about the liquidity, solvency and financial adaptability of an entity: this is provided by a statement of cash flows
- IAS 7 requires all companies to include a statement of cash flows in their published accounts
- Cash inflows and outflows must be presented under standard headings:
  - cash flows from operating activities
  - cash flows from investing activities
  - cash flows from financing activities
- IAS 7 also requires a note analysing changes in cash and cash equivalents
- There are two methods of calculating net cash flow from operating activities:
  - list and total the actual cash flows: the direct method
  - adjust profit for non-cash items: the indirect method
- IAS 7 allows either method
- Main advantages of cash flow information:
  - it shows an entity's liquidity, solvency and financial adaptability
  - it allows users to compare profit with net cash flow from operating activities
  - cash flow is difficult to manipulate
  - it is not affected by accounting policies or by estimates

KEY WORDS

Financial adaptability the ability to take effective action to alter the amount and timing of cash flows in order to respond to unexpected needs or opportunities

Statement of cash flows primary statement that summarises all movements of cash into and out of a business during the accounting period

Cash flows inflows and outflows of cash and cash equivalents

Cash cash in hand and demand deposits (normally) less overdrafts repayable on demand

Cash equivalents short-term, highly liquid investments that are readily convertible to known amounts of cash and which are subject to an insignificant risk of changes in value

Operating activities the principal revenue producing activities of the entity and other activities that are not investing or financing activities

Investing activities the acquisition and disposal of long-term assets and other investments not included in cash equivalents

Financing activities activities that result in changes in the size and composition of the contributed equity (share capital) and borrowings of the entity

Net cash flows the total cash flows reported under each of the standard headings in the cash flow statement

Gross cash flows the individual cash flows that make up the net cash flows reported under each of the headings in the cash flow statement

CHAPTER OVERVIEW cont.

- Limitations of cash flow information:
  - cash balances can be manipulated
  - businesses need to make profits as well as to generate cash: short term cash management may affect profit in the longer term
  - it is based on historical information
- To interpret a statement of cash flows: use simple observation; look at the net cash flow for the period; and at each category of cash flows in turn

HOW MUCH HAVE YOU LEARNED?

1 IAS 7 requires all companies to present a statement of cash flows. True or false?

2 Which of the following items does not meet the IAS 7 definition of cash?

A bank current account in foreign currency
B bank overdraft
C petty cash float
D short term deposit

3 Match the item with the correct part of the statement of cash flows.

a) increase in short term deposits
b) issue of ordinary share capital
c) receipt from sale of property, plant and equipment
d) tax paid

Heading	*Item*
Operating activities	
Investing activities	
Financing activities	
Increase/decrease in cash and cash equivalents	

4 Extracts from the statement of financial position of Dulwich Ltd are shown below:

	20X9	*20X8*
	£	£
Bank overdraft	–	3,000
Debenture loans	15,000	10,000
Share capital	20,000	15,000
Share premium	2,000	1,000

What is the cash flow from financing activities for the year ended 31 December 20X9?

5 There are two ways of reporting net cash flow from operating activities.

a) What are they?
b) Which presentation is required by IAS 7?

6 The following information relates to the property, plant and equipment of Bromley Ltd:

	20X2	*20X1*
	£	£
Cost	480,000	400,000
Accumulated depreciation	(86,000)	(68,000)
Carrying amount at 31 December	394,000	332,000

During the year ended 31 December 20X2 an asset which had originally cost £20,000 and had a carrying amount (net book value) of £8,000 was sold for £5,600.

What amount should be included in the statement of cash flows for the year ended 31 December 20X2 under the heading 'investing activities'?

7 The statement of financial position of Orion Ltd for the year ended 30 June 20X5 is provided below:

	20X5		*20X4*	
Assets	£'000	£'000	£'000	£'000
Non-current assets:				
Property, plant and equipment		2,030		1,776
Current assets:				
Inventory	1,009		960	
Trade and other receivables	826		668	
Cash	25		100	
		1,860		1,728
Total assets		3,890		3,504
Equity and liabilities				
Equity				
Share capital		1,200		1,200
Share premium		200		200
Retained earnings		1,171		1,028
		2,571		2,428
Non-current liabilities:				
Long term loan		610		460
Current liabilities				
Trade payables	641		563	
Tax liabilities	68		53	
		709		616
Total liabilities		1,319		1,076
Total equity and liabilities		3,890		3,504

Further information:

a) No non-current assets were sold during the year. The depreciation charge for the year amounted to £305,000.

b) The profit before tax was £270,000. Interest of £62,000 was charged in the year. The tax charge for the year was £68,000.

c) A dividend of £59,000 was paid during the year.

Prepare:

a) a reconciliation of profit from operations to net cash flow from operating activities, and
b) a statement of cash flows

for Orion Ltd for the year ended 30 June 20X5.

chapter 6: NON-CURRENT ASSETS

chapter coverage

This is the first of three chapters that deal with the requirements of accounting standards. In this chapter we will look at the accounting treatment of both tangible and intangible non-current assets, as set out in:

- IAS 16: *Property, plant and equipment*
- IAS 23: *Borrowing costs*
- IAS 40: *Investment property*
- IAS 38: *Intangible assets*
- IAS 36: *Impairment of assets*
- IFRS 5: *Non-current assets held for sale and discontinued operations*

Although you may be asked to account for any of these items, or to show how they are disclosed in the financial statements, you should remember that the most common type of Exam based Assessment task is to explain the required accounting treatment, usually to a non-accountant or someone with limited knowledge of accountancy. This means that you must understand the requirements of accounting standards and be prepared to apply them to a practical situation.

The topics that are to be covered are:

- recognising property, plant and equipment
- measurement after recognition
- depreciation
- disposals
- disclosures
- borrowing costs
- investment property
- intangible assets
- impairment of assets
- non-current assets held for sale

KNOWLEDGE AND UNDERSTANDING AND PERFORMANCE CRITERIA COVERAGE

knowledge and understanding

- the UK regulatory framework for financial reporting and the main requirements of relevant financial reporting standards

Performance criteria – element 11.1

- draft limited company financial statements from the appropriate information
- ensure that limited company financial statements comply with relevant accounting standards and domestic legislation and with the organisation's policies, regulations and procedures

student notes

RECOGNISING PROPERTY, PLANT AND EQUIPMENT

IAS 16 Property, plant and equipment

IAS 16 sets out the way in which items of property, plant and equipment should be treated in the financial statements. It applies to all items of property, plant and equipment except:

- items which are classified as held for sale, which are covered by IFRS 5; and
- investment properties, which are covered by IAS 40.

Property, plant and equipment are tangible items that:

- are held for use in the production or supply of goods or services, for rental to others, or for administrative purposes; and
- are expected to be used during more than one period.

In other words, property, plant and equipment includes all types of tangible non-current asset: land, buildings, machinery, computers, motor vehicles and office furniture.

Recognition

The cost of an item of property, plant and equipment is recognised as an asset if, and only if:

- it is probable that future economic benefits associated with the item will flow to the entity; and
- the cost of the item can be measured reliably.

This rule reflects the IASB's *Framework for the Preparation and Presentation of Financial Statements*. This defines an asset as a resource from which future economic benefits are expected to flow to an entity.

Measurement at recognition

When it is first recognised, an item of property, plant and equipment is measured at its cost.

The cost of an asset is its purchase price, including import duties and non-refundable purchase taxes, less any trade discounts or rebates.

student notes

Cost also includes any further costs directly attributable to bringing the item to the location and condition necessary for it to be capable of operating in the manner intended by management.

Directly attributable costs

Directly attributable costs may include:

- acquisition costs (e.g. stamp duty, import duties)
- wages and salaries paid to employees involved in constructing the item
- the cost of site preparation
- delivery and handling costs
- installation and assembly costs
- costs of testing whether the asset is functioning properly
- professional fees (e.g. legal fees, architects' fees).

Administrative and general overheads are not directly attributable costs and should not be included in the cost of an item.

Activity 1

A company purchased a building and converted it into offices for its own use. It incurred the following costs:

	£'000
Building	300
Legal fees (relating to the purchase)	5
Alterations (labour and materials)	50

The cost of the alterations included £5,000 relating to general overheads.

What amount should be capitalised in respect of the new offices?

Subsequent expenditure

During its life, an item of property, plant and equipment may need to be maintained, improved or upgraded.

- Subsequent expenditure that simply **services** the item should be recognised in the income statement as it is incurred. Examples of this kind of expenditure are the cost of repairs, maintenance and small parts.
- Subsequent expenditure should only be included in the cost of an item if it meets the recognition criteria above, ie, it will probably result in future economic benefits to the entity. This will be the case

where the expenditure **improves the performance** of an asset. Examples:

– the cost of modifying plant to increase its useful economic life or its capacity

– the cost of upgrading machine parts to achieve a substantial improvement in the quality of output.

student notes

MEASUREMENT AFTER RECOGNITION

Measuring assets

Measurement is the process of determining the monetary amounts at which items are recognised and carried in the financial statements.

An entity must select a basis on which to measure items, particularly assets.

The IASB *Framework* describes some possible measurement bases:

- **Historic cost**: assets are recorded at the amount of cash paid or the fair value of the consideration given to acquire them at the time of the acquisition.
- **Current cost**: assets are carried at the amount of cash that would have to be paid if the same or a similar asset was acquired currently.
- **Realisable value**: assets are carried at the amount of cash that could currently be obtained by selling the asset.
- **Present value**: assets are carried at the present discounted value of the future net cash inflows that the item is expected to generate in the normal course of business.

Historic cost is the most common. In practice, many entities combine historic cost with the other bases:

- Inventories are carried at the lower of cost and net realisable value.
- Many types of assets are carried at market value.
- Current cost accounting may be used to deal with the effects of inflation (this is very rare in the UK).

The alternative accounting rules

The Companies Act 2006 states that the current cost, market value or fair value of any non-current asset may be included in the statement of financial position instead of its historic cost.

student notes

These rules are known as the **alternative accounting rules** and the **fair value accounting rules**.

In practice, many companies adopt modified historic cost accounting: some assets (usually land and buildings) are included in the statement of financial position at current value or fair value while the remaining assets are included at historic cost.

The two measurement models in IAS 16

IAS 16 allows a choice after an item of property, plant and equipment is first recognised. An entity adopts one of two models:

- the **cost model**: an item is measured at (historic) cost less accumulated depreciation.
- the **revaluation model**: an item is measured at fair value less any subsequent accumulated depreciation.

IAS 16 states that if an item is revalued, the entire class of property, plant and equipment to which that asset belongs must be revalued.

A class of assets is a grouping of assets of a similar nature and use in the entity's operations. Examples of classes include: land; land and buildings; machinery; ships; aircraft; motor vehicles; furniture and fixtures; office equipment. For example, an entity could revalue all land and buildings or it could revalue land and leave all other assets at historic cost.

This means that similar items are treated consistently. It also means that entities cannot revalue items selectively. For example, an entity cannot revalue only those items that have increased in value while keeping the items that have fallen in value at cost.

This ensures that the financial statements provide useful information.

Fair value

Fair value is the amount for which an asset could be exchanged between knowledgeable, willing parties in an arm's length transaction. The fair value of an item of property, plant and equipment is normally its market value.

An entity can only adopt the revaluation model if the fair value of an item can be measured reliably.

- The fair value of land and buildings or plant and equipment is usually market value. Valuation of land and buildings is normally carried out by professionally qualified valuers.
- Some specialised items can be difficult to value. Because of their specialised nature, they are rarely, if ever, sold on the open market for a continuation of their existing use. Therefore there may be no

student notes

evidence of their market value. In this situation, fair value can be estimated using either depreciated replacement cost or the future income that the item will generate for the entity.

- Examples of specialised properties would include schools, universities, hospitals, oil refineries, power stations, museums.

Frequency of valuation

Using fair values provides users of the financial statements with relevant information. However, the information will not be useful if the valuations are not kept up to date.

IAS 16 does not require annual revaluations or set out a minimum time period between revaluations. It states that revaluations should be made with sufficient regularity to ensure that the carrying amount (or net book value) of an item does not differ materially from its actual fair value at the end of the reporting period.

This means that to some extent the frequency of revaluation depends on the judgement of management. Some items need to be revalued annually because their fair value changes significantly and often. Other items may only need to be revalued every three or five years.

Accounting for a revaluation

Revaluation gains are unrealised. Therefore they cannot be included in profit or loss, but must be taken directly to a separate revaluation reserve and reported as other comprehensive income.

The double entry to record a revaluation is:

DEBIT	Property, plant and equipment: Cost/valuation with the difference between fair value and historic cost
DEBIT	Property, plant and equipment: Accumulated depreciation with the total depreciation charged on the asset to date
CREDIT	Revaluation reserve with the difference between the revalued amount and net book value at historic cost

HOW IT WORKS

Upward Ltd purchased a freehold property for £400,000 on 1 January 20X1. At that date the property had a useful life of 50 years. On 31 December 20X3 the property was valued at £600,000 and the directors decided to incorporate this valuation in the financial statements for the year ended 31 December 20X3.

student notes

At 31 December 20X3, the carrying amount (net book value) of the property (at historic cost) is:

	£'000
Cost	400
Less accumulated depreciation (400 × 3/50)	(24)
	376

The double entry to record the revaluation is:

DEBIT	Freehold property: Cost/valuation	£200,000	
DEBIT	Freehold property: Accumulated depreciation	£24,000	
CREDIT	Revaluation reserve		£224,000

The note to the statement of financial position appears as follows:

Property, plant and equipment:

	Freehold land and buildings £'000
Cost at 1 January 20X3	400
Revaluation	200
Valuation at 31 December 20X3	600
Accumulated depreciation at 1 January 20X3	16
Charge for the year (400 / 50)	8
Revaluation	(24)
Accumulated depreciation at 31 December 20X3	–
Net carrying amount at 31 December 20X3	600
Net carrying amount at 1 January 20X3	384

The revaluation surplus of £224,000 is recognised in other comprehensive income and in the statement of financial position as a revaluation reserve within equity.

Activity 2

Walnut Ltd purchased a freehold property for £250,000 on 1 January 20X1. The useful life of the property was 40 years from that date. On 31 December 20X5 the property was revalued to £350,000.

What is the double entry to record the revaluation?

student notes

Revaluation losses

- If the asset was previously carried at historic cost, revaluation losses are recognised immediately in profit or loss.
- If the asset has previously been revalued upwards, revaluation losses are first set against the balance on the revaluation reserve relating to that asset. This means that losses are recognised in other comprehensive income until the carrying amount reaches depreciated historic cost. Any remaining loss is then recognised (taken to the income statement) in profit or loss.

DEPRECIATION

Depreciation is the systematic allocation of the depreciable amount of an asset over its useful life.

The purpose of depreciation is to allocate the cost (or fair value) of an asset to the accounting periods expected to benefit from its use. It is an application of the accruals concept.

Depreciation is not:

- a way of reflecting the fall in value of an asset over its life. The net realisable value (fair value less costs to sell) of an asset is not the same as its net book value.
- a means of ensuring that an asset can be replaced at the end of its life. The replacement cost of an asset normally exceeds the amount of depreciation provided, due to rising prices.

The basic principles

IAS 16 states that:

- the depreciation charge for each period should be recognised in profit or loss (ie, as an expense in the income statement).
- the depreciable amount of an asset should be allocated on a systematic basis over its useful life.

The **depreciable amount** is the cost of an asset (or, where an asset is revalued, the revalued amount) less its residual value.

Residual value is the estimated amount that an entity would currently obtain from disposal of the asset at the end of its useful life.

The **useful life** of an asset is the period over which it is expected to be available for use by an entity.

student notes

Choosing a method

The depreciation method used should reflect the pattern in which the asset's future economic benefits are expected to be consumed by the entity.

IAS 16 does not prescribe a method of depreciation. The directors must exercise their judgement in selecting a method.

To calculate depreciation, an entity must determine the useful life and residual value of an asset and the depreciation method to be used. An entity needs to consider:

- the expected usage of the asset by the entity (this may depend on the asset's expected capacity or physical output).
- the expected physical wear and tear (this may depend on repairs and maintenance expenditure and the way in which the asset is operated).
- technical or commercial obsolescence, for example arising from changes or improvements in production, or a change in the market demand for the product or service.
- legal or similar limits on the use of the asset, such as expiry dates of related leases.

The most common methods of depreciation are:

- the straight line method. This is the simplest to apply. It is also the most suitable method where the pattern of consumption of an asset's economic benefits is uncertain.
- the reducing balance method. This is suitable where an asset provides greater economic benefits when new than when older. For example, a machine may be less capable of producing a high quality product towards the end of its life because it breaks down more often, or because it is less technologically advanced than the latest model. Repair and maintenance costs are likely to increase as this type of asset grows older; therefore there is a more even allocation of total costs (depreciation and maintenance) over the life of the asset.
- the machine hour method. This is suitable where an asset is consumed primarily through use, rather than over time.

Depreciating an asset with different parts

An asset may consist of different parts with different useful lives. For example:

- Some items of property, plant and equipment need to have parts replaced every few years. For example, a furnace may require relining every five years.

student notes

- Some items need regular major inspections as a condition of continuing to operate them. For example, safety regulations may require an aircraft to be overhauled every three years.

Provided that the general recognition criteria are met, these costs should be recognised as part of the cost of the item. The carrying amount (the net book value) of the parts that are replaced or of the previous inspection is derecognised (disposed or scrapped).

Where the cost of a separate part of an asset is significant in relation to the total cost of the asset, each part must be depreciated separately over its individual useful life.

HOW IT WORKS

A machine is purchased for £700,000. It has an estimated useful life of 12 years. Part of the machine needs to be replaced every four years at an additional cost of £100,000. Depreciation is charged on a straight line basis over the machine's useful life.

The part of the machine that needs to be replaced is depreciated over four years, while the rest of the machine is depreciated over 12 years. Annual depreciation is:

	£'000
Part (100 ÷ 4)	25
Remainder (600 ÷ 12)	50
	75

At the beginning of Year 5 the part is replaced and the cost of the replacement part is treated as an addition. The replacement part is then depreciated over 4 years as before.

Year	*1*	*2*	*3*	*4*	*5*	*6*
	£'000	£'000	£'000	£'000	£'000	£'000
Cost						
B/f	700	700	700	700	700	700
Additions	–	–	–	–	100	–
Disposals	–	–	–	–	(100)	–
Cost c/f	700	700	700	700	700	700
Depreciation						
b/f	–	75	150	225	300	275
Charge	75	75	75	75	75	75
Disposals	–	–	–	–	(100)	–
Depreciation c/f	75	150	225	300	275	350
Carrying amount c/f	625	550	475	400	425	350

student notes

Changing the method of depreciation

The depreciation methods used should be reviewed at least at each year-end. If there has been a significant change in the expected pattern of consumption of the future economic benefits associated with the asset, the method should be changed to reflect the changed pattern.

As we saw in an earlier chapter, a change in the method of depreciation is a change in an accounting estimate, not a change in accounting policy. There is no prior period adjustment.

The carrying amount of the asset is depreciated using the new method over the asset's remaining useful life, beginning in the period in which the change is made.

Activity 3

On 1 January 20X1 Hazel Ltd purchased a machine for £20,000. The machine was depreciated over 10 years, using the straight line method.

On 1 January 20X3, the directors decided to change the method of depreciation, so that the machine was depreciated at 25% per annum on the reducing balance.

What is the depreciation charge for the year ended 31 December 20X3?

Review of useful life and residual value

The residual value and the useful life of an asset should be reviewed at least at each year-end. If expectations differ from previous estimates, the change is dealt with as a change in accounting estimate. It is not a change in accounting policy.

If a useful life is revised, the carrying amount of the asset at the date of revision should be depreciated over the revised remaining useful life.

A change in estimated residual value should be accounted for prospectively over the asset's remaining useful life.

Activity 4

On 1 January 20X1 Hazel Ltd purchased a machine for £20,000. The machine was depreciated over 10 years, using the straight line method.

On 1 January 20X3, the directors reviewed the useful life of the machine and came to the conclusion that it was only 5 years from that date.

What is the depreciation charge for the year ended 31 December 20X3?

Depreciation and revalued assets

student notes

Both the Companies Act and IAS 16 require that all items of property, plant and equipment are depreciated over their useful lives.

Where an asset has been revalued, the depreciation charge must be based on the **revalued amount**.

The only asset which should not be depreciated is land. This normally has an indefinite useful life (unless it is used for mining or similar activities).

Depreciation must be charged even where:

- the fair value of the asset exceeds its carrying amount; or
- the entity has repaired and maintained the asset so that its useful life has been extended.

In the past, many entities used one or both of these arguments to avoid charging depreciation on revalued buildings.

DISPOSALS

The carrying amount of an item of property, plant and equipment is derecognised (removed from the financial statements):

- on disposal; or
- when no future economic benefits are expected from its use or disposal.

The gain or loss on a derecognised asset is treated as follows:

- The gain or loss on derecognition of an item should be recognised in profit or loss (the income statement) of the period in which the derecognition occurs.
- If it is material it may need to be separately disclosed in the income statement.
- The gain or loss on the disposal (or derecognition) of an item is the difference between the net sale proceeds (if any) and the carrying amount (whether this is based on historical cost or on a valuation).
- Where there is a disposal of a revalued asset the gain or loss on revaluation has already been recognised in equity and in other comprehensive income (at the time of the revaluation). The gain or loss would be recognised twice if the gain or loss on disposal were based on the original cost of the asset.
- However, the gain is now realised. Therefore it is transferred from the revaluation reserve to retained earnings. The transfer does not

student notes

pass through profit or loss (the income statement) for the current year.

Activity 5

On 1 January 20X1 Cashew Ltd purchased a building for £300,000. The useful life of the building was 50 years from that date.

On 1 January 20X4, the building was revalued to £500,000. The useful life of the building was deemed to be 50 years from the date of valuation.

On 31 December 20X7, the building was sold for £700,000.

What is the profit on disposal?

DISCLOSURES

The following information should be disclosed for each class of property, plant and equipment:

- The measurement bases used for determining the gross carrying amount (ie, cost or fair value)
- The depreciation methods used;
- The useful lives or the depreciation rates used;
- Total depreciation charged for the period;
- The cost or revalued amount at the beginning of the accounting period and at the end of the reporting period;
- The cumulative amount of provisions for depreciation or impairment at the beginning of the accounting period and at the end of the reporting period;
- A reconciliation of the movements, separately disclosing additions, disposals, revaluations, transfers, depreciation and impairment losses in the accounting period; and
- The net carrying amount at the beginning of the reporting period and at the end of the reporting period.

The reconciliation note

This is an illustration of the way in which the reconciliation between amounts in the statement of financial position at the beginning and end of the year is normally presented. The separate classes of property, plant and equipment are shown in the column headings.

student notes

	Freehold land and buildings	Leasehold land and buildings Long leases	Short leases	Plant and machinery	Fixtures and fittings	Total
	£'000	£'000	£'000	£'000	£'000	£'000
Cost (or valuation)						
At beginning of year	X	X	X	X	X	X
Additions	X	–	X	–	X	X
Revaluation	X	–	–	–	–	X
Disposals	(X)	–	–	(X)	(X)	(X)
At end of year	X	X	X	X	X	X
Depreciation						
At beginning of year	X	X	X	X	X	X
Charge for year	X	X	X	X	X	X
Revaluation	(X)	–	–	–	–	(X)
Disposals	(X)	–	–	(X)	(X)	(X)
At end of year	X	X	X	X	X	X
Net carrying amount						
At end of year	X	X	X	X	X	X
At beginning of year	X	X	X	X	X	X

BORROWING COSTS

Sometimes entities borrow money in order to finance the construction of an asset.

Borrowing costs are interest and other costs incurred by an entity in connection with the borrowing of funds.

Accounting treatments

IAS 23 *Borrowing costs* states that where an entity incurs borrowing costs the following accounting treatment should be followed:

- Borrowing costs that are directly attributable to the acquisition, construction or production of a qualifying asset are capitalised as part of the cost of that asset.
- Other borrowing costs must be recognised as an expense in the period in which they are incurred.

student notes

A **qualifying asset** is an asset that necessarily takes a substantial period of time to get ready for its intended use or sale.

- Examples of qualifying assets are manufacturing plants and investment properties. Inventories are not normally qualifying assets. Assets that are ready for their intended use or sale when they are acquired are not qualifying assets.
- Directly attributable finance costs are those that would have been avoided if there had been no expenditure on the asset.

The amount to be capitalised

- If an entity borrows funds specifically for the purpose of obtaining a qualifying asset, the amount capitalised is the actual costs incurred.
- If an entity borrows funds generally and uses these to obtain a qualifying asset, the amount capitalised is the expenditure on the asset multiplied by the interest rate applicable to the entity's total borrowings. (A weighted average interest rate is used where the borrowings come from more than one source.)
- Capitalisation of borrowing costs should start when:
  - expenditures for the asset are being incurred; and
  - borrowing costs are being incurred; and
  - activities that are necessary to get the asset ready for use are in progress.
- Capitalisation of borrowing costs should cease when substantially all the activities necessary to prepare the asset for use or sale are complete.

INVESTMENT PROPERTY

As the name suggests, investment properties are held as investments, rather than for use in the entity's operating activities.

IAS 40 *Investment property* sets out the way in which these assets should be treated and disclosed in the financial statements.

The definition

student notes

IAS 40 defines an **investment property** as property (land or a building or both) held to earn rentals or for capital appreciation or for both, rather than for:

- use in the production or supply of goods or services or for administrative purposes; or
- sale in the ordinary course of business.

Examples of investment property:

- Land held for long term capital appreciation rather than for short term sale in the ordinary course of business
- Land held for a currently undetermined future use
- A building owned by the entity and leased out
- A building that is vacant but held to be leased out.

The following are not investment properties:

- Property still under construction
- Owner-occupied property.

Recognition

Investment property is recognised as an asset when, and only when:

- it is probable that the future economic benefits that are associated with the investment property will flow to the entity; and
- its cost can be measured reliably.

When an investment property is first recognised it is measured at its cost. Transaction costs (for example, legal fees and property transfer taxes) are included in the initial cost of an investment property.

Accounting treatment after initial recognition

There is a choice between two accounting treatments:

- the cost model;
- the fair value model.

All investment properties must be treated in the same way; it is not possible to use the cost model for some and the revaluation model for others.

student notes

The cost model

Investment properties are measured at their original cost less accumulated depreciation. The treatment is exactly the same as under the cost model in IAS 16.

The fair value model

The reasoning behind the fair value model is that investment properties are not 'consumed' in the business. Therefore it is not appropriate to depreciate them. The most useful information about investment properties is their fair value and changes in that fair value.

- All investment property is measured at fair value.
- Fair value is the price at which the property could be exchanged between knowledgeable, willing parties in an arm's length transaction (ie, normally open market value).
- Investment properties are not depreciated.
- Instead, properties are revalued at each year-end. Gains and losses arising from changes in fair value are recognised in profit or loss (in the income statement) for the period.

Disposals

An investment property is derecognised (removed from the statement of financial position) on disposal or when it is permanently withdrawn from use and no future economic benefits are expected from its disposal.

Gains and losses on disposal are calculated as the difference between the net disposal proceeds and the carrying amount of the asset. They are recognised in profit or loss (the income statement) in the period in which the disposal takes place.

Disclosures

An entity should disclose whether it applies the cost model or the fair value model.

student notes

INTANGIBLE ASSETS

Recognition

An **intangible asset** is an identifiable non-monetary asset without physical substance.

If an asset is identifiable, it is either:

- separable (capable of being separated from the rest of the business and sold or otherwise disposed of); or
- it arises from contractual or other legal rights, whether or not these rights are themselves separable or transferable.

Examples of intangible assets:

- Brand names
- Market and technical knowledge
- Franchises
- Licences
- Patents
- Computer software
- Customer lists
- Publishing titles; and
- Trademarks.

The basic principles are the same as for other non-current assets:

An intangible asset is recognised when, and only when:

- it is probable that the expected future economic benefits that are attributable to the asset will flow to the entity; and
- the cost of the asset can be measured reliably.

Most non-current assets generate economic benefits in the form of sales revenue from new products and services. An intangible asset can also generate economic benefits by reducing costs. For example, specialised technical knowledge can make a production process more efficient and lead to cost savings.

Activity 6

A company that develops and markets scientific equipment has several extremely well qualified and talented members of staff. The company's success is undoubtedly the result of their work. Can the company recognise the staff or their expertise as an asset in the company's statement of financial position?

student notes

Initial measurement

When an intangible asset is first recognised it is measured at cost.

Goodwill

Goodwill is the excess of the value of the business as a whole over the total value of its individual assets and liabilities.

You will already have met goodwill during your earlier studies. Goodwill is classified as an intangible asset.

For example, A Ltd buys an unincorporated business for £100,000. The fair values of its assets and liabilities are as follows:

	£'000
Property, plant and equipment	70
Net current assets	30
Long term liabilities	(10)
	90

As well as acquiring the assets and liabilities of the business for £90,000, A Ltd has acquired goodwill worth £10,000. Goodwill may arise as a result of a number of factors, such as the reputation of the business, the quality of its products, or the skill of its management. It cannot exist independently of the business.

There are two kinds of goodwill:

- internally generated goodwill (sometimes called inherent goodwill) and
- purchased goodwill.

Internally generated goodwill is the goodwill that a business generates over time. Almost all businesses have some internally generated goodwill.

Purchased goodwill is the difference between the cost of an acquired entity and the aggregate of the fair values of that entity's identifiable assets and liabilities.

In the example above, the business that A Ltd acquired has inherent goodwill. In the accounts of A Ltd this goodwill is purchased goodwill.

How goodwill is treated

IAS 38 states that internally generated goodwill should never be recognised as an asset. This is because it cannot be measured reliably; all methods of valuing it are subjective.

Purchased goodwill is recognised as an asset because it has a cost to the business that has acquired it. It can be measured reliably because there has

student notes

been a transaction which establishes its value as a fact at a particular point in time.

Purchased goodwill is outside the scope of IAS 38. It will be covered in more detail in the chapters on group accounts.

Research and development

Many companies spend large amounts on research and development projects. If these are successful, they result in new products or services that may provide significant income for many years to come.

Research and development expenditure may be an asset, rather than an expense, if it gives access to future economic benefits for the entity. There is an argument for treating it as an asset, capitalising it in the statement of financial position and matching it with the income that it produces in future accounting periods (applying the accruals concept).

On the other hand, it may be impossible to predict whether a project will give rise to future income or to precisely identify the future income if it is received. If this is the case the expenditure must be charged to profit or loss in the period in which it is incurred.

The research phase and the development phase

IAS 38 separates a research and development project into a **research phase** and a **development phase**.

- **Research** is original and planned investigation undertaken with the prospect of gaining new scientific or technical knowledge and understanding.
- **Development** is the application of research findings or other knowledge to a plan or design for the production of new or substantially improved materials, devices, products, processes, systems before the start of commercial production or use.

How the expenditure is treated

Research phase

At this stage it is impossible to be certain that the project will generate any future economic benefit.

Therefore expenditure on research is treated as an expense and recognised in profit or loss when it is incurred. No intangible asset is recognised.

student notes

Development phase

Development expenditure may result in identifiable income (economic benefits) in future periods. It should not be recognised as an asset unless it is reasonably certain that this will be the case.

IAS 38 states that an intangible asset arising from development should be recognised if an entity can demonstrate all of the following:

- The **technical feasibility** of completing the intangible asset so that it will be available for use or sale;
- Its **intention to complete** the intangible asset and use or sell it;
- Its **ability to use or sell** the intangible asset;
- **How** the intangible asset will **generate probable future economic benefits** (including the existence of a market for output of the asset or the asset itself; or, if it is to be used internally, the usefulness of the intangible asset);
- The **availability of adequate** technical, financial and other **resources** to complete the development and to use or sell the intangible asset;
- Its ability to **measure reliably** the expenditure attributable to the intangible asset during its development.

If any of these conditions are not met, the expenditure must be charged to profit or loss in the period in which it is incurred.

Activity 7

A company has incurred expenditure of £50,000 in investigating a new process. It is hoped that the new process can eventually be adapted and used to manufacture Product Z more efficiently than at present, resulting in considerable cost savings. The project is at a very early stage and the outcome is uncertain.

How should the expenditure be treated in the financial statements?

Other internally generated intangible assets

IAS 38 states that internally generated brands, mastheads, publishing titles, customer lists and items similar in substance should not be recognised as intangible assets.

student notes

Activity 8

Fifteen years ago, a company developed a brand of self-raising flour. The brand has now become a household name and has captured a substantial share of the market. One of the directors has claimed that it is worth at least £10 million to the company.

How should the brand be treated in the company's financial statements?

The cost of an internally generated intangible asset

The cost of an internally generated intangible asset includes all directly attributable costs necessary to create, produce and prepare the asset to be capable of operating in the manner intended by management.

Examples:

- Costs of materials and services
- Costs of employee benefits (eg, wages and salaries)
- Fees to register a legal right
- Amortisation (depreciation) of payments and licences that are used to generate the intangible asset.

The following should not be included in the cost of an internally generated intangible asset:

- Selling, administrative and other general overhead expenditure
- Inefficiencies and initial operating losses incurred before the asset achieves planned performance
- Expenditure on training staff to operate the asset.

Measurement after recognition

This is similar to the measurement of property, plant and equipment. After an intangible asset is first recognised, there is a choice between the cost model and the revaluation model.

The cost model

The intangible asset is carried at its cost less any accumulated amortisation (depreciation).

Cost is the amount of cash or cash equivalents paid or the fair value of other consideration given to acquire an asset at the time of its acquisition or construction.

student notes

The revaluation model

The intangible asset is carried at a revalued amount: its fair value at the date of revaluation less any subsequent accumulated amortisation.

Fair value is the amount for which the asset could be exchanged between knowledgeable, willing parties in an arm's length transaction.

- **Fair value** is determined by reference to an active market.
- An **active market** is a market in which all the following conditions exist:
  - the items traded are homogeneous (of the same kind);
  - willing buyers and sellers can normally be found at any time; and
  - prices are available to the public.
- Revaluations should be made with such regularity that at the year-end the carrying amount of the asset is not materially different from its fair value.
- If an intangible asset is revalued, all other assets in its class must also be revalued (unless there is no active market for those assets).

Revaluation gains and losses

The accounting treatment is similar to the treatment for gains and losses relating to property, plant and equipment.

- A revaluation gain is credited to equity. It is not included in profit or loss, but taken to a revaluation reserve and included in other comprehensive income.
- A revaluation loss is normally recognised in profit or loss (the income statement).
- If the intangible asset has previously been revalued upwards, a revaluation loss is debited to equity and set against the revaluation surplus relating to that asset. Any excess loss is recognised in the income statement.

The useful life of an intangible asset

Management need to assess the useful life of an intangible asset, which can be finite or indefinite.

- An intangible asset has an indefinite useful life when there is no foreseeable limit to the period over which the asset is expected to generate net cash inflows for the entity.

student notes

- All the relevant factors should be taken into account: expected usage; typical product life cycles; the likelihood of obsolescence; expected actions by competitors; whether the useful life of the asset is dependent on the useful life of other assets of the entity.

Where the useful life is finite

An intangible asset with a finite useful life is amortised on a systematic basis over its useful life.

- Amortisation begins when the asset is available for use (when it is in the location and condition necessary for it to be capable of operating in the manner intended by management).
- Amortisation ceases when the asset is derecognised (on disposal or where no future economic benefits are expected).
- The amortisation method used reflects the pattern in which the asset's future economic benefits are expected to be consumed. The straight line method is used if this pattern cannot be determined reliably.
- The amortisation charge for each period is included in the income statement.
- The residual value of the asset is normally assumed to be zero.
- The amortisation period and the amortisation method are reviewed at least at each year-end. Any change is dealt with as a change in accounting estimate, not a change in accounting policy.

Where the useful life is indefinite

An intangible asset with an indefinite useful life is not amortised.

Instead it remains in the statement of financial position but is reviewed for impairment (loss in value) annually and whenever there is an indication that it may be impaired. Impairment is covered in the next section.

The useful life of the asset is also reviewed each period to determine whether events and circumstances continue to support the previous assessment of an indefinite useful life. If the asset is then assessed as having a finite useful life, the change is accounted for as a change in accounting estimate.

student notes

IMPAIRMENT OF ASSETS

Impairment

When an asset is impaired, it has suffered a loss in value.

Impairment is a reduction in the recoverable amount of an asset below its carrying amount.

An **impairment loss** is the amount by which the carrying amount of an asset exceeds its recoverable amount.

IAS 36 *Impairment of assets* applies to all assets, including investments in other companies, except:

- inventories (see IAS 2)
- investment property measured at fair value (see IAS 40); and
- non-current assets held for sale (see IFRS 5).

When an impairment review must be carried out

IAS 36 states that assets should be reviewed for impairment if there is some indication that impairment has occurred, such as:

- a significant decline in an asset's market value during the period;
- evidence of obsolescence or physical damage to the asset;
- a significant adverse change in the business or the market in which the asset is involved (for example, the entrance of a major competitor);
- significant changes in the way in which the asset is used or will be used in the future (for example, plans to stop using it or to scrap it before the previously expected date);
- evidence that the economic performance of an asset is, or will be, worse than expected, for example:
  - cash outflows for maintaining the asset are significantly higher than originally budgeted;
  - cash flows or operating profit related to the asset are significantly worse than expected.

This list is not exhaustive. There might be other indications that an asset is impaired.

Certain assets must always be reviewed for impairment at least annually, even if there are no signs that the asset has become impaired:

student notes

- intangible assets with an indefinite useful life; and
- goodwill acquired in a business combination (see Chapter 10).

Carrying out an impairment review

To determine whether an asset is impaired, its carrying amount is compared with its recoverable amount.

- **Carrying amount** is the amount at which an asset is recognised after deducting any accumulated depreciation (amortisation) and accumulated impairment losses.

- An asset's **recoverable amount** is the higher of fair value less costs to sell or value in use.

- **Fair value less costs to sell** is the amount obtainable from the sale of an asset in an arm's length transaction between knowledgeable, willing parties, less the costs of disposal.

- **Value in use** is the present value of the future cash flows expected to be obtained from an asset (as a result of continuing to use it in the business, normally to produce goods or provide services for sale to customers).

If an asset is impaired, the entity can either sell the asset, or continue to use it in the business. IAS 36 assumes that an entity will always choose the course of action that will result in the most cash.

If the carrying amount exceeds the recoverable amount, the asset or goodwill is impaired and should be written down.

HOW IT WORKS

Cumin Ltd carries out impairment reviews on three assets. Details of the three assets are as follows:

	Carrying amount	*Fair value less costs to sell*	*Value in use*
	£'000	£'000	£'000
Asset A	20	18	25
Asset B	25	20	22
Asset C	30	40	38

Step 1 Determine recoverable amount (the higher of fair value less costs to sell and value in use)

- Asset A: £25,000 (value in use)
- Asset B: £22,000 (value in use)
- Asset C: £40,000 (fair value less costs to sell)

student notes

Step 2 Compare recoverable amount with carrying amount

- If recoverable amount is less than carrying amount, the asset is impaired.
- Only Asset B is impaired; recoverable amount is £22,000, £3,000 less than carrying amount.

Fair value less costs to sell

The best evidence of fair value less costs to sell is normally its market price in a binding sale agreement in an arm's length transaction. This is adjusted for any costs directly attributable to the disposal of the asset.

If there is no binding sale agreement, but the asset is traded in an active market, fair value less costs to sell is the asset's market price less the costs of disposal.

If there is no binding sale agreement or active market, fair value less costs to sell should be based on the best available evidence.

Examples of costs of disposal:

- Legal costs
- Stamp duty
- Cost of removing the asset
- Direct costs of bringing an asset into condition for sale.

Value in use

Estimating the value in use of an asset involves two steps:

- estimating the future cash inflows and outflows to be obtained from continuing use of the asset and from its ultimate disposal; and
- applying the appropriate discount rate to those future cash flows.

Estimates of the future cash flows should take into account any possible variations in the amount and timing of the future cash flows.

The discount rate used should reflect current market assessments of the time value of money and any risk (uncertainty) specific to the asset.

HOW IT WORKS

The idea behind the value in use calculation is that an asset generates income for an entity. The sooner the cash is received the more it is worth to the entity. Surplus cash can be invested to obtain interest, while reducing an overdraft

student notes

saves the entity interest. Discounting the cash flows adjusts them to reflect this.

You will **not** be asked to perform this kind of calculation in the assessment, but you could be asked to explain the reasoning behind it.

Suppose that A Ltd has an item of plant. The plant produces goods for sale to customers. A Ltd estimates that sales income from these goods will be as follows:

Year 1	£20,000
Year 2	£20,000
Year 3	£15,000

The current market rate of bank interest is 10% per annum.

	Cash inflow	*Discount rate (from tables)*	£
Year 1	20,000	0.909	18,180
Year 2	20,000	0.826	16,520
Year 3	15,000	0.751	11,265
			45,965

The value in use of the plant is the present value (the discounted value) of the total cash inflows that can be obtained by using it: £45,965.

Accounting for impairment losses

Where the recoverable amount of an asset is less than its carrying amount, the asset is impaired. The carrying amount of the asset must be reduced to its recoverable amount. The reduction is an impairment loss.

- Impairment losses are recognised in profit or loss (the income statement) if the asset has not previously been revalued.
- Impairment losses are recognised in other comprehensive income if the asset has previously been revalued above cost. The impairment loss is treated as a downward revaluation. Any impairment below depreciated historical cost is recognised in profit or loss.
- When an impairment loss on an asset is recognised, the remaining useful life should be reviewed and revised if necessary. The revised carrying amount should be depreciated over the revised estimate of the remaining useful life.

student notes

HOW IT WORKS

Juniper Ltd bought a machine on 1 January 20X1. The machine cost £60,000 and had a useful life of 6 years. It was depreciated using the straight line method.

On 1 January 20X3 an impairment review was carried out, and the recoverable amount of the plant was estimated at £30,000. Its useful life was reviewed and was estimated to be 2 years at that date.

At 1 January 20X3 the carrying amount of the machine is:

	£
Cost	60,000
Less: Accumulated depreciation (2 years)	(20,000)
	40,000

The recoverable value of the machine is £30,000 and so an impairment loss of £10,000 is recognised in the income statement. The impairment is effectively additional depreciation and so the double entry is:

DEBIT	Depreciation expense	£10,000	
CREDIT	Plant and machinery: Accumulated depreciation		£10,000

The remaining useful life of the machine is now two years and therefore the annual depreciation charge is now £15,000 (30,000 ÷ 2).

The total charge to profit or loss for the year ended 31 December 20X3 is £25,000 (impairment loss of £10,000 and depreciation of £15,000).

If the impairment loss is material, it may need to be disclosed separately in a note to the financial statements.

Activity 9

Coriander Ltd carries out an impairment review on a freehold property. You are provided with the following information:

	£'000
Carrying amount (based on a valuation)	150
Depreciated historic cost	100
Fair value less costs to sell	110
Value in use	100

How should the impairment loss be recognised in the financial statements?

Cash-generating units

student notes

Sometimes it is not possible to estimate the recoverable amount of an individual asset. Some assets, such as goodwill, do not generate cash inflows independently of other assets. This means that it is impossible to calculate value in use.

In this situation, assets are grouped together and the impairment review is carried out for each group of assets, or **cash-generating unit**.

A **cash-generating unit** is the smallest identifiable group of assets that generates cash inflows that are largely independent of the cash inflows from other assets or groups of assets.

A cash generating unit is normally a department or a single company within a group of companies.

Testing goodwill

Goodwill has to be tested for impairment annually. Because goodwill does not generate cash flows by itself, it must be allocated to a cash-generating unit. The impairment test is then carried out for the cash generating unit as a whole.

- The carrying amount of the unit is compared with the recoverable amount.
- If the recoverable amount of the unit is greater than the carrying amount, the unit and the goodwill are not impaired.
- If the carrying amount is greater than the recoverable amount of the unit, the unit is impaired.

Any impairment loss is then allocated between the assets in the cash-generating unit:

- first, to goodwill;
- then to the other assets in the unit on a pro-rata basis.

HOW IT WORKS

The carrying amounts of the assets in a cash generating unit are as follows:

	£
Goodwill	20,000
Other intangible assets	50,000
Property plant and equipment	150,000
	220,000

student notes

The recoverable amount of the unit is £180,000. Therefore there is an impairment loss of £40,000. This is allocated as follows:

	Before Impairment	*Impairment loss*	*After impairment*
	£	£	£
Goodwill	20,000	(20,000)	–
Other intangible assets	50,000	(5,000)	45,000
Property plant and equipment	150,000	(15,000)	135,000
	220,000	(40,000)	180,000

Disclosure

The following information must be disclosed for each class of assets:

- the amount of impairment losses recognised in profit or loss (in the income statement) for the period; and
- the line item of the income statement in which those impairment losses are included.

NON-CURRENT ASSETS HELD FOR SALE

At the year-end, an entity may have items of property, plant and equipment or other types of non-current asset that it intends to sell shortly after the year end. IFRS 5 *Non-current assets held for sale and discontinued operations* sets out the required accounting treatment for these items.

- An entity should classify a non-current asset as **held for sale** if it expects to obtain future income from the asset by selling it, rather than by continuing to use it in the business.
- An asset that is held for sale is measured at the lower of its carrying amount and its fair value less costs to sell. If fair value less costs to sell is lower than the carrying amount, the loss is treated as an impairment loss and recognised in profit or loss.
- An asset that is held for sale is not depreciated.
- Non-current assets held for sale are disclosed separately from other non-current assets in the statement of financial position.

In this way, users of the financial statements are made aware of any material disposals of assets that are about to take place.

CHAPTER OVERVIEW

- Non-current assets are recognised if: it is probable that future economic benefits associated with the item will flow to the entity; and the cost of the item can be measured reliably
- A non-current asset is initially measured at its cost
- After an item of property, plant and equipment is first recognised, it is either carried at cost (the cost model) or at fair value (the revaluation model). If an item is revalued, all assets of the same class must be revalued. Valuations must be kept up to date
- Double entry to record a revaluation:

  Debit Property, plant and equipment: Cost/valuation with the difference between fair value and historic cost

  Debit Property, plant and equipment: Accumulated depreciation with the total depreciation charged on the asset to date

  Credit Revaluation reserve with the difference between the revalued amount and carrying amount at historic cost
- Revaluation gains are reported in other comprehensive income and in equity (the revaluation reserve)
- The depreciable amount of an asset should be allocated on a systematic basis over its useful life
- Where an asset has been revalued, the depreciation charge must be based on the revalued amount

KEY WORDS

Property, plant and equipment tangible items that: are held for use in the production or supply of goods or services, for rental to others, or for administrative purposes; and are expected to be used during more than one period

Cost of an asset purchase price, including import duties and non-refundable purchase taxes, less any trade discounts or rebates, plus any further costs directly attributable to bringing the item to the location and condition necessary for it to be capable of operating in the manner intended by management

Alternative accounting rules Companies Act rules that allow companies to include assets in the statement of financial position at current cost or market value, rather than historic cost

Modified historic cost accounting where an entity measures some assets at fair value and others at historic cost

A class of assets a grouping of assets of a similar nature and use in the entity's operations

Fair value the amount for which an asset could be exchanged between knowledgeable, willing parties in an arm's length transaction

Depreciation the systematic allocation of the depreciable amount of an asset over its useful life

Depreciable amount the cost of an asset (or, where an asset is revalued, the revalued amount) less its residual value

Residual value the estimated amount that an entity would currently obtain from disposal of the asset at the end of its useful life

CHAPTER OVERVIEW cont.

- The gain or loss on the disposal of an item of property, plant and equipment is the difference between the net sale proceeds and the carrying amount (whether this is based on historical cost or on a valuation)
- Borrowing costs that are directly attributable to the acquisition or construction of a qualifying asset should be capitalised as part of the cost of the asset
- Investment properties should be included in the statement of financial position either at cost (following the cost model in IAS 16) or at fair value (the fair value model)
- If the fair value model is adopted, changes in the fair value of investment properties are recognised in profit or loss
- If an intangible asset is identifiable, it is either: separable; or it arises from contractual or other legal rights
- The following internally generated intangible assets are never recognised: goodwill, brands, mastheads, publishing titles, customer lists and similar items
- Expenditure on research is recognised in profit or loss when it is incurred
- Development expenditure should be recognised as an asset if all the following can be demonstrated:
  - technical feasibility of completing the asset;
  - intention and ability to complete the asset and to use or sell it;
  - how it will generate future economic benefits;
  - availability of adequate resources; and
  - ability to measure the expenditure reliably

KEY WORDS

Useful life the period over which an asset is expected to be available for use by an entity

Borrowing costs interest and other costs incurred by an entity in connection with the borrowing of funds

Qualifying asset an asset that necessarily takes a substantial period of time to get ready for its intended use or sale

Investment property property (land or a building or both) held to earn rentals or for capital appreciation or for both, rather than for: use in the production or supply of goods or services or for administrative purposes; or sale in the ordinary course of business

Intangible asset an identifiable non-monetary asset without physical substance

Goodwill the excess of the value of the business as a whole over the total value of its individual assets and liabilities

Internally generated goodwill the goodwill that a business generates over time

Research original and planned investigation undertaken with the prospect of gaining new scientific or technical knowledge and understanding

Development the application of research findings or other knowledge to a plan or design for the production of new or substantially improved materials, devices, products, processes, systems before the start of commercial production or use

Impairment a reduction in the recoverable amount of an asset below its carrying amount

Impairment loss the amount by which the carrying amount of an asset exceeds its recoverable amount

CHAPTER OVERVIEW cont.

- After initial recognition, intangible assets are carried either at cost (the cost model) or at fair value (the revaluation model). Revaluation gains are credited to equity
- If an intangible asset has a finite useful life, it should be amortised on a systematic basis over its useful life
- If an intangible asset has an indefinite useful life, it is not amortised. It is reviewed for impairment at least annually
- To determine whether an asset is impaired, its carrying amount (net book value based on cost or a valuation) is compared with its recoverable amount
- If recoverable amount is less than carrying amount, the asset is impaired and an impairment loss is recognised
- Impairment losses are recognised in profit or loss if the asset has not previously been revalued. Otherwise they are treated as downward revaluations
- Non-current assets held for sale are measured at the lower of carrying amount and fair value less costs to sell. They are separately disclosed in the statement of financial position

KEY WORDS

Carrying amount the amount at which an asset is recognised after deducting any accumulated depreciation (amortisation) and accumulated impairment losses

Recoverable amount the higher of fair value less costs to sell or value in use

Fair value less costs to sell the amount obtainable from the sale of an asset in an arm's length transaction between knowledgeable, willing parties, less the costs of disposal

Value in use the present value of the future cash flows expected to be obtained from an asset as a result of continuing to use it in the business

Cash-generating unit the smallest identifiable group of assets that generates cash inflows that are largely independent of the cash inflows from other assets or groups of assets

HOW MUCH HAVE YOU LEARNED?

1 Sage Ltd incurs expenditure of £5,000 on repainting the outside of an office building. How should this expenditure be treated in the financial statements?

2 Basil Ltd owns three properties:

	Cost	*Accumulated depreciation*	*Fair value*
	£'000	£'000	£'000
Property A	100	10	120
Property B	150	10	140
Property C	120	10	180

The properties are all currently carried in the company's statement of financial position at depreciated historic cost.

a) Property A and Property C can be carried at fair value, while Property B can be carried at historic cost. True or false?

b) Once the company has adopted a policy of revaluing property, plant and equipment, it must update the valuation annually. True or false?

c) Show the journal entry needed to incorporate the valuations in the financial statements of Basil Ltd.

3 What method of depreciation is required by IAS 16?

4 An item of plant cost £50,000. On 1 January 20X2 it is revalued to £60,000. Its remaining useful life was 30 years at that date. The plant is depreciated using the straight line method.

What is the depreciation charge for the year ended 31 December 20X2?

5 Fill in the gaps.

Investment property is property held to earn .... or for .... or for both, rather than for:

- use in the .... or for .... ; or
- .... in the ordinary course of business.

6 During the year ended 31 December 20X4, a company started two new research and development projects:

Project A: New adhesive. Expected to cost a total of £2,000,000 to complete. Future revenues from the sale of the product are expected to exceed £4,000,000. The completion date of the project is uncertain because external funding will have to be obtained before the work can be completed.

Project B: New type of cloth. Expected to cost a total of £900,000 to develop. Expected total revenues £2,500,000 once work completed – completion date expected to be early 20X5. Most of the expenditure on the project has now been incurred and the company expects to be able to fund the remainder from its ongoing operations.

How should the expenditure on these projects be treated in the financial statements for the year ended 31 December 20X4?

7 Which two of the following statements are correct?

A An intangible asset may have an indefinite useful life.
B An intangible asset should always be amortised over its useful life.
C Internally generated goodwill should never be recognised.
D No internally generated intangible asset may be recognised.

8 When should an impairment loss be recognised in other comprehensive income (and deducted from the revaluation reserve)?

chapter 7: INVENTORIES, TAXATION, PROVISIONS AND EVENTS AFTER THE REPORTING PERIOD

chapter coverage

This chapter covers the accounting treatment of inventories and certain liabilities. Lastly, we cover the treatment and disclosure of events that occur after the end of the reporting period (the year-end), but before the financial statements are finalised and approved by the directors.

As with the accounting treatment of non-current assets covered in the previous chapter, you must understand the requirements of the accounting standards and be prepared to explain them and apply them in a particular situation.

The topics that we shall cover are:

- accounting for inventories
- current tax
- deferred tax
- provisions, contingent liabilities and contingent assets
- events after the reporting period

KNOWLEDGE AND UNDERSTANDING AND PERFORMANCE CRITERIA COVERAGE

knowledge and understanding

- the UK regulatory framework for financial reporting and the main requirements of relevant financial reporting standards
- the presentation of corporation tax in financial statements

Performance criteria – element 11.1

- draft limited company financial statements from the appropriate information
- ensure that limited company financial statements comply with relevant accounting standards and domestic legislation and with the organisation's policies, regulations and procedures

student notes

ACCOUNTING FOR INVENTORIES

The way in which closing inventory is valued can have a significant impact on the financial statements as a whole.

- It is normally material in the context of an entity's statement of financial position. Because inventory is part of an entity's working capital, over or understating the figure may affect users' views of the liquidity and solvency of the entity.
- Closing inventory is deducted from purchases to arrive at cost of sales and therefore inventory valuation directly affects profits.

IAS 2 Inventories

Inventories can consist of:

- goods purchased for resale
- consumable stores (for example stationery)
- raw materials and components that will be used to manufacture products for sale;
- work in progress: products that are partly completed;
- amounts relating to long term contracts; and
- finished goods.

IAS 2 defines **inventories** as assets:

- held for sale in the ordinary course of business
- in the process of production for such sale; or
- in the form of materials or supplies to be consumed in the production process or in the rendering of services.

IAS 2 contains a basic rule about inventories:

- Inventories should be measured at the lower of cost and net realisable value.

Cost

- The cost of inventories comprises all costs of purchase, costs of conversion and other costs incurred in bringing the inventories to their present location and condition.

student notes

- Cost of purchase is the purchase price. It also includes import duties, transport and handling costs and any other directly attributable costs, less trade discounts, rebates and subsidies.

- Costs of conversion include direct labour, direct expenses, sub-contracted work, and any production or other overheads that are attributable to bringing the product or service to its present location and condition.

Notice that:

- Cost includes expenditure that is attributable to bringing the product to its present location and condition. For example, the cost of inventory includes transport costs and therefore the cost of identical items may be different if they are in different locations.

- It follows that costs that have not been incurred directly in bringing the inventory to its present condition and location are not included in the cost of inventory. For example, a manufacturer includes factory overheads in the cost of its finished goods, but does not include administrative overheads.

- Only costs incurred in the normal course of business are included. For example, if a van carrying items of raw material to the factory breaks down, the cost of repairing the van is not included in the cost of the raw materials.

Net realisable value

Net realisable value is the estimated selling price in the ordinary course of business less:

- the estimated costs of completion; and
- the estimated costs necessary to make the sale.

Net realisable value is likely to be less than cost where:

- there is an increase in costs or a fall in selling price;

- inventories have deteriorated physically;

- products become obsolete;

- it is part of the marketing strategy of the company to sell products at a loss;

- there are errors in production or purchasing.

student notes

IAS 2 states that:

- When inventories are sold, the carrying amount (cost or net realisable value) of the inventory is recognised as an expense in the period in which the related revenue is recognised.

Where inventory is written down to net realisable value, the loss is recognised in profit or loss in the period in which it is incurred.

As we have seen, inventories should be stated at the lower of cost and net realisable value.

- Closing inventory has been purchased in the current accounting period, but will not be sold until the following accounting period. If inventories are valued at cost, the cost of purchasing the inventory is carried forward to be matched with the sales revenue when it arises in the following period. This is an application of the accruals (or matching) concept.

- If inventories were valued at selling price (net realisable value), the entity would normally be taking a profit on the inventories before they were actually sold and the profit realised. This is not acceptable because it contravenes the matching concept and because the profit has not yet been realised.

- The exception to this rule is where net realisable value is lower than cost, in other words, where the entity expects to make a loss. If inventories are written down to net realisable value, the loss is taken in the period in which it arose. This is prudent, and means that closing inventories are not overstated.

Applying the lower of cost and net realisable value rule

The comparison between cost and net realisable value must be made for each individual item of inventory, or each group of similar items. It cannot be made for inventories as a whole.

student notes

Activity 1

Lewis Ltd sells three products, A, B and C. At the year-end, inventories of these are as follows:

	Cost	*Selling price*	*Selling costs*
	£	£	£
A	2,880	3,600	180
B	5,500	5,400	366
C	3,310	3,350	165

At what amount should inventory be valued for inclusion in the statement of financial position?

Methods of valuing inventories

Businesses normally purchase large quantities of identical items at regular intervals throughout the year. It is very unlikely that management knows the actual cost of each individual item in inventories at the year end.

There are a number of methods of arriving at the cost of closing inventory in this situation. The three most common are:

- **First in first out (FIFO):** this assumes that items are used in the order in which they were received from suppliers; the items in inventory are the most recent purchases.
- **Last in first out (LIFO):** this assumes that the most recent purchases are used first; the items in inventory are the earliest purchases.
- **Weighted average cost (AVCO):** after each purchase the weighted average cost of the inventory is calculated: the total cost of the items in inventory is divided by the total number of items in inventory; this average is taken as the cost of each item.

IAS 2 states that **either** the **first in first out (FIFO)** formula or the **weighted average cost** formula should be used.

- Last in first out (LIFO) is not allowed.
- The same method should be used for all inventories having a similar nature and use.

student notes

HOW IT WORKS

Rowling Ltd made the following purchases of inventory.

1 March	20 units @	£100 per unit
15 March	20 units @	£150 per unit

On 30 March it sold 30 units.

Value of closing inventory at 31 March:

FIFO

- The items sold are assumed to be the 20 units purchased on 1 March and 10 units purchased on 15 March.
- Therefore the items in inventory are 10 units purchased on 15 March.
- Value of inventory : £1,500 (10 x 150).

AVCO

- Total cost of inventory purchased in March is £5,000 (20 x 100 + 20 x 150).
- Cost per item is £125 (5,000 ÷ 40).
- Value of inventory : £1,250 (10 x 125).

CURRENT TAX

Companies pay corporation tax on their taxable profits. The current rate of tax for most companies is 30%; where profits are 'small' the rate is 19%.

You will not be asked to calculate corporation tax in the Assessment. You do need to know how to account for and disclose corporation tax in the financial statements once the amount of tax has been calculated.

student notes

Accounting for corporation tax

At the end of each accounting period, corporation tax is calculated on the profit for the year.

- The corporation tax charge is included in profit or loss (the income statement).
- The liability for corporation tax is included in current liabilities in the statement of financial position.

Activity 2

The corporation tax charge of X Ltd is £150,000 for the year ended 31 December 20X2. Show the journal entry that is needed to adjust the financial statements.

The corporation tax included in the financial statements is only an estimate of the amount to be paid. The company does not usually know the actual amount of corporation tax until after the year end, when this is agreed with Her Majesty's Revenue and Customs (HMRC).

The amount that is actually paid could be greater or smaller than the tax charge and the tax liability that have been included in the financial statements.

HOW IT WORKS

The following information relates to Pullman Ltd:

- Corporation tax for the year ended 31 March 20X2 is estimated as £38,000.
- During the year ended 31 March 20X3 the company agrees the amount at £42,000 and this is paid to HMRC.
- Corporation tax for the year ended 31 March 20X3 is estimated as £40,000.

The following adjustment is made to the accounts for the year ended 31 March 20X2:

DEBIT	Corporation tax charge (income statement)	£38,000	
CREDIT	Corporation tax payable (statement of financial position)		£38,000

Being the corporation tax charge for the year ended 31 March 20X2

student notes

On 1 April 20X2, opening liabilities include a balance of £38,000 for corporation tax. After the tax liability has been settled, the corporation tax account is as follows:

Corporation tax

	£		£
Bank	42,000	Balance b/f	38,000
		Balance c/f	4,000
	42,000		42,000
Balance b/f	4,000		

The debit balance of £4,000 is included in the trial balance when the accounts for the year ended 31 March 20X3 are prepared. It represents the difference between the estimate of £38,000 and the actual tax charge of £42,000.

After the year end adjustments have been made, the corporation tax account is as follows:

Corporation tax

	£		£
Balance b/f	4,000	Income statement	44,000
Balance c/f	40,000		
	44,000		44,000
		Balance b/f	40,000

The tax charge in the income statement is:

	£
Corporation tax based on profits for the year	40,000
Adjustment in respect of prior period (underprovision)	4,000
	44,000

The amount included in the statement of financial position is the corporation tax liability for the year ended 31 March 20X3: £40,000.

student notes

Activity 3

Tolkein Ltd estimated the corporation tax charge for the year ended 30 June 20X4 as £45,000. The actual amount payable was £43,000. The estimated corporation tax charge for the year ended 30 June 20X5 is £50,000.

What is:

a) the corporation tax charge in the income statement for the year ended 30 June 20X5; and

b) the corporation tax liability in the statement of financial position at that date?

IAS 12 Income taxes

IAS 12 sets out the way in which current tax must be treated in the financial statements.

- Unpaid current tax (for both current and previous periods) should be recognised as a liability.
- Current tax should be measured at the amounts expected to be paid (or recovered) using the tax rates and laws that have been enacted by the year-end. This means that if the rate of tax changes between the year end and the date on which the accounts are signed, the rates used are the rates in force at the year-end (the reporting date).
- The tax expense relating to the profit or loss for the period is presented in profit or loss.
- Any tax relating to a gain or loss that has been recognised in other comprehensive income should be separately disclosed in other comprehensive income.

HOW IT WORKS

student notes

At 31 March 20X3 the corporation tax account of Pullman Ltd is as follows:

Corporation tax

	£		£
Balance b/f	4,000	Income statement	44,000
Balance c/f	40,000		
	44,000		44,000
		Balance b/f	40,000

The way in which this information is disclosed in the financial statements is shown below:

Income statement for the year ended 31 March 20X3 (extract)

	£
Profit before tax	X
Tax (W)	(44,000)
Profit for the year	X

Working

	£
Corporation tax based on profits for the year	40,000
Adjustment in respect of prior period	4,000
	44,000

Statement of financial position at 31 March 20X3 (extract)

	£
Current liabilities:	
Tax liabilities	40,000

DEFERRED TAX

Temporary differences

The profit before taxation that is reported in the income statement is not the actual amount on which corporation tax is charged. There are two main reasons for this:

- **Permanent differences**: some items (such as entertainment expenditure) are not allowed as a deduction from income for tax purposes. They must be added back to reported profit when calculating the corporation tax charge for the year.

student notes

- **Temporary differences**: these are differences between the carrying amount of an asset or liability in the statement of financial position and its valuation for tax purposes (tax base). These differences will result in additional taxable amounts in future periods when the carrying amount of the asset or liability is recovered or settled.

Temporary differences can occur for a number of reasons. The commonest are:

- **Accelerated capital allowances**. Depreciation is not an allowable expense for tax purposes. Instead, a business claims capital allowances when assets are purchased. To calculate taxable profits, depreciation is added back to reported profit and capital allowances are deducted.

- **Revaluation gains**: when an asset is revalued upwards the gain is recognised immediately in the financial statements, but the extra tax is not payable until the gain is realised when the asset is sold.

Because of temporary differences, some items are charged to tax or allowed for tax in a period that is different from the one in which they are recognised in the accounts.

Definition of deferred tax

IAS 12 *Income taxes* defines **deferred tax liabilities** as the amounts of income taxes payable in future periods in respect of taxable temporary differences.

Deferred tax has also been defined as the estimated future tax consequences of transactions and events recognised in the financial statements of the current period.

Deferred tax is not a tax as such. Instead it is a way of dealing with the effect of timing differences on the corporation tax charge for the year. In simple terms, it applies the accruals concept to accounting for corporation tax.

HOW IT WORKS

On 1 January 20X1 a company buys a non-current asset for £150,000. The asset has a useful life of three years, with no residual value. On 31 December 20X3 the company sells the asset.

Profit before tax is £450,000 for each of the three years.

The rate of corporation tax is 30%. The company is able to claim a first year allowance of 100% on the asset. This means that it can deduct the entire cost of the asset from its taxable profit for the year in the year it buys the asset. The tax base of the asset is reduced to zero.

The carrying amount of the asset is as follows for the three years:

	20X1	*20X2*	*20X3*
	£'000	£'000	£'000
Cost	150	150	150
Less depreciation	(50)	(100)	(150)
Carrying amount	100	50	Nil
Tax base	Nil	Nil	Nil
Temporary difference	100	50	–
Corporation tax on the difference x 30%	30	15	–

The temporary difference reduces as the asset is depreciated. The tax effect of the difference is the deferred tax liability that should be recognised in the statement of financial position at the end of each year.

We can also consider the effect on the income statement. Profit chargeable to corporation tax is as follows for the three years:

	20X1	*20X2*	*20X3*	*Total*
	£'000	£'000	£'000	£'000
Profit before tax	450	450	450	1,350
Add back depreciation	50	50	50	150
Less capital allowances	(150)	–	–	(150)
Taxable profit	350	500	500	1,350
Corporation tax @ 30%	105	150	150	405

Without the adjustments for depreciation and capital allowances, the company would have paid corporation tax of £135,000 (450,000 × 30%) for each of the three years. The total tax paid during the period is exactly the same as it would have been without these adjustments; the timing of the payment is different. The corporation tax charge is lower in 20X1, but higher in 20X2 and 20X3.

The differences are:

	20X1	*20X2*	*20X3*	*Total*
	£'000	£'000	£'000	£'000
Profit before tax x 30%	135	135	135	405
Corporation tax	(105)	(150)	(150)	(405)
Tax effect of temporary timing differences	30	(15)	(15)	–

The tax effect of the temporary timing differences is the deferred tax charge or credit that should be recognised in profit or loss each year.

student notes

Accounting treatment

IAS 12 states that a deferred tax liability must be recognised for all taxable temporary differences.

- Deferred tax liabilities are reported under non-current liabilities in the statement of financial position.
- Increases and decreases in the deferred tax liability are recognised in profit or loss (the income statement) for the year, unless they relate to a gain or loss that has been recognised in other comprehensive income.
- All deferred tax recognised in profit or loss (the income statement) is included as part of the tax on profit or loss for the year.

HOW IT WORKS

You will not be asked to calculate deferred tax in the Assessment, but you may be asked to account for it.

In the previous example, the corporation tax charge for the year ended 31 December 20X1 was £105,000. Tax on the temporary difference was £30,000.

Therefore the company provides deferred tax of £30,000. The double entry to make the adjustment is:

DEBIT	Deferred tax (income statement)	£30,000
CREDIT	Deferred tax liability (statement of financial position)	£30,000

In the year ended 31 December 20X2 there is a credit to the income statement of £15,000:

DEBIT	Deferred tax liability (statement of financial position)	£15,000
CREDIT	Deferred tax (income statement)	£15,000

The same adjustment is made again for the year ended 31 December 20X3 and the provision for deferred tax reduces to nil.

student notes

Activity 4

At 31 December 20X4, Williams Ltd had the following balances in its trial balance:

	Dr	*Cr*
	£'000	£'000
Corporation tax	5	
Deferred tax liability		110

The corporation tax charge for the year has been estimated at £150,000. The deferred tax liability is to be increased by £20,000.

Show how this information would be reflected in the financial statements for the year ended 31 December 20X4.

PROVISIONS, CONTINGENT LIABILITIES AND CONTINGENT ASSETS

Provisions

The term 'provision' is often used in a very general way. For example, an entity makes 'provisions' for depreciation and doubtful debts. These are not really provisions at all, but the result of normal accounting estimates. The term has a much more precise meaning.

IAS 37 *Provisions, contingent liabilities and contingent assets* states that:

- a **provision** is a liability of uncertain timing or amount
- a **liability** is a present obligation arising from past events, the settlement of which is expected to result in an outflow of resources embodying economic benefits.

Uncertainty is what distinguishes a provision from another type of liability. For example, if an entity has a liability to pay a supplier, management usually knows how much it must pay and when. If a claim is made against an entity, management knows that it will possibly have to pay damages, but not the precise amount (because this normally depends on the outcome of a court case).

Financial statements must be reliable. This means that expenses and liabilities should not be understated. In addition, users of the financial statements need information about all potential liabilities of an entity, even if there is uncertainty.

student notes

On the other hand, if all potential liabilities were provided for, even where the likelihood of payment was remote, the financial statements would be equally misleading. Before the issue of IAS 37 provisions were sometimes used for profit smoothing (a form of 'creative accounting'). An entity would set up a large general provision for future expenditure or future losses (sometimes known as 'the big bath') in a year where it had made high profits. The provision was then released to the income statement in future years when profits were not as high, to make the results seem better than they really were.

For this reason, IAS 37 sets out conditions which must be met before a provision can be recognised.

Recognising a provision

IAS 37 states that a provision should only be recognised when:

- an entity has a present obligation as a result of a past event
- it is probable that an outflow of resources embodying economic benefits will be required to settle the obligation
- a reliable estimate can be made of the amount of the obligation.

If there is an **obligation** to transfer economic benefits an entity **cannot avoid making payment** in some form.

An obligation can be legal or constructive:

- A legal obligation arises as the result of a contract, legislation or other operation of law.
- A constructive obligation occurs where:
  - an entity indicates that it will accept certain responsibilities (for example, by past practice, published policies or statements)
  - as a result, the entity has created a valid expectation on the part of those other parties that it will discharge those responsibilities.

  For example, suppose that a shop has a policy of refunding the cost of goods purchased by dissatisfied customers. The shop makes customers aware of this policy. As a result, the shop has a constructive obligation to make refunds.

Other points to note:

- The obligation must be the result of a past event; in other words, the event giving rise to the obligation must have happened before the end of the reporting period.
- Probable means more likely than not.

- Only in extremely rare cases is it not possible to make a reliable estimate of the amount of an obligation.

student notes

Activity 5

A company guarantees to repair or replace items that become defective within three years from the date of sale. The chance of an individual item needing to be repaired or replaced are small. However, past experience suggests that it is probable that there will be some claims under the guarantee.

Should the company recognise a provision for the costs or repairing and replacing items under the guarantee?

Measuring a provision

IAS 37 states that:

- The amount recognised should be the best estimate of the expenditure required to settle the present obligation at the end of the reporting period (the year-end).
- Risks, uncertainties and future events should be taken into account.
- Where the effect of the time value of money is material, the amount of the provision should be the present value of the expenditures required to settle the obligation (the amount is discounted).
- A provision should be reviewed at the end of the reporting period and adjusted to reflect the current best estimate.
- A provision should only be used for expenditures for which it was originally recognised.

Specific situations

IAS 37 deals with specific situations in which excessive or unnecessary provisions were sometimes made in the past.

- A **restructuring** is a programme that is planned and controlled by management and materially changes either:
  - the scope of a business undertaken by an entity; or
  - the manner in which that business is conducted.
- Examples:
  - sale or termination of a line of business

student notes

- closure of business locations in a country or region or a relocation of business activities from one country or region to another
- changes in management structure
- fundamental reorganisations that have a material effect on the nature and focus of an entity's operations.

■ Provisions should not be recognised for restructuring unless the entity has a constructive obligation to restructure:

- it has a detailed formal plan for the restructuring; and
- it has raised a valid expectation in those affected that it will carry out the restructuring by starting to implement the plan or announcing its main features to those affected by it.

A management or board decision on its own is not sufficient.

■ A restructuring provision should include only the direct expenditures arising from the restructuring: those that are both:

- necessarily entailed by the restructuring; and
- not associated with the entity's ongoing activities.

For example, it should not include:

- the cost of retraining or relocating staff who will continue to be employed
- marketing; or
- investment in new systems.

This is because these costs relate to the future activities of the business and are not liabilities of the entity at the year-end.

■ Provisions should not be recognised for future operating losses. These do not meet the definition of a liability.

Contingent liabilities

A provision can only be recognised if the liability is probable (more likely than not to occur). Users of the financial statements also need information about possible liabilities.

A **contingent liability** is:

■ a possible obligation that arises from past events and whose existence will be confirmed only by the occurrence of one or more uncertain future events not wholly within the entity's control, or

student notes

- a present obligation that arises from past events but is not recognised because:
  - it is not probable that a transfer of economic benefits will be required to settle the obligation, or
  - the amount of the obligation cannot be measured with sufficient reliability.

IAS 37 states that contingent liabilities should not be recognised.

Instead, information about contingent liabilities is disclosed in the financial statements unless the possibility of a transfer of economic benefits is remote.

Contingent assets

A **contingent asset** is a possible asset that arises from past events and whose existence will be confirmed only by the occurrence of one or more uncertain future events not wholly within the entity's control.

For example, an entity makes a claim for damages. The outcome is uncertain, but if it is successful it will receive a significant amount of cash. The entity has a contingent asset.

IAS 37 states that:

- Contingent assets should not be recognised (they might never be realised and the financial statements would be misleading as a result).
- If the possibility of an inflow of economic benefits is probable information about the contingent asset should be disclosed.
- If the asset is virtually certain to be realised it should be recognised. It is not a contingent asset but an actual asset.

Disclosure

Provisions

For each class of provision, disclose:

- the carrying amount at the beginning and end of the period
- additional provisions made in the period
- amounts used during the period
- unused amounts reversed during the period.

student notes

Also disclose:

- a brief description of the nature of the obligation and expected timing of any resulting transfers of economic benefit
- an indication of the uncertainties about the amount or timing of those transfers of economic benefit.

Contingent liabilities and assets

For each class of contingent liability and for probable contingent assets disclose:

- a brief description of its nature
- an estimate of its financial effect
- an indication of the uncertainties relating to the amount or timing of any outflow.

Summary

Likelihood	Provision/contingent liability	Contingent asset
Virtually certain	Recognise provision*	Recognise: not a contingent asset
Probable	Recognise provision*	Disclose but do not recognise
Possible (or probable and not quantifiable)	Do not recognise Contingent liability: disclose	Do nothing

* Assuming there is a present obligation as a result of a past event, otherwise disclose.

EVENTS AFTER THE REPORTING PERIOD

Events after the reporting period are those events, both favourable and unfavourable, which occur between the end of the reporting period and the date on which the financial statements are authorised for issue.

Events after the reporting period may:

- affect amounts in the financial statements that are about to be approved, or

student notes

- have a significant effect on the entity's future performance and prospects.

IAS 10 *Events after the reporting period* distinguishes between:

- adjusting events, and
- non-adjusting events.

Adjusting events

Adjusting events are events after the reporting period which provide **evidence of conditions that existed at the end of the reporting period.**

Examples of adjusting events:

- Non-current assets: the subsequent determination of the purchase price or the proceeds of sale of assets purchased or sold before the year end.
- Property: a valuation which provides evidence of an impairment in value.
- Investment: the receipt of information in respect of an unlisted company which provides evidence of an impairment in the value of a long-term investment.
- Inventories: the receipt of proceeds of sales after the year-end or other evidence concerning the net realisable value of inventories.
- Receivables: the renegotiation of amounts owing by customers, or the insolvency of a customer.
- Claims: amounts received or receivable in respect of insurance claims which are in the course of negotiation at the year-end.
- Discoveries: discovery of errors or frauds which show that the financial statements were incorrect.

Non-adjusting events

Non adjusting events are events after the reporting period which are indicative of conditions which arose after the reporting period.

Examples of non-adjusting events:

- Business combinations
- Reconstructions and proposed reconstructions (such as discontinuing an operation)
- Issues of shares and debentures

student notes

- Purchases or sales of property and investments
- Losses of non-current assets or inventories as a result of catastrophe such as fire or flood
- Opening new trading activities or extending existing trading activities
- Closing a significant part of the trading activities if this was not anticipated at the year end
- Decline in the value of property and investment held as non-current assets, if it can be demonstrated that the decline occurred after the year end
- Changes in rates of foreign exchange, or rates of taxation
- Government action, such as nationalisation
- Strikes and other labour disputes
- Augmentation of pension benefits

The basic principle

Financial statements are prepared on the basis of conditions existing at the end of the reporting period.

- Where there are adjusting events after the reporting period the amounts recognised in the financial statements are adjusted.
- A material non-adjusting event after the reporting period should be disclosed where it could influence the economic decisions of users taken on the basis of the financial statements. The amounts in the financial statements should not be adjusted.

Disclosure

For each material non-adjusting event after the reporting period, the notes to the financial statements should disclose the following:

- the nature of the event; and
- an estimate of the financial effect, or a statement that it is not practicable to make such an estimate.

Separate disclosure of adjusting events is not normally required.

The date on which the financial statements were authorised for issue and who gave that authorisation should be disclosed in the financial statements.

student notes

Dividends

Equity (ordinary) dividends declared after the end of the reporting period should not be recognised as a liability. However, they should be disclosed in the notes to the financial statements.

Going concern

Some events after the reporting period could indicate that an entity may not be a going concern. For example, an entity could suffer significant losses shortly after the year-end (perhaps as a result of a serious accident or the loss of a major customer). This type of event would normally be non-adjusting, because it concerns conditions which did not exist at the end of the reporting period.

IAS 10 states that an entity should not prepare its financial statements on a going concern basis if this is not appropriate (for example, if management have no alternative but to cease trading). When an entity ceases to be a going concern, the effect is so pervasive that the amounts in the financial statements must reflect this.

Window dressing

An entity may deliberately attempt to artificially improve the appearance of its statement of financial position. For example, a company may repay a loan just before the year end and then take it out again after the year end. This form of 'creative accounting' is known as **window dressing**.

IAS 10 does not specifically deal with window dressing. However, the requirement to disclose non-adjusting events means that users should be made aware of any 'window dressing' that may have taken place.

Activity 6

Lessing Ltd has prepared financial statements for the year ended 31 December 20X4. The financial statements are due to be approved on 31 March 20X5.

On 20 January 20X5 Lessing Ltd sold land and buildings for £250,000. At 31 December 20X4 they had had a net book value of £100,000.

On 15 February 20X5 a major customer went into liquidation. The directors of Lessing Ltd were advised that they were unlikely to receive any amounts owing to them. At 15 February 20X5 the customer owed £20,000 of which £15,000 related to sales made before the year end.

How should these two events be treated in the financial statements for the year ended 31 December 20X4?

CHAPTER OVERVIEW

- Inventories should be stated at the lower of cost and net realisable value
- The comparison between cost and net realisable value must be made for each individual item of inventory, or each group of similar items
- Either FIFO or AVCO must be used to arrive at the cost of inventory
- The corporation tax charge is included in the income statement and described as 'tax expense'
- The liability for corporation tax is included in current liabilities
- Deferred tax is a way of dealing with the effect of timing differences on the corporation tax charge for the year. It applies the accruals concept
- Deferred tax should be recognised on all taxable temporary differences
- Deferred tax liabilities should be reported under non-current liabilities in the statement of financial position
- All deferred tax recognised in the income statement should be included within the heading 'tax expense'
- A provision should only be recognised when:
  - an entity has a present obligation as a result of a past event; and
  - it is probable that a transfer of economic benefits will be required to settle the obligation; and
  - a reliable estimate can be made of the amount of the obligation
- The amount recognised should be the best estimate of the expenditure required to settle the present obligation at the year-end

KEY WORDS

Inventories assets: held for sale in the ordinary course of business; in the process of production for such sale; or in the form of materials or supplies to be consumed in the production process or in the rendering of services

Net realisable value the estimated selling price in the ordinary course of business less: the estimated costs of completion; and the estimated costs necessary to make the sale

First in first out (FIFO) a method of valuing inventory that assumes that items are used in the order in which they were received from suppliers

Last in first out (LIFO) a method of valuing inventory that assumes that the most recent purchases are used first

Average cost (AVCO) a method of valuing inventory which divides the total cost of the items in inventory by the total number of items in inventory to arrive at the cost of each item

Permanent differences differences between taxable profit and reported profit which arise because some items are not allowed as a deduction from income for tax purposes

Temporary differences differences between taxable profit and reported profit which arise because some items are charged to tax or allowed for tax in a period that is different from the one in which they are recognised in the accounts

Deferred tax liabilities the amounts of income taxes payable in future periods in respect of taxable temporary differences

Provision a liability of uncertain timing or amount

Liability a present obligation arising from past events, the settlement of which is expected to result in an outflow of resources embodying economic benefits

CHAPTER OVERVIEW cont.

- Contingent liabilities should not be recognised. They should be disclosed in the financial statements unless the possibility of a transfer of economic benefits is remote
- Contingent assets should not be recognised. Probable contingent assets should be disclosed
- Financial statements should be prepared on the basis of conditions existing at the year-end
- A material adjusting event after the year-end requires changes in the amounts to be included in the financial statements
- A material non-adjusting event after the year-end should be disclosed

KEY WORDS

Legal obligation an obligation which arises as the result of a contract, legislation or other operation of law

Constructive obligation an obligation which occurs where: an entity indicates that it will accept certain responsibilities; and as a result, the entity has created a valid expectation that it will discharge those responsibilities

Restructuring a programme that is planned and controlled by management and materially changes either: the scope of a business undertaken by an entity; or the manner in which that business is conducted

Contingent liability a possible obligation that arises from past events and whose existence will be confirmed only by the occurrence of one or more uncertain future events not wholly within the entity's control; or a present obligation that arises from past events but is not recognised because: it is not probable that a transfer of economic benefits will be required to settle the obligation; or the amount of the obligation cannot be measured with sufficient reliability

Contingent asset a possible asset that arises from past events and whose existence will be confirmed only by the occurrence of one or more uncertain future events not wholly within the entity's control

Events after the reporting period those events, both favourable and unfavourable, which occur between the end of the reporting period and the date on which the financial statements are authorised for issue

Adjusting events events after the reporting period which provide evidence of conditions existing at the end of the reporting period.

Non adjusting events events after the reporting period which are indicative of conditions which arose after the end of the reporting period

Window dressing a form of creative accounting in which an entity enters into a transaction shortly before the year end and reverses it after the year end; the object is to improve the appearance of the statement of financial position

HOW MUCH HAVE YOU LEARNED?

1 Fill in the gaps.

The cost of inventories comprises all costs of ...., costs of .... and other costs incurred in bringing the inventories to their present .... and ....

2 A company started to trade on 1 April and made the following purchases of inventory:

	Units	*Price per unit*	
	£	£	
1 April	60	20	1,200
15 April	40	22	880
30 April	50	25	1,250
			3,330

On 30 April 125 units were sold. Total proceeds were £5,000.

Calculate gross profit for April under:

a) FIFO
b) average cost.

3 For the year ended 30 June 20X3, Angle Ltd estimated that the charge to corporation tax was £85,500. The deferred tax provision was increased by £25,400. The estimated charge for corporation tax provided in the accounts for the year ended 30 June 20X2 was £11,000 higher than the actual amount paid to HMRC during 20X2/20X3.

What is the charge for corporation tax that will be disclosed in the income statement for the year ended 30 June 20X3?

4 What are temporary differences?

5 Proper Ltd operates a chain of restaurants. During the year ended 31 December 20X5, the following events have occurred:

- After a private function in one of the restaurants, several people became ill, possibly as a result of food poisoning. Legal proceedings were started seeking damages from the company. At 31 December, the case had not yet been settled, but the directors were advised that the company would probably not be found liable.

- As a result of this incident, the directors have decided to retrain most of the catering staff to make sure that they are aware of health and hygiene issues. The staff training means that the restaurants will have to close temporarily and the resulting loss of income is expected to be material. At 31 December 20X5 no staff training had taken place and the directors had not announced their decision to anybody likely to be affected.

Should the company make a provision for expenditure relating to either of these items in the financial statements for the year ended 31 December 20X5?

6 Complete the table below.

Events after the reporting period

	Adjusting event	**Non-adjusting event**
Damage to inventory as a result of a flood	....	....
Insurance claim received	....	....
Issue of shares	....	....
Opening new trading activities	....	....
Sale of property	....	....

chapter 8: FURTHER ACCOUNTING STANDARDS

chapter coverage

This chapter starts by considering the problem of when to recognise items in the financial statements. This leads into a more detailed look at the concept of 'substance over form', which was briefly introduced in an earlier chapter. We then move on to consider two further accounting standards that are related to 'substance over form': IAS 17 *Leases* and IAS 18 *Revenue*.

In the Exam-based Assessment, you will not be asked to carry out detailed accounting for any of the items covered in this chapter. You do need to have an appreciation of the issues and an outline knowledge of the way in which these items are treated in the financial statements, as you may be asked to explain them briefly or to give simple advice on dealing with them.

The topics that are to be covered are:

- recognition in financial statements
- reporting the substance of transactions
- leases
- revenue

KNOWLEDGE AND UNDERSTANDING AND PERFORMANCE CRITERIA COVERAGE

knowledge and understanding

- the UK regulatory framework for financial reporting and the main requirements of relevant financial reporting standards

Performance criteria – element 11.1

- draft limited company financial statements from the appropriate information
- ensure that limited company financial statements comply with relevant accounting standards and domestic legislation and with the organisation's policies, regulations and procedures

RECOGNITION IN FINANCIAL STATEMENTS

student notes

The IASB's *Framework for the Preparation and Presentation of Financial Statements* provides rules as to when items (assets and liabilities, income and expenses) should be recognised in the financial statements. We looked at these in an earlier chapter.

The basic principle

An item that meets the definition of an element (eg, an asset or a liability) should be recognised if:

- it is **probable** that any future economic benefit associated with the item will flow to or from the entity; and
- the item has a cost or value that can be measured with **reliability**.

We have seen that many accounting standards incorporate this principle, for example:

- IAS 16 *Property, plant and equipment*
- IAS 38 *Intangible assets*
- IAS 37 *Provisions, contingent liabilities and contingent assets.*

Recognising gains and losses

The elements of financial statements were covered in an earlier chapter. Income (or gains) and expenses (or losses) are defined in relation to changes in assets and liabilities. This means that (assuming that there are no contributions from owners or distributions from owners):

- if net assets increase, income or a gain is recognised; and
- if net assets are reduced or eliminated, an expense or a loss is recognised.

In other words:

- CLOSING NET ASSETS – OPENING NET ASSETS = PROFIT/LOSS FOR THE PERIOD

REPORTING THE SUBSTANCE OF TRANSACTIONS

The concept of substance over form was introduced in an earlier chapter. The financial statements should report the commercial and economic substance of a transaction, rather than its strict legal form.

student notes

In most cases, the substance of a transaction and its legal form are the same, but some transactions are more complex. When substance and form are different, reporting the substance of the transaction rather than the legal form can have a dramatic effect on the financial statements.

HOW IT WORKS

A plc owns a freehold property with a book value of £500,000. It sells the property to B Bank plc for £600,000. A plc has agreed to repurchase the property from B Bank plc for £700,000 in five years' time. A plc continues to occupy the property.

There are two ways in which this transaction could be treated in the financial statements.

Reporting the legal form

A plc has sold the property to B Bank plc. B Bank plc is now the legal owner of the property, even though A plc is still occupying it.

- A plc makes a profit of £100,000 on disposal.
- Depreciation charges are reduced.
- Assets decrease by £500,000.
- Cash increases by £600,000.

Both profit and net assets increase as a result of the sale.

Reporting substance

A plc is occupying the property and will repurchase it in five years' time. A plc has not disposed of the property but has used it as security for a loan from the bank.

- The property remains in the statement of financial position and the company continues to charge depreciation.

- There is no profit on disposal.

- Cash increases by £600,000, but there is also a long term liability of £600,000.

- The difference of £100,000 between the sale proceeds and the repurchase price is effectively interest. This has to be charged to profit or loss over the period of the loan. Each year, liabilities will increase as a result of the accrual for interest.

Profit is reduced if the transaction is recorded as a loan. More importantly, long term liabilities are increased dramatically. This means that investors are

student notes

more likely to regard the company as a risky investment. It may be harder for A plc to raise additional finance as a result.

The problem

The above example illustrates the main reasons why entities wish to keep certain assets and liabilities 'off balance sheet'.

Substance over form is recognised as an accounting concept, but during the 1980s some entities began to devise complicated transactions so as to control assets and incur liabilities without having to include them on the statement of financial position. As a result, this form of 'creative accounting' (known as **off balance sheet financing**) became common.

In addition, the business environment has generally became more sophisticated during the last twenty years. As a result, companies enter into complex transactions without necessarily intending to mislead investors. Some of these transactions are still not covered by any specific accounting standard.

Activity 1

The example above deals with a sale and repurchase agreement. Give another example of a transaction or arrangement whose substance may be different from its legal form.

Substance over form and accounting standards

IAS 1 *Presentation of financial statements* contains a general requirement to report the substance of transactions:

- Fair presentation requires the faithful representation of the effects of transactions, other events and conditions in accordance with the definitions and recognition criteria for assets, liabilities, income and expenses set out in the *Framework*.

In addition, two other standards deal with substance over form in relation to specific types of transaction:

- IAS 17 *Leases*
- IAS 18 *Revenue*.

How to determine the substance of a transaction

An entity should identify whether the transaction has given rise to new assets or liabilities or whether it has increased or decreased existing assets or liabilities.

student notes

Where a transaction is routine it is usually fairly obvious whether an entity has an asset or a liability. In cases where substance and legal form are different an entity must often apply the strict definitions in the *Framework*:

- An **asset** is a resource controlled by the entity as a result of past events and from which future economic benefits are expected to flow to the entity.
- A **liability** is a present obligation of the entity arising from past events, the settlement of which is expected to result in an outflow of resources embodying economic benefits from the entity.
- An entity has an asset if it bears the risks inherent in the asset. **Risk** is uncertainty as to the amount of benefits. If an entity bears risks, there is potential for gain as well as exposure to losses.
- An entity **controls an asset** if it has the ability to obtain the future economic benefits relating to an asset and to restrict the access of others to those benefits.
- An entity has a liability if it is unable to avoid, legally or commercially, an outflow of benefits.

To report the substance of a transaction, an entity applies the rules in the *Framework*:

- An item is recognised if it meets the definition of an asset or a liability; and
- it is **probable** that any future economic benefit associated with the item will flow to or from the entity; and
- the item has a cost or value that can be measured with **reliability**.

The 'true' gains and losses resulting from the transaction will then be reported in the financial statements.

LEASES

A **lease** is a contract between a lessor and a lessee for the hire of a specific asset. The lessor retains ownership of the asset, but the lessee has the right to use the asset for an agreed period of time in return for the payment of specified rentals.

Many entities use leases to finance the purchase or use of non-current assets. By leasing an asset rather than buying it, an entity spreads the cash outflow over several accounting periods.

Types of lease

student notes

IAS 17 *Leases* classifies leases into two types.

A **finance lease** is a lease that **transfers substantially all the risks and rewards of ownership of an asset to the lessee**. Title (ownership) may or may not eventually be transferred. Although the lessor continues to own the asset, the substance of the contract is that the lessee has purchased the asset and has obtained a loan from the lessor to finance the purchase.

A lease is almost certainly a finance lease if all or some of the following apply:

- The lease transfers ownership of the asset to the lessee by the end of the lease term.
- The lease contract is for all or most of the asset's useful life, even if ownership is not transferred.
- At the inception (start) of the lease, the present value of the minimum lease payments amounts to at least substantially all of the fair value of the leased asset. The minimum lease payments are the total payments that the lessee will have to make under the terms of the lease.
- The leased assets are so specialised that only the lessee can use them without major modifications.
- The lessee is responsible for repairs, maintenance and insurance.

A lease could be a finance lease if the following applies:

- if the lease is cancelled, the lessee bears any losses incurred by the lessor as a result of the cancellation.
- after the initial lease term ends, the lessee has the option of continuing to lease the asset for a secondary period at a rent that is substantially lower than the market rent.

However, IAS 17 is clear that the key factor is the transfer of the risks and rewards of ownership.

An **operating lease** is a lease other than a finance lease. An operating lease is similar to a rental agreement.

IAS 17 requires entities to account for the substance of a lease contract rather than its legal form. This means that finance leases and operating leases are treated differently in the financial statements.

student notes

Activity 2

Witney Ltd leases an item of plant. Under the terms of the lease, Witney Ltd makes payments of £20,000 each year for five years. The present value of the minimum lease payments is £95,500. The plant has a useful life of five years and would cost £98,000 to purchase outright.

Is this an operating lease or a finance lease?

Land and buildings

Land and buildings are often leased together under the same agreement.

- Land normally has a very long useful life. This means that when land is leased, the agreement often covers only a very small part of its useful life, so that the risks and rewards of ownership are not transferred to the lessee. Leases of land are normally operating leases.
- Leases of buildings may be either finance leases or operating leases.
- For accounting purposes, the land element and the buildings element must be separated. Each part is then classified as a finance lease or an operating lease independently of the other.

Accounting for finance leases in the financial statements of the lessee

You will **not** be asked to do any accounting for leases in the Exam-based Assessment, but you do need to understand how they are treated in the financial statements.

At the start of the lease

- The leased asset is recognised in the lessee's statement of financial position at its **fair value**, or, if this is lower, the **present value of the minimum lease payments**.
- The lessee also recognises a liability for the loan. This is the same amount as the value of the asset.
- **Fair value** is the amount for which an asset could be exchanged, or a liability settled, between knowledgeable, willing parties in an arm's length transaction. In practice, this is usually the same as the purchase price of the asset.
- **Minimum lease payments** are the payments that the lessee is, or can be, required to make over the lease term.
- To arrive at the present value of the minimum lease payments, the payments are discounted using the **interest rate implicit in the**

student notes

lease, or, if this is not possible, the lessee's **incremental borrowing rate**.

- The **interest rate implicit in the lease** is the discount rate that, at the inception of the lease, causes the total present value of the minimum lease payments to be equal to the fair value of the leased asset.
- The idea here is that the lease is really a loan for the sum of money that the lessee would need to buy the asset outright (its fair value). The fair value of the asset is the capital amount of the loan and the lessor charges interest on this at a rate that takes account of the time value of money.
- The lessee's **incremental borrowing rate** is the rate of interest that the lessee would have to pay on a similar lease or on a similar sum of money over a similar term.

Over the term of the lease

- The asset is depreciated over its **useful life**. The depreciation rate and method used must be the same as those used for similar assets that are owned by the entity.
- The useful life of a leased asset is the shorter of the normal useful life of a similar asset and the lease term.
- The total payments under the lease are usually more than the value of the leased asset in the statement of financial position. The difference is the lease interest.
- The lease payments are split between capital and interest. As each instalment is paid, the capital portion reduces the outstanding liability, while the interest is charged in the income statement.

Accounting for operating leases in the financial statements of the lessee

- The lease payments are charged to profit or loss (the income statement) on a straight line basis. (The asset is not recognised in the statement of financial position.)
- Information about the operating lease is disclosed in the notes to the financial statements.

Accounting for finance leases in the financial statements of the lessor

At the start of the lease

- The lessor recognises a receivable in the statement of financial position.

student notes

- This is measured at the present value of the total minimum lease payments receivable from the lessee.
- The leased asset itself is not recognised, because the substance of the agreement is that ownership has been transferred to the lessee.

Over the term of the lease

- The amounts receivable from the lessee are split between capital and interest. The capital portion reduces the receivable in the statement of financial position and the interest portion is recognised in the income statement.

Accounting for operating leases in the financial statements of the lessor

- Ownership of the asset is not transferred to the lessee.
- The lessor recognises the leased asset in the statement of financial position and depreciates it over its useful life in the usual way. The depreciation rate and method used must be the same as those used for similar assets owned by the lessor.
- Income from the lease is recognised in profit or loss on a straight line basis over the lease term.

REVENUE

Revenue is an entity's income from its main operating activities.

IAS 18 *Revenue* defines it more formally as:

- The gross inflow of economic benefits during the period arising in the course of the ordinary activities of the entity, when those inflows result in increases in equity, other than increases relating to contributions from equity shareholders (increases in share capital).

Activity 3

A company sells an item of property at a profit. Should the income be treated as revenue?

IAS 18 applies to:

- the sale of goods
- the rendering of services; and
- the use by others of entity assets yielding interest, royalties and dividends.

student notes

The basic principle

Revenue is measured at the fair value of the consideration received or receivable.

For example, where an entity makes a sale the amount recognised is the amount invoiced. This is the amount of cash that the entity will eventually receive.

Sale of goods

Revenue from the sale of goods is recognised when all the following conditions have been satisfied:

- The entity has transferred to the buyer the significant risks and rewards of ownership of the goods;
- The entity retains neither continuing managerial involvement to the degree usually associated with ownership nor effective control over the goods sold;
- The amount of revenue can be measured reliably;
- It is probable that the economic benefits associated with the transaction will flow to the entity; and
- The costs incurred or to be incurred in respect of the transaction can be measured reliably.

Notice that IAS 18 uses the same recognition criteria as the *Framework:* there must be a probable inflow of economic benefits; and these must be capable of being measured reliably.

Activity 4

A customer orders some goods from Bampton Ltd which have to be specially manufactured for it. Because of the amount of work involved, the customer pays Bampton Ltd in full at the time the goods are ordered.

How should Bampton Ltd treat this payment in its financial statements?

Rendering of services

When the outcome of a transaction involving the rendering of services can be estimated reliably, revenue associated with the transaction is recognised by reference to the stage of completion of the transaction at the end of the reporting period.

student notes

The outcome of a transaction can be estimated reliably when:

- the amount of revenue can be measured reliably;
- it is probable that the economic benefits associated with the transaction will flow to the entity;
- the stage of completion of the transaction at the end of the reporting period can be measured reliably; and
- the costs incurred for the transaction and the costs to complete the transaction can be measured reliably.

Dividends

Revenue from dividends is recognised when:

- it meets the normal recognition criteria:
  - it is probable that the economic benefits associated with the transaction will flow to the entity; and
  - the amount of the revenue can be measured reliably; and
- the shareholder's right to receive payment is established.

CHAPTER OVERVIEW

- Financial statements should report the commercial and economic substance of a transaction, rather than its strict legal form
- To determine the substance of a transaction an entity should identify whether the transaction has increased or decreased its assets or liabilities
- An entity has an asset if it bears the risks inherent in the asset
- An entity has a liability if there is some circumstance in which the entity is unable to avoid an outflow of benefits
- To report the substance of a transaction the entity must follow the recognition rules in the *Framework*
- IAS 17 requires entities to account for the substance of a lease contract rather than its legal form
- A lease is either an operating lease or a finance lease. The classification of a lease determines the accounting treatment
- If the lease is a finance lease, the lease is treated as if the lessee has purchased an asset and financed the purchase by taking out a loan. The leased asset and the liability for the loan are recognised in the lessee's statement of financial position. The income statement includes depreciation and interest on the loan
- If the lease is an operating lease, the lease payments are charged to the lessee's income statement as rental and the leased asset is not recognised in the statement of financial position
- A lessor recognises a finance lease as an amount receivable and recognises finance income over the term of the lease

KEY WORDS

Off balance sheet financing a form of creative accounting where an entity accounts for the legal form of a complicated transaction rather than its commercial substance. In this way, an entity controls assets and has liabilities without including them in the statement of financial position

Risk uncertainty as to the amount of benefits. The term includes both potential for gain and exposure to loss

Control of an asset the ability to obtain the future economic benefits relating to an asset and to restrict the access of others to those benefits

Lease a contract for the hire of a specific asset. The lessor retains ownership of the asset, but the lessee has the right to use the asset for an agreed period of time in return for the payment of specified rentals

Hire purchase contract a contract for the hire of an asset. Legal title normally passes to the hirer when all instalments have been paid

Finance lease a lease that transfers substantially all the risks and rewards of ownership of an asset to the lessee

Operating lease a lease other than a finance lease; similar to a rental agreement

Minimum lease payments the total payments that the lessee is required to make over the lease term

Interest rate implicit in the lease the discount rate that, at the inception of the lease, causes the total present value of the minimum lease payments to be equal to the fair value of the leased asset

Incremental borrowing rate the rate of interest that the lessee would have to pay on a similar lease or on a similar sum of money over a similar term

CHAPTER OVERVIEW cont.

- If a lessor has an operating lease, it continues to recognise the asset and to depreciate it as normal. Income from the lease is recognised in the income statement
- Revenue is measured at the fair value of the consideration received or receivable
- Revenue from the sale of goods is recognised when:
  - the entity has transferred the significant risks and rewards of ownership of the goods;
  - the entity no longer has effective control over the goods sold;
  - the amount of revenue and the related costs of the transaction can be measured reliably; and
  - it is probable that the economic benefits associated with the transaction will flow to the entity
- When the outcome of a transaction involving the rendering of services can be estimated reliably, revenue associated with the transaction is recognised by reference to the stage of completion of the transaction at the year-end

KEY WORDS

Revenue the gross inflow of economic benefits during the period arising in the course of the ordinary activities of the entity, when those inflows result in increases in equity, other than increases relating to contributions from equity shareholders

HOW MUCH HAVE YOU LEARNED?

1 Two conditions must be met before a new asset or liability is recognised. What are they?

2 Which accounting standard requires an entity to report the substance of transactions?

3 A company's financial statements include the following note:

Profit from operations:

Profit from operations is stated after charging the following:

Depreciation:	owned assets	X
	leased assets	X

Assuming that the company has followed the correct accounting treatment set out in IAS 17, which type of lease agreement has it entered into?

4 Fill in the gaps.

.... is the gross inflow of .... during the period arising in the course of the .... of the entity.

chapter 9: INTERPRETING FINANCIAL STATEMENTS

chapter coverage

The objective of financial statements is to enable users to make economic decisions. This chapter concentrates on the start of the decision making process: analysing and interpreting the information in financial statements.

The topics that we shall cover are:

- different types of limited company compared
- ratio analysis
- profitability
- liquidity
- efficiency
- gearing
- interpreting ratios
- writing reports
- limitations of ratio analysis

KNOWLEDGE AND UNDERSTANDING AND PERFORMANCE CRITERIA COVERAGE

knowledge and understanding

- analysing and interpreting the information contained in financial statements
- computing and interpreting accounting ratios

Performance criteria – element 11.2

- identify the general purpose of financial statements used in limited companies
- identify the elements of financial statements used in limited companies
- identify the relationships between the elements of limited company financial statements
- interpret the relationship between elements of limited company financial statements using ratio analysis
- identify unusual features or significant issues within financial statements of limited companies
- draw valid conclusions from the information contained within financial statements
- present issues, interpretations and conclusions clearly to the appropriate people

DIFFERENT TYPES OF LIMITED COMPANY

student notes

Objectives

It is important to understand that different types of company have different objectives.

- **Public companies and large private companies:** to provide a return to investors by maximising profit.
- **Owner-managed businesses (small private companies, partnerships and sole traders):** to make sufficient profit to support the owners and their dependents.

Sources of finance

- **Public companies and large private companies:** ordinary shares (equity); preference shares; debentures and other types of loan (debt).
- **Owner managed businesses:** ordinary shares; owners' capital; loans (normally from the bank).

Stewardship responsibilities

- **Public companies and large private companies** are managed by directors on behalf of shareholders.
- **Owner managed businesses:** strictly speaking, management have no stewardship responsibilities. Many small businesses are financed by debt and therefore they could be said to be 'accountable' to lenders.

The persons to whom management has stewardship responsibilities (who are also likely to be the main providers of finance) are normally the most important users of an entity's financial statements.

Activity 1

The IASB's *Framework* identifies the groups of people who are interested in financial statements. What are they?

student notes

What decisions do users of financial statements need to make?

The main objective of financial statements is to help users make economic decisions.

- **Public companies and large private companies:** investors and potential investors need to decide whether to hold or sell their investment, or whether to invest in the company at all. These users are most interested in the profitability of the entity and in its efficiency (the way in which it has used its resources to generate profit).

- **Owner managed businesses:** the main external users are Her Majesty's Revenue and Customs (HMRC) and lenders:

  - HMRC needs to be satisfied that the business has paid the right amount of tax, based on its profit for the period. It is interested in the profit figure and in the make-up of revenue and expenses.

  - Lenders need to be satisfied that the loan will be repaid when it is due. Potential lenders need to decide whether to lend to the business and on what terms. These users are interested in an entity's cash flows and in its ability to meet its debts as they fall due, both in the short term and in the longer term (its liquidity and solvency).

In the exam based assessment, you may be asked to prepare a report which interprets information in the financial statements. Ask yourself:

- who is the report intended for?
- what are they most interested in?
- what decision do they need to make?

RATIO ANALYSIS

Ratio analysis is a technique used to interpret financial information. It involves calculating ratios by comparing one figure in the financial statements with another.

For example, revenue is £100,000 and gross profit is £25,000. The gross profit margin is 25%.

However, this tells us very little on its own. Is a gross profit margin of 25% good or bad? The ratios must be compared with other information:

- The previous year's financial statements (is the gross profit margin better or worse than last year?)

- Budgeted financial statements (is gross profit more or less than forecast?)
- The financial statements of another company (is the gross profit margin better or worse than that of a competitor?)
- Average figures for the industry (how profitable is the company in relation to the industry as a whole?).

Types of ratios

Ratios can be used to assess:

- profitability
- liquidity
- efficient use of resources
- gearing.

The income statements and statements of financial position below will be used to illustrate the ratio calculations.

Example financial statements

Income statements for the year ended 31 December 20X8

	Smith Ltd	*Jones Ltd*
	£'000	£'000
Continuing operations		
Revenue	2,200	3,000
Cost of sales	(770)	(2,100)
Gross profit	1,430	900
Operating expenses	(1,320)	(600)
Profit from operations	110	300
Finance cost	(10)	(15)
Profit before tax	100	285
Tax	(35)	(85)
Profit for the year attributable to equity holders	65	200

student notes

Statements of financial position at 31 December 20X8

	Smith Ltd £'000	*Jones Ltd* £'000
Assets		
Non-current assets:		
Property, plant & equipment	440	660
Current assets:		
Inventories	170	110
Receivables	220	100
Cash	–	20
	390	230
Total assets	830	890
Equity and liabilities		
Equity:		
Share capital	100	100
Retained earnings	230	440
	330	540
Non-current liabilities	140	170
Current liabilities:		
Trade payables	220	90
Tax liabilities	30	90
Bank overdraft	110	–
	360	180
Total liabilities	500	350
Total equity and liabilities	830	890

Return on capital employed

Return on capital employed (ROCE) is regarded as the key measure of a business' profitability. It measures the profit (the return) that a business generates from the resources available to it (its capital employed). **Capital employed** is equity plus non-current liabilities or can also be calculated as total assets less current liabilities.

$$\text{ROCE} = \frac{\text{Profit before interest and tax (profit from operations)}}{\text{Capital employed}}$$

	Smith Ltd	*Jones Ltd*
ROCE	$\frac{110}{330+140} \times 100\% = 23.4\%$	$\frac{300}{540+170} \times 100\% = 42.2\%$

Notice that both interest and long term liabilities are included in the calculation. ROCE measures the total return made by the company on both debt and share capital, not simply the return to shareholders.

A variation of ROCE measures the return to shareholders only:

$$\text{Return on equity} = \frac{\text{Profit after tax}}{\text{Equity}}$$

This ratio is also known as return on shareholders' equity (capital) or return on owners' equity.

	Smith Ltd	*Jones Ltd*
ROE	$\frac{65}{330} \times 100\% = 19.7\%$	$\frac{200}{540} \times 100\% = 37.0\%$

In this ratio interest is deducted, as we are only concerned with the profit for the shareholders.

Net profit margin

Net profit margin measures the overall profitability of a business. It is normally calculated on operating profit, but may be calculated on profit before tax if these are different.

$$\text{Net profit margin} = \frac{\text{Profit before interest and tax}}{\text{Revenue}}$$

	Smith Ltd	*Jones Ltd*
Net profit margin	$\frac{110}{2,200} \times 100\% = 5\%$	$\frac{300}{3,000} \times 100\% = 10\%$

Gross profit margin

Gross profit margin measures gross profit as a percentage of sales.

$$\text{Gross profit margin} = \frac{\text{Gross profit}}{\text{Revenue}}$$

	Smith Ltd	*Jones Ltd*
Gross profit margin	$\frac{1,430}{2,200} \times 100\% = 65\%$	$\frac{900}{3,000} \times 100\% = 30\%$

student notes

Expenses ratio

The **expenses ratio** (sometimes called **expenses/sales**) measures operating expenses as a percentage of sales. For this purpose, operating expenses are expenses other than those included in cost of sales (often shown in the income statement as distribution costs and administrative expenses). It follows that if a business has a high expenses ratio it normally has a low net profit margin.

$$\text{Expenses ratio} = \frac{\text{Operating expenses}}{\text{Revenue}}$$

	Smith Ltd	*Jones Ltd*
Expenses ratio	$\frac{1,320}{2,200} \times 100\% = 60\%$	$\frac{600}{3,000} \times 100\% = 20\%$

Asset turnover

Asset turnover measures the efficiency with which a business uses its resources (its net assets, in other words capital employed) to generate sales.

$$\text{Asset turnover} = \frac{\text{Revenue}}{\text{Capital employed}}$$

	Smith Ltd	*Jones Ltd*
Asset turnover	$\frac{2,200}{330+140} = 4.7$ times	$\frac{3,000}{540+170} = 4.2$ times

The relationship between the ratios

A business' return on capital employed (ROCE) has two components:

- its profitability (measured by net profit margin)
- its use of assets (measured by asset turnover).

The relationship between the three ratios is:

$$\frac{\text{Profit before interest and tax}}{\text{Revenue}} \times \frac{\text{Revenue}}{\text{Capital employed}} = \frac{\text{Profit before interest and tax}}{\text{Capital employed}}$$

student notes

The nature of the business often affects the components of ROCE. For example, a manufacturing business and a business that provides services could both have the same ROCE, made up in different ways:

	Net profit margin	×	Asset turnover	=	ROCE
■ Manufacturer	10%	×	2.5	=	25%
■ Service provider	5%	×	5	=	25%

The service provider appears to make more efficient use of assets than the manufacturer because a manufacturer needs to invest in plant and equipment in order to generate revenue. Service industries normally have few non-current assets relative to their revenue; they rely on the expertise of their staff to generate profit.

Activity 2

The summarised statement of financial position of Brookstream Ltd is shown below:

	£'000	£'000
Assets		
Non-current assets		1,400
Current assets		400
Total assets		1,800
Equity:		
Share capital		200
Share premium		100
Retained earnings		600
		900
Non-current liabilities	600	
Current liabilities	300	
Total liabilities		900
Total equity and liabilities		1,800

Sales revenue for the year was £2 million and profit from operations was £300,000.

Calculate the following ratios:

a) Return on capital employed (ROCE)
b) Net profit margin
c) Asset turnover

student notes

LIQUIDITY

A business' **liquidity** is its ability to meet its debts as they fall due.

Current ratio

This is an overall measure of a business' liquidity. It shows the extent to which current liabilities are covered by either cash or assets that can be converted into cash within a reasonably short time.

$$\textbf{Current ratio} = \frac{\text{Current assets}}{\text{Current liabilities}}$$

	Smith Ltd	*Jones Ltd*
Current ratio	$\frac{390}{360} = 1.1$	$\frac{230}{180} = 1.3$

Quick (acid test) ratio

This ratio measures the immediate solvency of a business by showing the extent to which its current liabilities are covered by cash and amounts receivable. Inventories are excluded from the calculation because they are less liquid than receivables. Inventories must be sold and converted into receivables before they can eventually be converted into cash.

$$\textbf{Quick ratio} = \frac{\text{Current assets} - \text{inventories}}{\text{Current liabilities}}$$

	Smith Ltd	*Jones Ltd*
Quick ratio	$\frac{220}{360} = 0.6$	$\frac{120}{180} = 0.7$

Activity 3

The following information has been extracted from the statement of financial position of Gloryline Ltd:

	£'000
Inventories	4,750
Receivables	11,350
Cash	2,900
Trade payables	7,400
Other current liabilities	2,100

Calculate the current ratio and the quick ratio.

student notes

EFFICIENCY

This group of ratios measures the ability of a business to control its working capital. They are also used to analyse liquidity because they provide information about the individual components of working capital: inventories, receivables and payables.

If a business has a relatively high level of inventories and receivables it has cash tied up which cannot be used immediately. This means that:

- the business may not be able to meet its debts promptly
- it may miss opportunities for growth (for example, it may be more difficult to purchase new plant and equipment which might generate more revenue)
- lack of cash may mean that the business has a bank overdraft or has to take out a loan. Profit is then reduced by interest charges.

If a business has a relatively low level of trade payables, it may be paying its debts more quickly than is strictly necessary.

A business can improve its cash flow (and possibly avoid a bank overdraft) by:

- keeping inventory levels as low as possible;
- collecting cash from customers promptly (by offering prompt payment discounts or by good credit control);
- delaying payments to suppliers.

However:

- a business must carry enough inventory to meet customer demand;
- customers must be allowed a reasonable amount of credit;
- suppliers must be paid within a reasonable amount of time.

In practice, a business has to balance the need for cash against the need to maintain good relationships with customers and suppliers (in order to continue to generate sales and profits).

Inventory turnover

This shows how rapidly a business's inventory is sold on average during the year; or alternatively, the extent to which inventory levels are justified relative to sales.

$$\textbf{Inventory turnover} = \frac{\text{Cost of sales}}{\text{Inventories}}$$

student notes

	Smith Ltd	Jones Ltd
Inventory turnover	$\frac{770}{170} = 4.5$ times	$\frac{2{,}100}{110} = 19.1$ times

An alternative calculation is inventory days, or the average number of days for which a business holds an item of inventory.

$$\textbf{Inventory days} = \frac{\text{Inventory}}{\text{Cost of sales}} \times 365$$

	Smith Ltd	Jones Ltd
Inventory days	$\frac{170}{770} \times 365 = 81$ days	$\frac{110}{2{,}100} \times 365 = 19$ days

Receivables days

This is the average period taken to collect receivables.

$$\textbf{Receivables days} = \frac{\text{Receivables}}{\text{Revenue}} \times 365$$

	Smith Ltd	Jones Ltd
Receivables days	$\frac{220}{2{,}200} \times 365 = 36$ days	$\frac{100}{3{,}000} \times 365 = 12$ days

Payables days

This is the average period taken to pay suppliers.

$$\textbf{Payables days} = \frac{\text{Trade payables}}{\text{Cost of sales}} \times 365$$

	Smith Ltd	Jones Ltd
Payables days	$\frac{220}{770} \times 365 = 104$ days	$\frac{90}{2{,}100} \times 365 = 16$ days

Technically, payables days should be based upon purchases rather than cost of sales, but the purchases figure is not normally available from a set of financial statements. Therefore cost of sales is used as an approximation.

student notes

Activity 4

Trading account for the year ended 30 June 20X5:

	£'000	£'000
Sales		6,900
Opening inventory	900	
Purchases	4,500	
Closing inventory	(1,200)	
Cost of sales		(4,200)
Gross profit		2,700

What is inventory turnover?

GEARING

The ratios

Gearing ratios measure the extent to which a company is financed by debt rather than by shareholders' equity. Debt usually means long term liabilities: loan stock (debentures) and long term loans.

There are two main calculations:

- **Gearing** (sometimes called capital gearing) = $\dfrac{\text{Debt}}{\text{Capital employed}}$

- **Debt to equity** = $\dfrac{\text{Debt}}{\text{Share capital and reserves}}$

There are several possible variations. For example, if a company has a substantial bank overdraft, this may be included in debt.

In the exam, it will usually be obvious which ratio you are to calculate; if not, you will get credit for any sensible calculation.

	Smith Ltd	*Jones Ltd*
Gearing	$\dfrac{140}{330+140} \times 100\% = 30\%$	$\dfrac{170}{540+170} \times 100\% = 24\%$
Debt to equity	$\dfrac{140}{330} \times 100\% = 42\%$	$\dfrac{170}{540} \times 100\% = 31\%$

student notes

Gearing and risk

A company with a high proportion of debt to equity is said to be **highly geared.** If a company is highly geared:

- Interest charges mean that less profit is available to pay dividends to ordinary shareholders. As a result, the company may be less attractive to investors and potential investors.
- It may be difficult to raise additional finance, because banks and other potential lenders are normally reluctant to lend to a company that is already heavily in debt.
- If the company makes losses, there is a greater likelihood that it will face severe problems as a result. If interest payments cannot be met, loan creditors can demand repayment of the entire loan. This may lead to the company going into liquidation.

HOW IT WORKS

A highly geared company is perceived as a risky investment. Consider the three companies below:

	A plc	*B plc*	*C plc*
	£'000	£'000	£'000
10% loan stock	Nil	1,000	2,000
Ordinary share capital	1,000	1,000	1,000
Reserves	1,000	1,000	1,000
	2,000	2,000	2,000
Gearing	0%	33%	50%

	A plc	*B plc*	*C plc*
	£'000	£'000	£'000
Profit from operations	1,000	1,000	1,000
Interest payable	–	(100)	(200)
Profit before tax	1,000	900	800
Tax at 30%	(300)	(270)	(240)
Profit available for shareholders	700	630	560

Suppose that profit from operations falls by 50%. This is the effect on ordinary shareholders:

	A plc	*B plc*	*C plc*
	£'000	£'000	£'000
Profit from operations	500	500	500
Interest payable	–	(100)	(200)
Profit before tax	500	400	300
Tax at 30%	(150)	(120)	(90)
Profit available for shareholders	350	280	210
Decrease in profits available to shareholders	50%	55%	62.5%

Suppose that profit from operations increases by 50%.

	A plc	*B plc*	*C plc*
	£'000	£'000	£'000
Profit from operations	1,500	1,500	1,500
Interest payable	–	(100)	(200)
Profit before tax	1,500	1,400	1,300
Tax at 30%	(450)	(420)	(390)
Profit available for shareholders	1,050	980	910
Increase in profits available to shareholders	50%	55%	62.5%

Risk is uncertainty as to the amount of benefits. If a company is highly geared, profits available for shareholders (and therefore dividends) may fluctuate considerably as the result of a relatively small change in the level of profit from operations.

Interest cover

This shows the extent to which interest payments are 'covered' by profit from operations; or whether a business is generating enough profit to meet its interest costs comfortably.

$$\textbf{Interest cover} = \frac{\text{Profit before interest and tax (profit from operations)}}{\text{Finance costs (interest payable)}}$$

	Smith Ltd	*Jones Ltd*
Interest cover	$\frac{110}{10}$ = 11 times	$\frac{300}{15}$ = 20 times

student notes

INTERPRETING RATIOS

Ratio calculations are the first step in interpreting financial statements. The calculations themselves do not provide firm answers. Rather, they focus attention on significant aspects of an entity's performance and position.

There is no such thing as an 'ideal' ratio. Whether a particular ratio is a sign of strength or weakness may depend on a number of factors, including:

- whether the ratio is improving or deteriorating
- any other information that is available (including possible reasons for a result)
- the nature of the business.

For example, it is often said that the quick ratio should be greater than 1. A company has a quick ratio of 0.5. Does this mean that the company has severe liquidity problems?

Not necessarily: either of the following could apply:

- The company is a retailer. All sales are for cash; there are no trade receivables. The average quick ratio in the industry is 0.4.
- The quick ratio for the previous year was 0.2. Other information suggests that the company has had severe liquidity problems, but it is recovering.

In the Exam-based Assessment, you will probably be asked to calculate specific ratios and to comment on them. As well as making observations ('revenue has increased during the year') it is important that you attempt to **interpret** the ratios, for example, by suggesting reasons why revenue might have increased, based on any other relevant information you are given.

HOW IT WORKS

The following information relates to two companies. The ratios have been calculated for the year ended 31 December 20X8. The two companies operate in the same line of business.

	Smith Ltd	*Jones Ltd*
ROCE	23.4%	42.2%
Gross profit margin	65%	30%
Net profit margin	5%	10%
Expenses ratio	60%	20%
Asset turnover	4.7 times	4.2 times
Current ratio	1.1	1.3
Quick ratio	0.6	0.7

student notes

	Smith Ltd	*Jones Ltd*
Inventory turnover	4.5 times	19.1 times
Receivables days	36 days	12 days
Payables days	104 days	16 days
Gearing	30%	24%
Interest cover	11 times	20 times

Profitability

- Smith Ltd has the higher gross profit margin, 60% compared with Jones Ltd's 30%.
- However, overall Jones Ltd is performing much better than Smith Ltd, with ROCE of 42.2% compared with 23.4%.
- Asset turnover for the two companies is roughly comparable, so the difference in ROCE is largely a reflection of net profit margin. Smith Ltd has a net profit margin of 5%, only half that of Jones Ltd.
- The difference in gross profit margin may indicate that the two companies have different strategies. Smith Ltd may be concentrating on low volume, high margin sales, while Jones Ltd may be selling its products very cheaply in order to generate more revenue.
- Smith Ltd incurs much higher operating expenses than Jones Ltd, as shown by the expenses ratio, which is three times that of Jones Ltd. This may be because it is less efficient at controlling administrative costs. Alternatively it may have incurred high 'one off' costs, such as legal fees, during the year.

Liquidity and working capital management (efficiency)

- The current ratios are 1.1:1 and 1.3:1 respectively. Both companies are likely to be able to meet their current liabilities in the near future.
- However, Smith Ltd has an acid test ratio of 0.6:1 and Jones Ltd's position is only slightly better. This suggests potential liquidity problems for both companies, or a type of business which tends to have a low quick ratio (see above).
- Smith Ltd has a bank overdraft of £110,000, which suggests possible cash flow problems.
- Jones Ltd appears to be much better at managing its working capital than Smith Ltd.

student notes

- Smith Ltd's inventory turnover is 4.5 times compared with 19 times for Jones Ltd.
- Smith Ltd takes over three months on average to pay its suppliers. In contrast, Jones Ltd's average supplier payment period is less than one month. Jones Ltd evidently has sufficient cash to pay its suppliers promptly.
- Smith Ltd takes just over one month on average to collect receivables. Most companies allow roughly 30 days credit, but this compares badly with the performance of Jones Ltd (which has an average collection period of just under two weeks). Jones Ltd's efficiency in this area may have contributed to its positive cash balance of £20,000.

■ All the above information seems to indicate that Smith Ltd is suffering liquidity problems.

Gearing

■ Although Smith Ltd is more highly geared than Jones Ltd, neither company's gearing ratio seems to be unduly high.

■ Neither company appears to be having difficulty in generating enough profit to cover interest charges on their loans (interest cover is 11 times and 20 times respectively).

Conclusion

On the basis of the information provided, Jones Ltd appears to be more profitable and to be in a stronger financial position than Smith Ltd. Jones Ltd has a low acid test ratio, but there are no other signs of trading problems.

In contrast, Smith Ltd's financial position gives cause for concern. There are several signs that it may be experiencing liquidity problems. In addition, there are indications that working capital could be better managed.

Activity 5

A business normally allows customers 30 days credit. However, the information in the latest annual accounts suggests that the average collection period is actually 45 days.

A major customer went into liquidation during the year and the debt was written off. Could this be a reason for the difference?

Suggest one other possible reason to explain the difference.

student notes

WRITING REPORTS

In the Exam-based Assessment, you may be asked to set out your comments in the form of a report.

Format

- Begin your report with a heading showing:
  - the addressee
  - the author
  - the date
  - the subject.
- Example:

> **REPORT**
>
> **To:** The Chief Accountant
>
> **From:** An accounting technician
>
> **Subject:** Analysis of the financial statements of Smith Ltd and Jones Ltd
>
> **Date:** 23 June 20X2

- Start with an introductory comment. This should set out the scope of your report and can normally be based on the wording of the task. For example:

  As requested, I have analysed the performance and financial position of Smith Ltd and Jones Ltd as shown by their accounts for the year ended 31 December 20X1.
- In the main body of the report, group your comments under headings (for example, profitability, liquidity, working capital management, gearing). The wording of the task may suggest suitable headings. For example, it may ask for comments on specific areas or ratios. Ask yourself:
  - who is the report addressed to?
  - what are they interested in?
  - what decision do they need to make?
- You may already have calculated the ratios as part of a separate task. If not, set them out in an appendix to your main report.
- Assessment tasks almost always ask for recommendations, for example, which of the two companies is the more profitable. Draw a conclusion, based on your observations and reasoning in the main part of the report.

student notes

Further information

In the Exam-based Assessment, ratio analysis is normally based on a statement of financial position and income statement. This information is very limited. For this reason, the conclusions drawn can often only be very tentative. Ratio analysis often poses questions, rather than providing definitive answers.

You may be asked to suggest further information that you would need before reaching a decision.

Suppose that a company wishes to acquire another company. The two possibilities are Smith Ltd and Jones Ltd in the example above. On the basis of the analysis, Jones Ltd appears to be the safer choice. However, the following further information would be useful for both companies:

- Comparative figures for at least the previous year (and preceding periods if possible;)
- Notes to the financial statements;
- The directors' report, auditor's report and any other non-financial information that is available. (There is unlikely to be any further information because both companies are private companies. The published annual report of a public company includes a Chairman's Statement and normally includes an Operating and Financial Review, both of which may help to explain the view given by the financial statements);
- Budgeted figures for the current year (with actual figures for the period to date if these are available);
- Average figures for the industry.

In addition, the following specific information is needed:

- Analysis of cost of sales and operating expenses for both companies. This may help to explain the differences in gross profit margin and net profit margin and in particular the reason why Smith Ltd's operating expenses are so high.
- Statements of cash flow. These may help to explain the differences in liquidity and working capital management. They should also help to explain the reason for Smith Ltd's bank overdraft (which may be unusually high at the year end for a particular reason, for example, major purchases of non-current assets or inventories).
- Repayment dates and terms for the long term loans. If the loans have to be repaid in the near future, Smith Ltd will probably then have severe liquidity problems and even Jones Ltd may have difficulty in finding the necessary cash.

student notes

- Details of movements in property, plant and equipment during the year. These might help to explain the reason for Smith Ltd's low ROCE. ROCE has been calculated on the closing capital employed. If Smith Ltd has purchased assets just before the year end, the new assets will be included in capital employed, even though they will have generated very little if any profit during the year. As a result, ROCE will appear artificially low.

LIMITATIONS OF RATIO ANALYSIS

Ratio analysis is a useful technique, but as we have seen, it does not provide all the answers. Nor does it replace simple observation. For example, if revenue has increased, or the company has made an operating loss this should be immediately obvious, without calculations. Ratios should always be interpreted in the context of the accounts as a whole and of any other information that is available.

Ratio analysis also has some serious limitations.

General limitations

- Financial statements are based on historical information. They may be several months out of date by the time that they are published. Very recent or forecast information is more useful for decision making.
- Most ratios are calculated on closing figures taken from the statement of financial position. This means that ROCE, asset turnover and the working capital ratios may not compare like with like (because the figures in the income statement are for the whole period).
- Businesses can use 'window dressing' to improve the appearance of the statement of financial position. For example, they can order goods to be delivered just after the year-end so that inventories and payables are lower than usual or they can collect debts just before the year-end so that cash is higher than usual and receivables are lower than usual. (IAS 10 requires this type of transaction to be disclosed in the notes to the financial statements.)
- Some businesses are seasonal. This means that the choice of reporting date can be crucial, as the financial position varies according to the time of year.
- Financial statements only include information which can be measured in money terms. For example, they do not normally contain information about:
  - an entity's effect on the natural environment
  - its effect on the community

student notes

- the human resources available to it (its management and employees)
- some internally generated intangible assets, such as brand names.

These factors can have an important effect on an entity's performance. For example, consumers may choose to buy goods from entities that have been seen to adopt 'green' policies. (Many large public companies now publish information about the effect of their activities upon the natural environment and upon the wider community.)

- Ratios are normally based on historic cost accounts. This means that they ignore the effect of inflation and trends can be distorted. An entity may appear to be more profitable than is actually the case in real terms.

Comparisons between different businesses

Ratios for an individual business are often compared with ratios for a similar business, or with industry averages. These comparisons can be misleading.

- Businesses may use different accounting policies. For example, some businesses revalue non-current assets, while others carry them at historic cost. This can have a significant effect on key ratios.
- Businesses within the same industry can operate in completely different markets. They may also adopt different strategies. For example, some food stores may specialise in quality (relatively few sales at high margins), while other stores may concentrate on high volume, low-margin sales.
- Size differences may affect the way in which a business operates. A large company can often achieve economies of scale that are not available to a smaller business. For example, it may make use of trade discounts for bulk buying. Large companies are likely to have a different approach to managing working capital. They may be able to take advantage of extended credit terms and they may only hold fast-moving inventory lines. They may also adopt a more aggressive policy towards customers than would be the case in a small family business.
- Ratios may not always be calculated according to the same formula. For example, there are several possible variations on the calculation of gearing.

Activity 6

Harkeats Ltd revalues some of its properties upwards. How does this affect its key ratios?

CHAPTER OVERVIEW

- Different types of limited company have different objectives
- The most important users of an entity's financial statements are usually the persons to whom management has stewardship responsibilities and/or the main providers of finance
- Ratio analysis is used to interpret financial information. Ratios are normally compared with other information (eg, the previous years' financial statements, industry averages)
- Return on capital employed (ROCE) measures the profit that a business generates from the resources available to it
- Net profit margin measures the overall profitability of a business
- Gross profit margin measures gross profit as a percentage of sales
- The expenses ratio measures operating expenses as a percentage of sales
- Asset turnover measures the efficiency with which a business uses its resources to generate sales
- The current ratio shows the extent to which a business' current liabilities are covered by current assets
- The quick ratio measures the immediate solvency of a business by showing the extent to which its current liabilities are covered by cash and receivables
- Inventory turnover shows how rapidly a business' inventory is sold on average during the year
- Receivables days is the average period taken to collect receivables
- Payables days is the average period taken to pay suppliers

KEY WORDS

Ratio analysis a technique used to interpret financial information. It involves calculating ratios by comparing one figure in the financial statements with another

Capital employed capital and reserves (equity) plus long term liabilities

Return on capital employed (ROCE)

$$\frac{\text{Profit before interest and tax (profit from operations)}}{\text{Capital employed}}$$

Return on shareholders' equity

$$\frac{\text{Profit after tax}}{\text{Share capital and reserves}}$$

Net profit margin

$$\frac{\text{Profit before interest and tax}}{\text{Revenue}}$$

Gross profit margin $\frac{\text{Gross profit}}{\text{Revenue}}$

Expenses ratio $\frac{\text{Operating expenses}}{\text{Revenue}}$

Asset turnover $\frac{\text{Revenue}}{\text{Capital employed}}$

Liquidity the ability of an entity to meet its debts as they fall due

Current ratio $\frac{\text{Current assets}}{\text{Current liabilities}}$

Quick ratio $\frac{\text{Current assets} - \text{inventory}}{\text{Current liabilities}}$

Inventory turnover $\frac{\text{Cost of sales}}{\text{Inventory}}$

CHAPTER OVERVIEW cont.

- Gearing ratios measure the extent to which a company is financed by debt rather than by shareholders' equity
- Interest cover shows the extent to which interest payments are 'covered' by profit from operations
- There is no such thing as an 'ideal' ratio. Whether a particular ratio is a sign of strength or weakness may depend on a number of factors
- Ratios should always be interpreted in the context of the accounts as a whole and of any other information that is available
- Ratio analysis has some serious limitations. Comparisons with ratios for a similar business or with industry averages can be misleading

KEY WORDS

Inventory days $\dfrac{\text{Inventory}}{\text{Cost of sales}} \times 365$

Receivables days $\dfrac{\text{Receivables}}{\text{Revenue}} \times 365$

Payables days $\dfrac{\text{Trade payables}}{\text{Purchases/cost of sales}} \times 365$

Gearing (capital gearing) $\dfrac{\text{Debt}}{\text{Capital employed}}$

Debt to equity $\dfrac{\text{Debt}}{\text{Share capital and reserves}}$

Highly geared having a high proportion of debt compared with equity

Interest cover $\dfrac{\text{Profit before interest and tax (profit from operations)}}{\text{Interest payable}}$

HOW MUCH HAVE YOU LEARNED?

1 Gross profit is £20,000 and operating expenses are £10,000. The gross profit margin is 25%. What is the net profit margin?

2 If return on capital employed is 20% and the net profit margin is 10%, what is asset turnover?

3 Which ratios would be of most interest to lenders and potential lenders?

4 Fill in the gaps.

.... = Revenue / ....

.... = Current assets / ....

Receivables days = ... / .... × 365

Gearing = ... / ....

5 The summarised statement of financial position of Bellbrock Ltd is shown below:

	£'000	£'000
Non-current assets		57,000
Current assets		22,800
		79,800
Equity:		
Ordinary shares		10,000
Revaluation reserve		4,600
Retained earnings		11,400
		26,000
Non-current liabilities	39,000	
Current liabilities	14,800	
		53,800
		79,800

What is the gearing ratio?

6 The following information relates to X Ltd.

During the year ended 31 December 20X3 sales were £100,000. The gross profit margin was 25%. Operating expenses amounted to £20,000. The rate of corporation tax is 30% on profit from operations.

The company has an issued share capital of 5,000 £1 ordinary shares. The directors did not declare any dividends for the year ended 31 December 20X3.

At 31 December 20X3 closing inventory represented 36.5 days' sales and this was three times as much as opening inventory. The receivables payment period was 40 days and payables represented 30 days' purchases.

The ratio of current assets to liabilities was 1.6:1.0. Current assets includes a bank balance of £1,541.

The non-current assets were equal to 25% of total assets. There are no long term liabilities.

Prepare an income statement for X Ltd for the year ended 31 December 20X3 and a statement of financial position at that date, in as much detail as possible from the above information. These need not be in a format suitable for publication. Where necessary, round your workings to the nearest £1.

chapter 10: GROUP ACCOUNTS: THE CONSOLIDATED STATEMENT OF FINANCIAL POSITION

chapter coverage

The next two chapters explain how to prepare simple accounts for a group of companies.

A group consists of a parent company and one or more subsidiary companies controlled by the parent. As well as its own financial statements, the parent prepares financial statements for the group as a single entity. These are known as consolidated financial statements.

This chapter concentrates on the consolidated statement of financial position.

The topics that we shall cover are:

- groups
- the consolidated statement of financial position
- intra-group adjustments

KNOWLEDGE AND UNDERSTANDING AND PERFORMANCE CRITERIA COVERAGE

knowledge and understanding

- the UK regulatory framework for financial reporting and the main requirements of relevant financial reporting standards
- preparing financial statements in proper form
- the general principles of consolidation

Performance criteria – element 11.1

- draft limited company financial statements from the appropriate information
- ensure that limited company financial settlements comply with relevant accounting standards and domestic legislation and with the organisation's regulations, policies and timescales

student notes

GROUPS

A **group** of companies consists of a **parent (holding) company** and all its **subsidiaries**. The parent controls the subsidiaries.

The individual companies within the group are separate legal entities. Each group company prepares its own financial statements.

In the accounts of the parent:

- investments in subsidiaries are included in the statement of financial position at cost (or fair value), under non-current assets;
- dividends receivable from subsidiaries are included in the income statement.

Consolidated financial statements

The individual accounts of a parent do not reflect the commercial reality of the situation.

- Because the parent can control the subsidiary, it has the benefits and risks attaching to the subsidiary's assets and liabilities, even though it may not directly own them.
- The parent is directly affected by the subsidiary's results, because it can appropriate the subsidiary's profits as dividends.

In practice, the parent and the subsidiary operate as a single economic entity: the group.

The Companies Act and IAS 27 *Consolidated and separate financial statements* both require a parent to prepare consolidated financial statements for its group.

Consolidation is the process of adjusting and combining financial information from the individual financial statements of a parent and its subsidiary to prepare **consolidated financial statements** that present financial information for the group as a single economic entity.

IAS 27 *Consolidated and separate financial statements* and IFRS 3 *Business combinations* apply to all situations in which a parent and one or more subsidiaries come together to form a group.

A **business combination** is a transaction or other event in which an acquirer obtains control of one or more businesses.

There are several ways in which a business combination can occur, but the most common way is that one company acquires equity shares in another company.

- Equity shares can be purchased for cash, for other assets, or for equity shares in the acquirer.
- A subsidiary is normally a company, but it could be a partnership or another type of unincorporated body.

student notes

Control

A **parent** is an entity that has one or more subsidiaries.

A **subsidiary** is an entity that is controlled by another entity (the parent).

Control is the power to govern the financial and operating policies of an entity so as to obtain benefits from its activities.

Control is presumed to exist where the parent owns more than half the voting power of an entity, unless it can be clearly demonstrated that such ownership does not constitute control.

Control also exists when the parent owns half or less of the voting power of an entity when there is:

- power over more than half of the voting rights by virtue of an agreement with other investors;
- power to govern the financial and operating policies of the entity under a statute or an agreement;
- power to appoint or remove the majority of the members of the board of directors; or
- power to cast the majority of votes at meetings of the board of directors.

In practice, if a company holds more than 50% of the equity (ordinary) shares in another company it is normally able to control that company. You should assume that this is the case unless you are told otherwise.

However, it is important to remember that a company may be able to control another company even though it owns less than 50% of its issued equity share capital.

Activity 1

Moat Ltd owns 6,000 'A' £1 ordinary shares in Grange Ltd. The share capital of Grange Ltd consists of:

	£'000
Ordinary voting 'A' shares	10,000
Ordinary non-voting 'B' shares	20,000

Is Grange Ltd a subsidiary of Moat Ltd?

student notes

THE CONSOLIDATED STATEMENT OF FINANCIAL POSITION

The basic idea

To prepare a consolidated statement of financial position:

- add together the individual assets and liabilities of the parent and the subsidiary
- make adjustments to cancel out intra-group items.

HOW IT WORKS

On 1 January 20X0 P Ltd acquired 100% of the issued ordinary share capital of S Ltd. S Ltd was incorporated on that date. At 31 December 20X0, individual company statements of financial position were as follows:

	P Ltd	*S Ltd*
	£'000	£'000
Property, plant and equipment	25,000	4,000
Investment in S Ltd	5,000	–
Net current assets	20,000	6,000
	50,000	10,000
Share capital	20,000	5,000
Retained earnings	30,000	5,000
	50,000	10,000

Step 1 Cancel P Ltd's investment in S Ltd against the share capital of S Ltd.

Consolidation has the effect of replacing the cost of the investment with the net assets that it represents.

P Ltd bought the whole of the share capital of S Ltd for £5,000,000 its nominal value. The two items cancel exactly.

Step 2 Add the individual assets and liabilities of P Ltd and S Ltd together.

student notes

The share capital of the subsidiary never appears in the consolidated statement of financial position.

Consolidated statement of financial position at 31 December 20X0

	£'000
Property, plant & equipment (25,000 + 4,000)	29,000
Current assets (20,000 + 6,000)	26,000
	55,000
Share capital (P Ltd only)	20,000
Retained earnings (30,000 + 5,000)	35,000
	55,000

Dealing with goodwill

In practice, where a parent acquires a subsidiary the cost of the investment is almost always more than the total fair value of the subsidiary's individual assets and liabilities. The difference represents goodwill.

IFRS 3 defines *goodwill* more formally as: an asset representing the future economic benefits arising from other assets acquired in a business combination that are not individually identified and separately recognised.

IFRS 3 states that goodwill acquired in a business combination must be recognised as an asset.

- Unlike many other intangible assets, goodwill is not amortised.
- Instead it is carried in the statement of financial position at its cost less any accumulated impairment losses.
- It must be tested for impairment annually, or more frequently if there are any indications that it might be impaired.
- IAS 36 *Impairment of assets* explains how to carry out an impairment review (see Chapter 6).

HOW IT WORKS

On 1 January 20X0, P acquired 100% of the issued ordinary share capital of S Ltd. S was incorporated on that date. At 31 December 20X0, the individual company statements of financial position were as follows:

student notes

	P Ltd	*S Ltd*
	£'000	£'000
Property, plant and equipment	25,000	4,000
Investment in S Ltd	10,000	–
Current assets	20,000	6,000
	55,000	10,000
Share capital	20,000	5,000
Retained earnings	35,000	5,000
	55,000	10,000

Calculate goodwill:

	£'000
Cost of investment in S Ltd	10,000
Less: net assets acquired	(5,000)
	5,000

The individual assets and liabilities are added together to produce the consolidated statement of financial position.

Consolidated statement of financial position at 31 December 20X0

	£'000
Intangible assets: goodwill	5,000
Property, plant & equipment (25,000 + 4,000)	29,000
Current assets (20,000 + 6,000)	26,000
	60,000
Share capital (P Ltd only)	20,000
Retained earnings (35,000 + 5,000)	40,000
	60,000

Impairment of goodwill

In the example above, P Ltd would have reviewed the goodwill for impairment at 31 December 20X0 (a year after acquisition). We assumed that the goodwill was not impaired.

If goodwill is impaired, intangible assets and the retained earnings reserve are both reduced by the amount of the impairment loss.

student notes

HOW IT WORKS

Suppose that in the example above, goodwill had been tested for impairment and found to have suffered an impairment loss of 20% of its original cost.

Calculate goodwill:

	£'000
Cost of investment in S Ltd	10,000
Less: net assets acquired	(5,000)
	5,000
Less: impairment (20% x 5,000)	(1,000)
	4,000

Consolidated retained earnings are also reduced by £1,000,000.

Consolidated statement of financial position at 31 December 20X0

	£'000
Intangible assets: goodwill (5,000 – 1,000)	4,000
Property, plant & equipment (25,000 + 4,000)	29,000
Net current assets (20,000 + 6,000)	26,000
	59,000
Share capital (P Ltd only)	20,000
Retained earnings (35,000 + 5,000 – 1,000)	39,000
	59,000

Activity 2

Thatch Ltd acquired 600 £1 ordinary shares in Straw Ltd for £4,000,000 on 1 January 20X2. At that date, the capital and reserves of Straw Ltd were:

	£'000
Share capital (£1 ordinary shares)	1,000
Retained earnings	5,000
	6,000

Calculate goodwill on acquisition.

Pre-acquisition profits and post-acquisition profits

A parent may acquire a subsidiary that has already been trading for some time. This means that the parent's interest includes retained profits, as well as share capital.

student notes

Consolidated accounts only include profits made by the group. Profits made by the subsidiary before the acquisition were not made by the group; instead they represent the net assets acquired.

Pre-acquisition profits must be excluded from the consolidated retained earnings reserve.

HOW IT WORKS

On 1 January 20X4 A Ltd acquired 100% of the issued ordinary share capital of B Ltd. On that date, the retained earnings reserve of B Ltd was £10,000,000. At 31 December 20X4, the statements of financial position of A Ltd and B Ltd were as follows:

	A Ltd	*B Ltd*
	£'000	£'000
Property, plant and equipment	50,000	10,000
Investment in B Ltd	25,000	–
Net current assets	25,000	15,000
	100,000	25,000
Share capital	25,000	10,000
Retained earnings	75,000	15,000
	100,000	25,000

Step 1 Calculate goodwill

The net assets acquired consist of B Ltd's share capital plus its retained profits at the date of acquisition.

	£'000	£'000
Cost of investment		25,000
Less: net assets acquired		
Share capital	10,000	
Retained earnings	10,000	
		(20,000)
		5,000

Step 2 Calculate the consolidated retained earnings reserve

This consists of the retained earnings of A Ltd, plus the post-acquisition profits of B Ltd.

	£'000	£'000
A Ltd		75,000
B Ltd: At 31 December 20X4	15,000	
Less: At acquisition	(10,000)	
		5,000
		80,000

student notes

Step 3 Prepare the consolidated statement of financial position

Consolidated statement of financial position at 31 December 20X4

	£'000
Intangible assets: goodwill	5,000
Property, plant and equipment	60,000
Net current assets	40,000
	105,000
Share capital	25,000
Retained earnings (as above)	80,000
	105,000

Activity 3

The following information relates to Church Ltd and Steeple Ltd:

	Church Ltd	*Steeple Ltd*
	£'000	£'000
Share capital (£1 ordinary shares)	480	400
Retained earnings at 1 January 20X5	1,080	600
Profit for the year ended 31 December 20X5	96	50

On 1 January 20X5 Church Ltd purchased 100% of the ordinary share capital of Steeple Ltd for £1,000,000.

What are consolidated reserves at 31 December 20X5?

Non-controlling interests

The consolidated statement of financial position includes 100% of the subsidiary's individual assets and liabilities. This reflects the fact that the parent controls the subsidiary and therefore controls its assets.

Suppose that the parent owns 80% of the subsidiary's equity share capital. This means that it controls 100% of the subsidiary's assets and liabilities, but it only owns 80% of them.

Equity (share capital and reserves) is analysed to show:

- the group's share
- the share owned by other shareholders.

The part of the equity share capital and reserves not owned by the parent is the **non-controlling interest**.

student notes

IFRS 3 contains a more formal definition:

- **Non-controlling interest** is the equity in a subsidiary not attributable, directly or indirectly, to a parent.

The non-controlling interest in the net assets of the subsidiary is shown on a separate line within equity:

	£
Equity attributable to owners of the parent	
Share capital	X
Retained earnings	X
	X
Non-controlling interest	X
Total equity	X

The sub-total below retained earnings shows the equity that 'belongs' to the parent.

Calculating goodwill where there is a non-controlling interest

In simple terms, goodwill is the difference between the cost of the parent's investment in a subsidiary and the fair value of the net assets acquired.

Where there is a non-controlling interest, goodwill is calculated as:

	£
Cost of investment	X
Plus: non-controlling interest	X
Less: net assets acquired	(X)
Goodwill	X

IFRS 3 allows the non-controlling interest to be measured as either:

- The proportionate share of the fair value of the subsidiary's net assets, or
- Fair value

Unusually, an entity does not have to choose one method and then apply it to every business combination. For example, if A plc acquired 80% of the shares in B Ltd and then 75% of the shares in C Ltd it could measure the non-controlling interest in B Ltd at the proportionate share of B Ltd's net assets and the non-controlling interest in C Ltd at fair value.

The first method (proportionate share of subsidiary's net assets) is the method that is normally used and this is the method that you will almost certainly be asked to use in the Exam-based Assessment.

In the examples in this book, you should assume that non-controlling interests are measured at the proportionate share of the subsidiary's net assets unless you are told otherwise.

student notes

HOW IT WORKS

On 1 January 20X4 A Ltd acquired 8,000,000 ordinary shares in B Ltd. On that date, the retained earnings reserve of B Ltd was £10,000,000. At 31 December 20X4, the statements of financial position of A Ltd and B Ltd were as follows:

	A Ltd	*B Ltd*
	£'000	£'000
Property, plant and equipment	50,000	10,000
Investment in B Ltd	25,000	–
Net current assets	25,000	15,000
	100,000	25,000
Share capital (£1 ordinary shares)	25,000	10,000
Retained earnings	75,000	15,000
	100,000	25,000

Step 1 Establish the group structure

A Ltd owns 80% (8,000/10,000) of the equity share capital of B Ltd.

Step 2 Calculate goodwill

Because there is a non-controlling interest, goodwill is calculated as the cost of the investment **plus the non-controlling interest**, less the net assets acquired.

The non-controlling interest (NCI) is measured as the non-controlling interest's share of B Ltd's net assets at the date of acquisition.

	£'000	£'000
Cost of investment		25,000
Plus: non-controlling interest:		
Net assets acquired:		
Share capital	10,000	
Retained earnings	10,000	
Group share (80%)	20,000	4,000
		(20,000)
		9,000

Where this method of measuring non-controlling interest is used, goodwill can also be calculated as the cost of the investment less the group share of the net assets acquired:

student notes

	£'000	£'000
Cost of investment		25,000
Less: net assets acquired		
Share capital	10,000	
Retained earnings	10,000	
	20,000	(16,000)
		9,000

Step 3 Calculate the consolidated retained earnings reserve

The consolidated retained earnings reserve only includes the **group share** of post-acquisition profits.

	£'000	£'000
A Ltd		75,000
B Ltd: At 31 December 20X4	15,000	
Less: At acquisition	(10,000)	
Group share (80%)	5,000	4,000
		79,000

Step 4 Calculate non-controlling interest

This is the non-controlling interest's share of the net assets of B Ltd at the reporting date.

	£'000
Share capital	10,000
Retained earnings	15,000
	25,000
Non-controlling interest (20%)	5,000

Step 5 Prepare the consolidated statement of financial position

Consolidated statement of financial position at 31 December 20X4

	£'000
Intangible assets: goodwill (Step 2)	9,000
Property, plant and equipment	60,000
Net current assets	40,000
	109,000
Share capital	25,000
Retained earnings (Step 3)	79,000
	104,000
Non-controlling interest (Step 4)	5,000
	109,000

Measuring non-controlling interest at fair value

student notes

The fair value of the non-controlling interest is normally the market price of the shares held by non-controlling shareholders at the acquisition date.

Suppose that A plc acquires 800,000 of the 1,000,000 £1 ordinary shares in B plc. At the date of acquisition, the market price of B plc's shares is £1.50 each. The fair value of the non-controlling interest is £300,000 (20% x 1,000,000 x £1.50).

IFRS 3 allows this method, as well as the more traditional one described above, because it can be argued that the shareholders making up the non-controlling interest have also purchased goodwill in the subsidiary. Any goodwill in the subsidiary would have been reflected in the price that they paid for their shares. Some people believe that the subsidiary's goodwill should be treated in exactly the same way as the other assets and liabilities acquired by the parent. In other words, the consolidated statement of financial position should recognise **all** the subsidiary's goodwill, not just the goodwill acquired by the parent.

It is very unlikely that you will be asked to apply the fair value method in the Exam-based Assessment, but you may be asked to explain it.

HOW IT WORKS

The facts are the same as in the example above, except that the non-controlling interest in B Ltd is measured at fair value.

On 1 January 20X4 A Ltd acquired 8,000,000 ordinary shares in B Ltd. On that date, the retained earnings reserve of B Ltd was £10,000,000. At 31 December 20X4, the statements of financial position of A Ltd and B Ltd were as follows:

	A Ltd	*B Ltd*
	£'000	£'000
Property, plant and equipment	50,000	10,000
Investment in B Ltd	25,000	–
Net current assets	25,000	15,000
	100,000	25,000
Share capital (£1 ordinary shares)	25,000	10,000
Retained earnings	75,000	15,000
	100,000	25,000

student notes

The fair value of the non-controlling interest in B Ltd is £5,000,000.

Step 1 Establish the group structure

A Ltd owns 80% of B Ltd.

Step 2 Calculate goodwill

	£'000
Cost of investment	25,000
Plus: non-controlling interest at fair value	5,000
Less: net assets acquired	(20,000)
	10,000

This is the total amount of goodwill in B Ltd: the goodwill owned by A Ltd plus the goodwill owned by the non-controlling interest.

Notice that this is less than the figure of £11,250,000 (100/80 x £9,000,000) that would result if we simply 'grossed up' the goodwill 'owned' by the parent (see the example above). This is because A Ltd has paid a higher price for its shares than the various shareholders making up the non-controlling interest. A Ltd's 8 million shares are worth more, per share, than the 2 million shares held by the non-controlling interests because the size of the shareholding enables it to exercise control. A Ltd has paid a 'control premium'.

Step 3 Calculate the consolidated retained earnings reserve

This is the same figure as before: £79,000,000.

Step 4 Calculate non-controlling interest

As before, this is the non-controlling interest's share of the net assets of B Ltd at the reporting date. But because the fair value method has been used, this figure must include the additional goodwill 'owned' by the non-controlling interest.

The non-controlling interest's goodwill is calculated below:

	£'000
Fair value at acquisition	5,000
Non-controlling interest's share of subsidiary's net assets acquired (20% x 20,000)	(4,000)
Additional goodwill	1,000

student notes

This additional goodwill is added on to the non-controlling interest's share of the subsidiary's net assets at the reporting date, which is calculated in exactly the same way as before:

	£'000
Share capital	10,000
Retained earnings	15,000
	25,000
Non-controlling interest (20%)	5,000
Plus goodwill	1,000
	6,000

Step 5 Prepare the consolidated statement of financial position

Consolidated statement of financial position at 31 December 20X4

	£'000
Intangible assets: goodwill (Step 2)	10,000
Property, plant and equipment	60,000
Net current assets	40,000
	110,000
Share capital	25,000
Retained earnings (Step 3)	79,000
	104,000
Non-controlling interest (Step 4)	6,000
	110,000

student notes

Reflecting fair values

The subsidiary's statement of financial position normally shows its assets and liabilities at their original cost to the subsidiary. This is not necessarily the same as their cost to the parent and the group.

Suppose that P Ltd acquires 100% of the shares in S Ltd. The statement of financial position of S Ltd includes a freehold property which it purchased for £100,000 some years ago. The market value of the property (its fair value) is now £150,000.

The statement of financial position of S Ltd records the property at (say) £90,000 (original cost less accumulated depreciation). However, the price that P Ltd has paid for its investment in S Ltd reflects the fact that the fair value of the property is now £150,000. It would be incorrect to include the property in the consolidated statement of financial position at £90,000.

IFRS 3 states that the identifiable assets and liabilities of a subsidiary that are acquired by a parent should be recognised in the consolidated financial statements at their **fair values** at the date of the acquisition.

- **Fair value** is the amount for which an asset could be exchanged, or a liability settled between knowledgeable, willing parties in an arm's length transaction.

There are two reasons why fair value adjustments are required:

- The consolidated statement of financial position includes all the assets and liabilities controlled by the group (the parent's own assets and liabilities plus the assets and liabilities of the subsidiary). The group has purchased these assets and liabilities and so the consolidated statement of financial position should reflect their cost to the group.

- Goodwill is calculated as the difference between the cost of the investment in the subsidiary and the total fair values of the identifiable assets and liabilities acquired. If the subsidiary's assets and liabilities are not adjusted to fair value, goodwill will be over-stated.

Note that fair value adjustments **only** affect the consolidated accounts. The subsidiary continues to record assets at their book values in its own accounts.

The cost of an investment in a subsidiary (cost of a business combination) must also be recognised at its fair value.

student notes

HOW IT WORKS

On 1 January 20X6, P Ltd acquired 100% of the ordinary shares in S Ltd. At that date the reserves of S Ltd were £140,000,000. On 31 December 20X6, the summarised statements of financial position of the two companies were as follows:

	P Ltd	*S Ltd*
	£'000	£'000
Net assets	540,000	252,000
Investment in S Ltd	280,000	
	820,000	252,000
Share capital	400,000	50,000
Retained earnings	420,000	202,000
	820,000	252,000

At 1 January 20X6 the fair values of the assets and liabilities of S Ltd were equal to their book values with one exception. A freehold property that originally cost £100,000,000 and had a net book value of £90,000,000 had a fair value of £120,000,000. Depreciation on the property is charged at 2% of cost per annum.

Step 1 Calculate goodwill

The net assets acquired must be increased by £30,000,000 (the difference between the book value and the fair value of the freehold property).

	£'000	£'000
Cost of investment		280,000
Net assets acquired:		
Ordinary share capital	50,000	
Reserves at acquisition	140,000	
Fair value adjustment (120,000 – 90,000)	30,000	
		(220,000)
		60,000

Step 2 Calculate group net assets (excluding goodwill)

These include S Ltd's freehold property and therefore the total must take account of:

- the fair value adjustment of £30,000,000

student notes

- additional depreciation on the revalued amount of £400,000 (20,000,000 × 2%)

	£'000	£'000
P Ltd		540,000
S Ltd:		
Book values	252,000	
Fair value adjustment	30,000	
Additional depreciation	(400)	
		281,600
		821,600

Step 3 Calculate consolidated reserves

The fair value adjustment of £30,000,000 is included in pre-acquisition reserves, but the additional depreciation affects post-acquisition results.

	£'000	£'000
P Ltd		420,000
S Ltd:		
At 31 December 20X6 (202,000 + 30,000 – 400)	231,600	
At acquisition (140,000 + 30,000)	(170,000)	
		61,600
		481,600

Consolidated statement of financial position at 31 December 20X6

	£'000
Goodwill	60,000
Other net assets	821,600
	881,600
Share capital	400,000
Reserves	481,600
	881,600

Recognising the subsidiary's identifiable assets and liabilities

At the acquisition date, a parent (an acquirer) should recognise:

- all the subsidiary's identifiable assets that it has acquired;
- all the liabilities that it has assumed; and
- any non-controlling interest

student notes

in the consolidated financial statements, provided that they meet the definitions of assets and liabilities in the *Framework for the Preparation and Presentation of Financial Statements*:

- An asset is recognised if it is probable that any associated future economic benefits will flow to the acquirer; and its fair value can be measured reliably.
- A liability is recognised if it is probable that an outflow of resources embodying economic benefits will be required to settle the obligation; and its fair value can be measured reliably.

This means that there are two exceptions to the normal rules for recognising assets and liabilities:

- Intangible assets acquired are normally recognised even if they are not included in the subsidiary's statement of financial position because they were internally generated. (IAS 38 prohibits the recognition of most internally generated assets).
- IFRS 3 states that contingent liabilities of the subsidiary are recognised if they exist at the date of the acquisition. (IAS 37 normally prohibits their recognition).

INTRA-GROUP ADJUSTMENTS

Group companies normally enter into transactions with each other. These may include:

- sales by one group company to another
- loans by one group company to another
- receipts and payments of dividends.

Consolidated accounts reflect the financial performance and position of the group as if it were a single economic entity. Therefore:

- the effect of any intra-group transactions must be eliminated from the consolidated accounts (because the group cannot trade with itself)
- any balances due to or from another group company must be eliminated from the statement of financial position (because the group cannot owe or be owed money to or from itself).

Intra-group balances

If one group company sells goods to another there may be trade receivables and trade payables that relate to group companies at the year end.

These are cancelled against each other on consolidation.

student notes

Activity 4

X Ltd owns 80% of the equity share capital of Y Ltd. X Ltd has trade receivables of £20,000 and Y Ltd has trade receivables of £15,000. The trade receivables of Y Ltd include an amount of £1,500 which is due from X Ltd.

What is the amount for trade receivables included in the consolidated statement of financial position at 30 June 20X4?

Intra-group sales

Suppose that P Ltd sells goods costing £10,000 to its subsidiary S Ltd for £20,000.

- The revenue of P Ltd and the cost of sales of S Ltd both increase by £20,000.
- P Ltd makes a profit of £10,000 on the sale.

At the year-end S Ltd still has half the goods in inventory.

- Although P Ltd has made a profit of £10,000 as a result of the sale, **the group** has only made a profit of £5,000.
- The goods which S Ltd still has in inventory are valued at their cost to S Ltd: £10,000. The cost of the inventory **to the group** is the price that P Ltd originally paid for the goods: £5,000.
- From the perspective of the group, both inventory and profits are overstated.

Only realised profits can be included in the income statement. Therefore the following adjustment must be made in the consolidated statement of financial position:

DEBIT	Consolidated retained earnings	£5,000	
CREDIT	Inventory		£5,000

It is unlikely that you will be asked to account for unrealised profits on intra-group sales. However, you may be asked to explain how to do so and why this is necessary.

student notes

HOW IT WORKS

Perch Ltd acquired 80% of the equity share capital of Sild Ltd many years ago. At the date of acquisition the retained earnings reserve of Sild Ltd was £200,000. The statements of financial position of the two companies at 31 December 20X7 are shown below:

	Perch Ltd	*Sild Ltd*
	£'000	£'000
Assets		
Non-current assets		
Property, plant and equipment	1,000	600
Investment in S Ltd	400	–
	1,400	600
Current assets:		
Inventory	200	150
Trade and other receivables	200	100
Cash	60	40
	460	290
Total assets	1,860	890
Equity and liabilities		
Equity		
Share capital	500	100
Retained earnings	1,160	640
	1,660	740
Current liabilities		
Trade payables	200	150
Total equity and liabilities	1,860	890

The following information is relevant:

- During the year, Perch Ltd sold goods costing £20,000 to Sild Ltd at a mark-up of 20%. At 31 December 20X7 three-quarters of these goods were still included in the inventory of Sild Ltd.

Step 1 Calculate goodwill

	£'000	£'000
Cost of investment		400
Non-controlling interest:		
Share capital	100	
Retained earnings	200	
	300	
NCI above (20%)		60
Less: net assets acquired		(300)
		160

student notes

Step 2 Calculate the provision for unrealised profit

Profit on goods sold to Sild Ltd (20,000 × 20%)	£4,000
Unrealised profit on goods remaining in inventory (4,000 × 75%)	£3,000

Adjustment required:

DEBIT	Consolidated retained earnings £3,000	
CREDIT	Inventory	£3,000

Step 3 Calculate the consolidated retained earnings

	£'000	£'000
Perch Ltd		1,160
Less: provision for unrealised profit		(3)
Sild Ltd	640	
Less: pre-acquisition	(200)	
	440	
Group share (80%)		352
		1,509

Step 4 Calculate the non-controlling interest

	£'000
Net assets of Sild Ltd at 31 December 20X7:	
Share capital	100
Retained earnings	640
	740
Non-controlling interest (20%)	148

Step 5 Prepare the consolidated statement of financial position

	£'000	£'000
Assets		
Non-current assets		
Intangible: Goodwill (Step 1)		160
Non-current assets		1,600
		1,760
Current assets:		
Inventory (200 + 150 – 3)	347	
Trade and other receivables	300	
Cash	100	
		747
Total assets		2,507
Equity and liabilities		
Equity attributable to owners of the parent		
Share capital		500
Retained earnings (Step 3)		1,509
		2,009
Non-controlling interest (Step 4)		148
		2,157

student notes

Current liabilities:	
Trade payables	350
Total equity and liabilities	2,507

Activity 5

Kilvert Ltd owns 60% of the issued share capital of Woodford Ltd. At the year end, their statements of financial position showed inventories of £100,000 and £50,000 respectively. Kilvert Ltd sells goods to Woodford Ltd at a mark-up of 25% on cost. At the year-end, goods which had been purchased from Kilvert Ltd for £30,000 remained in the inventory of Woodford Ltd.

At what value should inventories appear in the consolidated statement of financial position of the group?

Sales from the subsidiary to the parent

Suppose that in the example above, Sild Ltd sells the goods to Perch Ltd.

- The unrealised profit arises in the accounts of Sild Ltd, instead of the accounts of Perch Ltd.
- The adjustment for unrealised profit affects both the group and the non-controlling interest.

HOW IT WORKS

During the year, Sild Ltd sold goods costing £20,000 to Perch Ltd at a mark-up of 20%. At 31 December 20X7 three-quarters of these goods were still included in the inventories of Perch Ltd.

As before:

- Profit on goods sold to Perch Ltd (20,000 × 20%) £4,000
- Unrealised profit on goods remaining in inventory (4,000 × 75%) £3,000

Adjustment required:

DEBIT	Consolidated retained earnings (3,000 × 80%)	£2,400	
DEBIT	Non-controlling interest (3,000 × 20%)	£600	
CREDIT	Inventories		£3,000

CHAPTER OVERVIEW

- A group of companies consists of a parent (holding) company and one or more subsidiaries under the control of the parent
- A parent must prepare consolidated financial statements for its group
- An entity is a subsidiary of another (the parent) if that other entity can control it
- Control exists where:
  - the parent owns more than half the voting power of an entity; or where it has:
    - power over more than half of the voting rights by virtue of an agreement with other investors;
    - power to govern the financial and operating policies of the entity under a statute or an agreement;
    - power to appoint or remove the majority of the members of the board of directors; or
    - power to cast the majority of votes at meetings of the board of directors.
- To prepare a consolidated statement of financial position:
  1 Calculate the proportion of the subsidiary's shares owned by the parent
  2 Calculate goodwill: cost of investment plus non-controlling interest less net assets acquired
  3 Calculate consolidated retained earnings reserve: parent plus group share of post acquisition reserves of subsidiary
  4 Calculate non-controlling interest: non-controlling interest's share of net assets of subsidiary at year end
  5 Complete the consolidated statement of financial position by adding the parent's assets and liabilities and the subsidiary's assets and liabilities together, line by line

KEY WORDS

Consolidation the process of adjusting and combining financial information from the individual financial statements of a parent and its subsidiary to prepare consolidated financial statements

Consolidated financial statements the financial statements of a group presented as those of a single economic entity

Business combination a transaction or other event in which an acquirer obtains control of one or more businesses

Parent an entity that has one or more subsidiaries

Subsidiary an entity that is controlled by another entity (the parent)

Control the power to govern the financial and operating policies of an entity or business so as to obtain benefits from its activities

Goodwill an asset representing the future economic benefits arising from other assets acquired in a business combination that are not individually identified and separately recognised.

Non-controlling interest the equity in a subsidiary not attributable to the parent

Fair value the amount for which an asset could be exchanged, or a liability settled between knowledgeable, willing parties in an arm's length transaction

CHAPTER OVERVIEW cont.

- Goodwill is recognised as an asset and carried at cost. It must be reviewed for impairment at least annually
- Non-controlling interest at acquisition is normally measured at the proportionate share of the fair value of the subsidiary's net assets.
- The identifiable assets and liabilities of a subsidiary are included in the consolidated financial statements at their fair values at the date of the acquisition
- Adjustment to eliminate unrealised profit on intra-group sales:

  Sale from parent to subsidiary

  DEBIT Consolidated retained earnings
  CREDIT Inventories

  Sale from subsidiary to parent

  DEBIT Consolidated retained earnings (group share)
  DEBIT Non-controlling interest (non-controlling interest's share)
  CREDIT Inventories

HOW MUCH HAVE YOU LEARNED?

1 A plc owns the following investments in other companies:

- B Ltd: 15% of the ordinary shares and 80% of the preference shares.
- C Ltd: 80% of the ordinary shares.
- D Ltd: 45% of the ordinary shares.
- E Ltd: 25% of the ordinary shares and 60% of the loan stock.

A plc has the right to appoint three of the four directors of D Ltd.

Which of the four companies are subsidiaries of A plc?

2 Fill in the gaps.

Control is presumed to exist where the parent owns .... the voting power of an entity, unless it can be clearly demonstrated that such ownership ....

Control also exists when the parent owns half or less of the voting power of an entity when there is:

- power over .... of the .... by virtue of an agreement with other investors;
- power to govern the .... and .... of the entity under a statute or an agreement;
- power to appoint or remove the majority of the .... ; or
- power to cast the .... at meetings of the board of directors.

3 The summarised consolidated statement of financial position of Left plc and Right plc at 31 December 20X9 were as follows:

	Left plc	*Right plc*
	£'000	£'000
Net assets	30,000	10,000
Investment in Right plc	8,000	–
	38,000	10,000
Share capital	10,000	5,000
Reserves	28,000	5,000
	38,000	10,000

On 1 January 20X9 Left plc bought 95% of the share capital of Right plc for £8,000,000 in cash. At that date the reserves of Right plc were £2,000,000.

Calculate:

a) consolidated reserves
b) goodwill
c) non-controlling interest

at 31 December 20X9.

4 Why should the assets and liabilities of an acquired subsidiary be adjusted to fair value before they are included in the consolidated statement of financial position?

5 The following statements of financial position relate to Salt Ltd and its subsidiary, Pepper Ltd, at 31 March 20X7:

	Salt Ltd £'000	*Pepper Ltd* £'000
Assets		
Non-current assets:		
Property, plant and equipment	8,000	6,000
Investment in Pepper Ltd	4,000	–
	12,000	6,000
Current assets:		
Inventories	2,400	1,440
Trade and other receivables	2,640	2,400
Cash and cash equivalents	480	360
	5,520	4,200
Total assets	17,520	10,200
Equity and liabilities		
Equity		
Share capital (£1 ordinary shares)	5,000	1,000
Retained earnings	7,960	6,200
	12,960	7,200
Non-current liabilities	1,200	1,080
Current liabilities:		
Trade payables	2,500	1,700
Tax liabilities	860	220
	3,360	1,920
Total liabilities	4,560	3,000
Total equity and liabilities	17,520	10,200

The following information is relevant:

1) Salt Ltd purchased 800,000 ordinary shares in Pepper Ltd on 1 April 20X5 when the retained earnings reserve of Pepper Ltd was £2,500,000.

2) At 31 March 20X7, the payables of Salt Ltd included £960,000 which was due to Pepper Ltd.

Required

Prepare the consolidated statement of financial position of the Salt Ltd group at 31 March 20X7.

chapter 11: GROUP ACCOUNTS: FURTHER ASPECTS

chapter coverage

This chapter explains how to prepare a consolidated income statement and looks at a number of further aspects of group accounts.

The topics that we shall cover are:

- the consolidated income statement
- the consolidated statement of changes in equity
- group accounts: further points
- associates

KNOWLEDGE AND UNDERSTANDING AND PERFORMANCE CRITERIA COVERAGE

knowledge and understanding

- the UK regulatory framework for financial reporting and the main requirements of relevant financial reporting standards
- preparing financial statements in proper form
- the general principles of consolidation

Performance criteria – element 11.1

- draft limited company financial statements from the appropriate information
- ensure that limited company financial statements comply with relevant accounting standards and domestic legislation and with the organisation's policies, regulations and procedures

student notes

THE CONSOLIDATED INCOME STATEMENT

The basic idea

As for the consolidated statement of financial position, there are basically two steps:

- add together the income statements of the parent and the subsidiary; and
- make adjustments to cancel out intra-group items.

HOW IT WORKS

P Ltd has owned 80% of the share capital of S Ltd for many years. The individual company income statements for the year ended 31 December 20X0 are shown below:

	P Ltd	*S Ltd*
	£'000	£'000
Revenue	100,000	50,000
Cost of sales	(50,000)	(25,000)
Gross profit	50,000	25,000
Operating expenses	(30,000)	(10,000)
Profit from operations	20,000	15,000
Investment income	4,000	–
Profit before tax	24,000	15,000
Tax	(7,000)	(4,000)
Profit for the year	17,000	11,000

During the year, S Ltd paid a dividend of £5,000,000.

Step 1 Add together the income statements of the parent and the subsidiary, line by line, from revenue to profit for the year

- This reflects the fact that the parent **controls** 100% of the results of the subsidiary, even though it only owns 80% of the equity shares.
- The investment income is P Ltd's share of S Ltd's dividend (80% × 5,000,000). This is not included in the consolidated income statement. Intra-group dividends are eliminated on consolidation.

student notes

	£'000
Revenue	150,000
Cost of sales	(75,000)
Gross profit	75,000
Operating expenses	(40,000)
Profit before tax	35,000
Tax	(11,000)
Profit for the year	24,000

Step 2 Deal with the non-controlling interest

- The non-controlling interest is the non-controlling interest's share of profit for the year in the accounts of the subsidiary.
- Profit for the year is analysed between profits owned by the non-controlling interest and profits owned by the group. The analysis is shown at the foot of the consolidated income statement.

Attributable to:

	£'000
Equity holders of the parent	21,800
Non-controlling interest (20% × 11,000)	2,200
	24,000

Consolidated income statement for the year ended 31 December 20X0

	£'000
Revenue	150,000
Cost of sales	(75,000)
Gross profit	75,000
Operating expenses	(40,000)
Profit before tax	35,000
Tax	(11,000)
Profit for the year	24,000

Attributable to:

	£'000
Equity holders of the parent	21,800
Non-controlling interest (20% × 11,000)	2,200
	24,000

Goodwill

Any impairment loss is normally included in administrative expenses.

student notes

Intra-group dividends and interest

Interest payable by one group company to another is cancelled against interest receivable in the income statement of the other company.

Dividends are dealt with as follows:

- The parent's share of the dividend paid by the subsidiary is cancelled against dividends receivable in the accounts of the parent.
- The non-controlling interest's share of the dividend paid by the subsidiary is paid from the non-controlling interest's share of the subsidiary's profit for the year. This has already been deducted.
- Therefore **only dividends paid by the parent** are deducted from consolidated retained earnings (and shown in the statement of changes in equity).

HOW IT WORKS

P Ltd has owned 80% of the share capital of S Ltd for many years. Information relating to the two companies for the year ended 31 December 20X0 is shown below:

	P Ltd	*S Ltd*
	£'000	£'000
Retained earnings at 1 January 20X0	43,000	24,000
Profit for the year	17,000	11,000
Dividends	(10,000)	(5,000)
Retained earnings at 31 December 20X0	50,000	30,000

- At the date of acquisition, the retained earnings reserve of S Ltd was £10,000,000.
- Profit for the year attributable to the owners of the parent is £21,800,000.

Step 1 Calculate consolidated retained earnings brought forward

- This is done in exactly the same way as the calculation of the consolidated retained earnings reserve in the consolidated statement of financial position.
- The retained earnings reserve carried forward can also be calculated as proof.

student notes

Retained earnings brought forward at 1 January 20X0

	£'000	£'000
P Ltd		43,000
S Ltd: At 1 January 20X0	24,000	
Less: At acquisition	(10,000)	
Group share (80%)	14,000	11,200
		54,200

Retained earnings carried forward at 31 December 20X0 (proof)

	£'000	£'000
P Ltd		50,000
S Ltd: At 31 December 20X0	30,000	
Less: At acquisition	(10,000)	
Group share (80%)	20,000	16,000
		66,000

Step 2 Movements on the consolidated retained earnings reserve

	£'000
Retained earnings at 1 January 20X0	54,200
Profit attributable to equity holders of the parent	21,800
Dividends (parent only)	(10,000)
Retained earnings at 31 December 20X0	66,000

Activity 1

Thatch Ltd owns 75% of the issued share capital of Slate Ltd.

Extracts from income statements for the year ended 30 June 20X9:

	Thatch Ltd	*Slate Ltd*
	£'000	£'000
Profit from operations	685	90
Dividends received from Slate Ltd	15	–
Profit before tax	700	90
Tax	(150)	(30)
Profit for the year	550	60

Show the figures that would appear in the consolidated income statement for the group for the year ended 30 June 20X9.

student notes

Intra-group sales

Suppose that P Ltd sells goods costing £10,000 to its subsidiary S Ltd for £20,000.

- The revenue of P Ltd and the cost of sales of S Ltd both increase by £20,000.

- P Ltd makes a profit of £10,000 on the sale.

At the year-end S Ltd still has half the goods in inventory.

From the perspective **of the group**:

- Revenue and cost of sales are both overstated by £10,000.
- Profit is overstated by £5,000 (10,000 ÷ 2).

Where one company sells goods to another two adjustments must be made to the consolidated income statement:

- intra-group sales and purchases are cancelled against each other; and

- the unrealised profit is removed.

HOW IT WORKS

Arden Ltd has owned 75% of the share capital of Baker Ltd for many years. The individual company income statements for the year ended 31 December 20X1 are shown below:

	Arden Ltd	*Baker Ltd*
	£'000	£'000
Revenue	6,000	3,000
Cost of sales	(4,000)	(2,000)
Gross profit	2,000	1,000
Operating expenses	(1,000)	(500)
Profit before tax	1,000	500
Tax	(300)	(100)
Profit for the year	700	400

- During the year, Arden Ltd made sales totalling £1,000,000 to Baker Ltd. Arden Ltd made a gross profit of 30% on these sales. All the goods were still in the inventory of Baker Ltd at 31 December 20X1.

student notes

Intra-group sales

To cancel the sale from Arden Ltd to Baker Ltd:

DEBIT	Revenue	£1,000,000	
CREDIT	Cost of sales		£1,000,000

To eliminate the unrealised profit of £300,000 (1,000,000 × 30%):

DEBIT	Consolidated retained earnings reserve	£300,000	
CREDIT	Closing inventory		£300,000

Closing inventory is **deducted** from cost of sales. Therefore the reduction in closing inventory **increases** cost of sales.

Method of working

Add the income statements of Arden Ltd and Baker Ltd together line by line, making adjustments to cancel:

- intra-group sales
- intra-group interest and dividends (if any)

Consolidated income statements for the year ended 31 December 20X1

	£'000
Revenue (6,000 + 3,000 – 1,000)	8,000
Cost of sales (4,000 + 2,000 – 1,000 + 300)	(5,300)
Gross profit	2,700
Operating expenses (1,000 + 500)	(1,500)
Profit before tax	1,200
Tax (300 + 100)	(400)
Profit for the year	800
Attributable to:	
Equity holders of the parent	700
Non-controlling interest (25% × 400)	100
	800

Intra-group sales from the subsidiary to the parent

Where the subsidiary sells goods to the parent, the profit on sale arises in the subsidiary's accounts. The adjustment to remove the unrealised profit must be allocated between the group and the non-controlling interest:

student notes

DEBIT	Consolidated retained earnings reserve (with the group share)
DEBIT	Non-controlling interest (with the non-controlling interest's share)
CREDIT	Closing inventory

HOW IT WORKS

During the year, Baker Ltd made sales totalling £1,000,000 to Arden Ltd. Baker Ltd made a gross profit of 30% on these sales. All the goods were still in the inventory of Arden Ltd at 31 December 20X1.

To cancel the sale from Baker Ltd to Arden Ltd:

DEBIT	Revenue	£1,000,000	
CREDIT	Cost of sales		£1,000,000

To eliminate the unrealised profit of £300,000:

DEBIT	Consolidated retained earnings (75% × 300,000)	£225,000	
DEBIT	Non-controlling interest (25% × 300,000)	£75,000	
CREDIT	Closing inventory		£300,000

Non-controlling interest:

	£'000
Share of subsidiary's profit after tax (25% × 400)	100
Less: share of unrealised profit (25% × 300)	(75)
	25

Consolidated income statement for the year ended 31 December 20X1

	£'000
Revenue (6,000 + 3,000 – 1,000)	8,000
Cost of sales (4,000 + 2,000 – 1,000 + 300)	(5,300)
Gross profit	2,700
Operating expenses (1,000 + 500)	(1,500)
Profit before tax	1,200
Tax (300 + 100)	(400)
Profit for the year	800
Attributable to:	
Equity holders of the parent	775
Non-controlling interest (25% × (400 – 300)	25
	800

student notes

Activity 2

Timber Ltd is an 80% subsidiary of Wood Ltd. During the year, Timber Ltd sold goods that originally cost £30,000 to Wood Ltd for £40,000. At the year end, half those goods remained in inventory.

What adjustments must be made to the consolidated income statement as a result of this transaction?

THE CONSOLIDATED STATEMENT OF CHANGES IN EQUITY

The basic idea

The consolidated statement of changes in equity is the 'bridge' between the consolidated income statement and the consolidated statement of financial position. It shows:

- equity at the beginning of the period; plus
- profit for the period, as shown in the consolidated income statement; which is
- equity at the end of the period, as shown in the consolidated statement of financial position.

analysed between the amounts 'belonging' to the group and the amounts 'belonging' to the non-controlling interest.

Illustration

In the Assessment, you will be given a pro-forma to follow:

Consolidated statement of changes in equity for the year ended...

	Equity holders of the parent	Non-controlling interest	Total equity
	£	£	£
Balance at the beginning of the period	X	X	X
Changes in equity for the period			
Profit for the period	X	X	X
Balance at the end of the period	X	X	X
	X	X	X

student notes

HOW IT WORKS

Extracts from the consolidated financial statements of the Cinnamon group are shown below:

Consolidated statement of financial position at 31 December

	20X9 £'000	20X8 £'000
Equity		
Share capital	15,000	15,000
Share premium	5,000	5,000
Retained earnings	25,500	18,250
Equity attributable to owners of the parent	45,500	38,250
Non-controlling interest	5,500	4,000
Total equity	51,000	42,250

Consolidated income statement for the year ended 31 December 20X9

	£'000
Profit for the year	8,750
Attributable to:	£'000
Equity holders of the parent	7,250
Non-controlling interest	1,500
	8,750

The consolidated statement of changes in equity is as follows:

Consolidated statement of changes in equity for the year ended 31 December 20X9

	Equity holders of the parent £'000	Non-controlling interest £'000	Total equity £'000
Balance at 1 January 20X9 (consolidated statement of financial position)	38,250	4,000	42,250
Changes in equity for the period			
Profit for the year (consolidated income statement)	7,250	1,500	8,750
Balance at 31 December 20X9 (consolidated statement of financial position).	45,500	5,500	51,000

student notes

In the Assessment, you will be given some of these balances and asked to calculate others. Remember that:

- opening equity + profit for the year = closing equity
- closing equity – profit for the year = opening equity.

Activity 3

Chervil plc acquired 60% of the equity share capital of Lovage Ltd on 1 April 20X7. The summarised statements of financial position of the two companies at 31 March 20X9 are set out below:

Statement of financial position at 31 March 20X9

	Chervil plc	Lovage Ltd
	£'000	£'000
Non-current assets:		
Property, plant and equipment	42,691	35,460
Investment in Lovage Ltd	28,000	-
	70,691	35,460
Current assets	20,497	8,880
	91,188	44,340
Share capital	30,000	7,500
Retained earnings	18,995	25,190
	48,995	32,690
Non-current liabilities	32,000	8,000
Current liabilities	10,193	3,650
	91,188	44,340

Additional information

- There have been no changes to the share capital since acquisition. No dividends were paid or proposed by either company in the current year.
- The balance on retained earnings of Lovage Ltd on 1 April 20X7 was £22,500,000.
- Goodwill arising on the acquisition of Lovage Ltd has been impaired during the current year. The impairment is estimated to be 15% of the goodwill.
- The consolidated profit for the year is £8,366,000 of which £1,076,000 relates to the non-controlling interest in Lovage Ltd.

Prepare the summarised consolidated statement of financial position for the Chervil plc group at 31 March 20X9 and the consolidated statement of changes in equity for the year ended 31 March 20X9.

student notes

GROUP ACCOUNTS: FURTHER POINTS

Scope of consolidated accounts

IAS 27 states that the consolidated financial statements must include **all** subsidiaries of the parent.

Subsidiaries cannot be excluded because they are held for resale or because their activities are very different from those of the parent.

Accounting policies

Consolidated financial statements must be prepared using uniform accounting policies for similar transactions and other events in similar circumstances.

If a subsidiary uses different accounting policies from the parent its financial statements are adjusted before consolidation.

The purchase method

When two companies combine to form a group, one company (the parent) acquires (takes over) the other (the subsidiary). The shareholders of the parent become the ultimate shareholders of the subsidiary and the parent exercises control over the subsidiary. Almost all business combinations are **acquisitions**.

The way in which consolidated financial statements are prepared reflects the idea of an acquisition. It presents the financial statements from the point of view of the acquirer (the parent). The method used is called the **purchase method** or the **acquisition method**. All the examples in this book use the purchase method.

In theory, there is another, very rare type of business combination. Two companies combine in order to share their resources and neither company controls the other (although technically one company is the parent and the other is the subsidiary). This form of combination is a **merger** or a **uniting of interests**. When a combination is treated as a uniting of interests a different method of consolidation is used: the **pooling of interests method**.

IFRS 3 states that an entity should account for each business combination by using the **acquisition method**.

In other words, the pooling of interests method is prohibited.

student notes

Separate financial statements

Separate financial statements are the parent's individual financial statements. They show the parent as a separate entity.

- Separate financial statements recognise the parent's investment in the subsidiary as a non-current asset in the statement of financial position.
- The investment is measured either at **cost** or at **fair value**.

ASSOCIATES

A company can have three types of investment in another company:

- a simple investment: the investor has little or no influence;
- a subsidiary: the investor has control; and
- an associate: the investor does not have control, but can exercise significant influence.

Definition

- An **associate** is an entity (other than a subsidiary) in which another entity (the investor) has **significant influence**.
- **Significant influence** is the power to participate in the financial and operating policy decisions of the investee.

If an investor holds 20% or more of the voting power of the investee it is normally presumed that the investor has significant influence.

In most cases, a holding of between 20% and 50% of the equity share capital of a company gives significant influence (but not control). However:

- It is possible for an investor to exercise significant influence with a shareholding of less than 20%. For example, it might have the right to appoint and remove directors.
- It is possible for an investor to have a shareholding of more than 20% without being able to exercise significant influence. For example, the remainder of the shares might be held by another company.

IAS 28 *Investments in associates* explains that an investor usually has significant influence if:

- it is represented on the board of directors;
- it takes part in policy making processes, including decisions about dividends and other distributions;

student notes

- there are material transactions between the investor and the investee;
- there is interchange of management personnel;
- it provides essential technical information to the investee.

The accounting treatment of associates

In the investing company's separate financial statements:

- associates are included in the statement of financial position as a non-current asset investment and shown either at cost or fair value; and
- the income statement includes dividends received from associates.

If the investing company prepares group accounts, associates are not consolidated, as this would imply that the investor has control over their assets and liabilities. However, they are too significant to be treated as simple investments.

IAS 28 states that the **equity method** should be used.

- At acquisition, the investment is recognised at cost.
- In subsequent periods the value of the investment is adjusted for changes in the investor's share of the net assets of the associate (which are post acquisition profits and losses).
- The investor's share of the associates' profit or loss is included in the income statement.
- The financial statements must be prepared using uniform accounting policies for both investor and associate.

In the consolidated statement of financial position

The investment in the associate is recognised as a non-current asset investment and disclosed as a separate line item.

The carrying amount of the investment is:

- the group share of the net assets of the associate; plus
- any goodwill arising on the acquisition.

Goodwill is the cost of the investment less the parents' (groups') share of the net assets acquired.

In the consolidated income statement

The group share of the associates' profit after tax is included as a separate line item above profit before tax.

HOW IT WORKS

Python Ltd, which has one wholly owned subsidiary, acquired 40% of the issued ordinary share capital of Adder Ltd on 1 January 20X1, when the retained earnings reserve of Adder Ltd stood at £1,000,000. The accounts of Python Ltd and its subsidiary and Adder Ltd for the year ended 31 December 20X1 are shown below:

Income statements for the year ended 31 December 20X1

	Python Group	*Adder Ltd*
	£'000	£'000
Revenue	10,000	2,000
Cost of sales	(7,000)	(1,000)
Gross profit	3,000	1,000
Operating expenses	(2,000)	(500)
Profit before tax	1,000	500
Tax	(300)	(100)
Profit for the year	700	400

Statement of financial position at 31 December 20X1

	Python Group	*Adder Ltd*
	£'000	£'000
Assets		
Non-current assets		
Property, plant and equipment	10,000	2,000
Investment in Adder Ltd	1,500	–
	11,500	2,000
Current assets:		
Inventories	1,500	400
Trade and other receivables	1,600	500
Cash and cash equivalents	200	100
	3,300	1,000
Total assets	14,800	3,000

Equity and liabilities		
Equity		
Share capital	5,000	1,000
Retained earnings	7,300	1,400
	12,300	2,400
Current liabilities:		
Trade and other payables	2,000	500
Tax liabilities	500	100
	2,500	600
Total equity and liabilities	14,800	3,000

Step 1 Calculate goodwill

	£'000	£'000
Cost of investment		1,500
Less: net assets acquired:		
Share capital	1,000	
Retained earnings	1,000	
	2,000	
Group share (40%)		(800)
		700

Step 2 Calculate the group's share of the net assets of the associate

	£'000
Group share of net assets at year end (40% × 2,400)	960
Add: goodwill	700
	1,660

Alternative calculation (proof):	
Cost of investment	1,500
Add: share of associate's profit since acquisition (40% × 400)	160
	1,660

Step 3 Calculate consolidated retained earnings reserve

	£'000
Python Group	7,300
Add: share of associate's profit since acquisition (40% × 400)	160
	7,460

Step 4 Prepare the consolidated financial statements

Consolidated income statement for the year ended 31 December 20X1

	£'000
Revenue	10,000
Cost of sales	(7,000)
Gross profit	3,000
Operating expenses	(2,000)
Share of profit of associates (40% × 400)	160
Profit before tax	1,160
Tax	(300)
Profit for the year	860

Consolidated statement of financial position at 31 December 20X1

	£'000	£'000
Assets		
Non-current assets:		
Property, plant and equipment		10,000
Investment in associate (Step 2)		1,660
		11,660
Current assets:		
Inventories	1,500	
Trade and other receivables	1,600	
Cash and cash equivalents	200	
		3,300
Total assets		14,960
Equity		
Equity attributable to owners of the parent		
Share capital		5,000
Retained earnings (Step 3)		7,460
		12,460
Current liabilities:		
Trade and other payables	2,000	
Tax liabilities	500	2,500
Total equity and liabilities		14,960

Activity 4

Plaster Ltd purchased a 30% interest in Paint Ltd for £500,000 on 1 April 20X6 when the total net assets of the company amounted to £1,000,000. Since acquisition Paint Ltd has made profits amounting to £250,000 and at 31 March 20X8, the total net assets of the company amounted to £1,250,000.

At what amount will the investment in Paint Ltd be shown in the group statement of financial position of Plaster Ltd at 31 March 20X8?

CHAPTER OVERVIEW

- To prepare a consolidated income statement:
  - Add together the income statements of the parent and the subsidiary, line by line
  - Split the profit for the year between the parent and the non-controlling interest
- Where one company sells goods to another two adjustments must be made to the consolidated income statement:

  1 To eliminate the sale:

  DEBIT Revenue
  CREDIT Cost of sales

  2 To eliminate unrealised profit:

  Sale from parent to subsidiary

  DEBIT Consolidated retained earnings reserve
  CREDIT Closing inventories (ie reduce cost of sales)

  Sale from subsidiary to parent

  DEBIT Consolidated retained earnings reserve (group share)
  DEBIT Non-controlling interest (NCI's share)
  CREDIT Closing inventories (ie reduce cost of sales)
- Consolidated financial statements must include all subsidiaries of the parent
- Uniform accounting policies must be used
- All business combinations must be accounted for by applying the acquisition method

KEY WORDS

Acquisition a business combination in which one company (the parent) acquires and controls the other (the subsidiary)

Purchase method method of preparing consolidated financial statements which presents the financial statements from the point of view of the acquirer (the parent). It is the method normally used

Uniting of interests (sometimes called a merger) a business combination in which two companies combine to share their resources and neither company controls the other

Pooling of interests method method of preparing consolidated financial statements used to account for a uniting of interests

Separate financial statements the parent's individual financial statements, showing the parent as a separate entity

Associate an entity (other than a subsidiary) in which another entity (the investor) has significant influence

Significant influence the power to participate in the financial and operating policy decisions of the investee

Equity method a method of accounting in which the group share of the net assets of an investment are recognised in the consolidated statement of financial position and the group share of its results are recognised in the consolidated income statement

- In separate financial statements, the parent's investment in the subsidiary is measured either at cost or at fair value
- Associates are included in the consolidated financial statements using the equity method
- The consolidated statement of financial position includes the group share of the associate's net assets
- The consolidated income statement includes the group share of the associates' profit after tax

HOW MUCH HAVE YOU LEARNED?

1 Why must adjustments be made in group accounts when one group company sells goods to another?

2 Stansfield Ltd is a 75% subsidiary of Purton Ltd. An extract from its income statement is shown below:

	£'000
Profit before tax	7,500
Tax	(2,000)
Profit for the year	5,500

During the year, Purton Ltd sold goods to Stansfield Ltd. As a result, inventories in the consolidated statement of financial position have been reduced to reflect unrealised profit of £12,000.

What is the figure for non-controlling interests in the consolidated income statement for the year?

3 Denston Ltd has owned 60% of the share capital of Hawkedon Ltd and 30% of the share capital of Clare Ltd for many years. Revenue for the year ended 30 September 20X9 for each of the three companies was as follows:

	£
Denston Ltd	950,000
Hawkedon Ltd	500,000
Clare Ltd	300,000

What figure for revenue will be reported in the consolidated income statement for the year ended 30 September 20X9?

A £1,250,000
B £1,340,000
C £1,450,000
D £1,540,000

4 Fill in the gaps.

An .... is an entity (other than a subsidiary) in which another entity (the investor) has ....

.... is the power to participate in the .... and .... decisions of the investee.

5 The income statements of Thames Ltd and Stour Ltd for the year ended 31 December 20X3 are shown below.

	Thames Ltd	*Stour Ltd*
	£000	£000
Continuing operations		
Revenue	2,280	1,200
Cost of sales	(1,320)	(660)
Gross profit	960	540
Operating expenses	(360)	(180)
Profit from operations	600	360
Investment income	85	–
Profit before tax	685	360
Tax	(240)	(120)
Profit for the year attributable to equity holders	445	240

The following information is relevant:

1) The issued share capital of Stour Ltd consists of 100,000 ordinary shares of £1 each.

2) Thames Ltd acquired 85,000 of the ordinary shares of Stour Ltd on 1 January 20X0.

3) During the year, Stour Ltd made sales totalling £600,000 to Thames Ltd. All these goods had been sold by 31 December 20X3.

Required

Prepare the consolidated income statement of the group for the year ended 31 December 20X3.

6 On 31 December 20X8 Thomas plc acquired 60% of the equity share capital of Percy Ltd for £7,200,000. No goodwill arose on the acquisition. The income statements of both companies for the year ended 31 December 20X9 are shown below:

	Thomas plc	Percy Ltd
	£'000	£'000
Continuing operations		
Revenue	39,500	13,250
Cost of Sales	(21,200)	(5,250)
Gross Profit	18,300	8,000
Distribution costs	(7,320)	(3,150)
Administrative expenses	(2,950)	(3,240)
Profit from operations	8,030	1,610
Finance costs	(430)	(210)
Profit before tax	7,600	1,400
Tax	(2,220)	(420)
Profit for the year from continuing operations	5,380	980

Additional information:

- During the year, Percy Ltd sold goods to Thomas plc for £2,500,000. All these goods had been sold by the year-end.
- The equity (share capital, share premium and retained earnings) of both companies at 1 January 20X9 (the date on which Percy Ltd was acquired) was £23,000,000 for Thomas plc and £12,000,000 for Percy Ltd.
- All the assets in Percy Ltd were deemed to be at their fair value at the acquisition date.

Required

Prepare the consolidated income statement and the consolidated statement of changes in equity of the Thomas plc Group for the year ended 31 December 20X9.

ANSWERS TO CHAPTER ACTIVITIES

CHAPTER 1 Introduction to financial statements

1 Users most likely to be interested in the accounts of a small family-owned company:

- Lenders (if the business is financed by borrowings, for example, from a bank)
- Government and its agencies (the Inland Revenue)

2 There is a potential conflict between caution (usually called prudence) and neutrality (lack of bias), both qualities that information must have if it is to be reliable. It is possible to make excessively prudent estimates, so that liabilities and losses are overstated and assets and gains are understated. Financial statements prepared in this way would not be neutral. Again, a compromise must be made between the two aspects of reliability.

3 Examples:

- Purchases are adjusted for opening and closing inventories (stock) to arrive at the cost of sales (to match the cost of sales to the sales made during the period)

- Non-current (fixed) assets are depreciated (to match the cost of an asset to the accounting periods expected to benefit from its use)

4 Examples:

- Inventory (stock) is valued at the lower of cost or net realisable value
- Allowance is made for doubtful debts

5 Error a) is certainly not material in the context of total sales revenue. However, it could be material if net profit has also been overstated by £1,000 (this is 5% of total net profit).

Error b) represents 6% of the company's net assets. Whether this is material depends on the total non-current asset figure (which is probably much larger than £500,000) and also on whether the error has affected net profit. If the £30,000 has been treated as an expense instead of being capitalised, net profit has been reduced by more than half.

6 Possible examples of non-current assets: land and buildings; plant and machinery; motor vehicles; fixtures and fittings; brand names; long-term investments.

Possible examples of current assets: inventories (stocks); receivables (debtors); prepayments; bank account; petty cash; short-term investments.

7 Owners contribute to ownership interest (capital) by introducing further finance (for example, by paying the proceeds of a legacy into the business bank account).

In the accounts of a sole trader, distributions to owners are described as drawings.

CHAPTER 2 Introduction to limited companies

1 **Amelia**
Income statement for the year ended 30 June 20X1

	£	£
Sales		350,000
Opening stock	12,700	
Purchases	219,000	
Carriage inwards	1,000	
	232,700	
Less: closing stock	(14,900)	
Cost of sales		(217,800)
Gross profit		132,200
Carriage outwards	1,200	
Wages and salaries	55,000	
Rent and rates (9,600 – 900)	8,700	
Heat and light (4,500 + 700)	5,200	
Depreciation – equipment (91,000 × 10%)	9,100	
– motor vehicles (39,000 × 20%)	7,800	
Sundry expenses	7,300	
		(94,300)
Net profit for the year		37,900

Amelia
Statement of financial position as at 30 June 20X1

	£	£
Fixed assets		
Equipment (91,000 – 20,500 – 9,100)		61,400
Motor vehicles (39,000 – 8,000 – 7,800)		23,200
		84,600
Current assets		
Stock	14,900	
Debtors	48,000	
Prepayments	900	
Cash at bank (4,800 + 500)	5,300	
	69,100	
Current liabilities		
Creditors	33,000	
Accruals	700	
	33,700	
Net current assets		35,400
		120,000
Capital		
Balance at 1 July 20X0		97,700
Add profit for the year		37,900
		135,600
Less: drawings		(15,600)
Balance at 30 June 20X1		120,000

2 There are several reasons why the directors of the company would not wish to distribute the whole of the profit after tax as dividend:

- It would be unwise to pay out all the company's profits as dividends. The directors should ensure that some profits are retained in the business to enable it to continue to operate and to finance future growth (for example, by financing the purchase of new non-current assets).
- The Companies Act 2006 places restrictions on the amount of profits that can be distributed.
- The company may not have sufficient cash to pay the whole amount.

3 Total interest charge (12% × 200,000) £24,000

Adjustment to be made at the year-end:

DEBIT	Interest payable	£10,000	
CREDIT	Accruals		£10,000

Being five months' interest (12% × 200,000 × 5/12)

The interest account then appears as:

Debenture interest

		£			£
31 Jan	Bank	12,000	1 Jan	Balance b/f	10,000
31 July	Bank	12,000	31 Dec	Income statement	24,000
31 Dec	Balance c/f (accurals)	10,000			
		34,000			34,000
			1 Jan	Balance b/f	10,000

4 **Income statement for the year ended**

	£'000
Revenue	3,534
Cost of sales (228 + 2,623 – 264)	(2,587)
Gross profit	947
Distribution costs (W)	(157)
Administrative expenses (W)	(416)
Profit from operations	374
Finance costs	(24)
Profit before tax	350
Tax	(105)
Profit for the year	245

Working

	Distribution costs £'000	*Administrative expenses* £'000	*Total* £'000
Directors' salaries		32	32
Wages and salaries:			
sales staff	131		131
office staff		197	197
Advertising and marketing costs	16		16
Office expenses		128	128
Light and heat		16	16
Depreciation:			
freehold buildings		2	2
fixtures and fittings		36	36
delivery vans	10		10
Audit fees		5	5
	157	416	573

5 Double entry:

		£	£
DEBIT	Bank	£125,000	
CREDIT	Share capital		£125,000

Being the issue of 250,000 50p ordinary shares at par.

6

	£
Share capital (25p ordinary shares)	135,000
Share premium	27,000
Retained earnings	170,000
	332,000

Working

	Number of shares	*Share capital* £	*Share premium* £
Original	400,000	100,000	30,000
Rights issue (1 for 5)	80,000	20,000	12,000
	480,000	120,000	42,000
Bonus issue (1 for 8)	60,000	15,000	(15,000)
	540,000	135,000	27,000

CHAPTER 3 Published financial statements of limited companies

1 An item that meets the definition of an element should be recognised if:

- it is probable that any future economic benefit associated with the item will flow to or from the entity; and
- the item has a cost or value that can be measured with reliability.

The key word here is 'probable'. The advertising campaign is intended to generate sales income, but it is very difficult to predict whether it actually will do this in practice. No asset should be recognised; the £100,000 should be treated as an expense in the period in which it is incurred.

2 If the definition were not so specific, preparers of accounts might be able to use the required disclosure to give a more favourable view of the company's performance than is actually the case.

For example, if closing a loss making division had merely been discussed (rather than actually put into effect), it might be possible to argue that it was a discontinuing operation and to present its results separately from those of the rest of the entity. This would give users the impression that the entity's performance might improve in future periods.

3 ■ It is often said that the duty to publish annual accounts and to make all the legally required disclosures is the 'price' of limited liability. As the shareholders are only liable for the amount that they have invested, the level of disclosure gives creditors some protection.

■ However, the main reason for the high level of disclosure is to enable investors and potential investors to assess the stewardship of the directors and to make economic decisions about their investment.

CHAPTER 4 Reporting financial performance

1 Is the gain part of the company's performance? Yes. The building is part of the resources of the company, which have increased in value. In theory it could now be sold for more than its original cost, resulting in extra income and a cash inflow.

Should the gain be included in the income statement? No. The gain is not yet realised (the cash has not yet been received). It is not certain that the gain ever will be realised. The company may not sell the building, or the market may collapse so that the building falls in value in the future.

2 Characteristics of reliable information:

- faithful representation of financial position, financial performance and cash flow
- reflection of the economic substance of transactions (substance over form)
- neutrality
- prudence
- completeness

3 This is a change in accounting estimate. It does not involve a change to recognition, presentation or measurement basis. (Compare this with the next example, which is a change in accounting policy: this is a change from no depreciation to depreciation, rather than simply a change in the way that depreciation is calculated.)

4 This is is not a prior period error, because the doubtful debt allowance was an accounting estimate based on the information available at the time (see the definition). Routine adjustments and corrections to previous accounting estimates should not normally be treated as prior period errors.

The shortfall would only be a prior period error if there had been misuse of information that was available before the financial statements were authorised for issue. This would be the case, if, for example, the directors knew that one of their major customers was about to go into liquidation and they ignored this when making the provision.

5 **Statement of comprehensive income for the year ended 31 December 20X3**

	£'000
Profit for the year	609
Other comprehensive income for the year:	
Gain on property revaluation	125
Total comprehensive income for the year	734

Statement of changes in equity for the year ended 31 December 20X3

	Total equity £'000
Balance at 1 January 20X3	2,020
Changes in equity for 20X3	
Total comprehensive income for the year	734
Dividends	(100)
Issue of share capital (200,000 x 1.50)	300
Balance at 31 December 20X3	2,954

CHAPTER 5 The statement of cash flows

1 A loan creditor needs to be able to assess whether or not the company can (a) pay the interest on the loan and (b) repay the principal of the loan when it falls due. Cash flow information is more relevant than the level of the company's profits (although without profits there can be no cash in the longer term).

2 The answer is D: repayment of loans.

Cash received from the sale of property, plant and equipment is reported under 'cash flows from investing activities'

Equity dividends paid are normally reported under 'cash flows from financing activities', but may also be included under 'cash flows from operating activities'.

Interest received is reported under 'cash flows from investing activities'.

3

	£
Profit from operations	20,000
Depreciation	5,000
Decrease in inventory (5,100 – 5,800)	700
Increase in receivables (7,500 – 7,000)	(500)
Decrease in payables (5,700 – 6,000)	(300)
Cash generated from operations	24,900

4 Statement of cash flows

	£	£
Net cash from operating activities		39,000
Investing activities:		
Purchase of property, plant and equipment	(65,000)	
Proceeds on disposal of property, plant and equipment	10,000	
Dividends received	4,000	
Net cash used in investing activities		(51,000)
Financing activities:		
Proceeds of share issue	50,000	
Repayment of long-term loan	(20,000)	
Dividends paid	(8,000)	
Net cash from financing activities		22,000
Increase in cash and cash equivalents for the period		10,000
Cash and cash equivalents at the beginning of the period		7,000
Cash and cash equivalents at the end of the period		17,000

Working

Net cash from operating activities

Cash generated from operations	56,000
Interest paid	(3,000)
Tax paid	(14,000)
	39,000

5 There has been a decrease in cash of £238,000 and this has reduced the company's cash balance from £240,000 to only £2,000.

However, there are many positive signs:

- Cash generated from operations is more than £5,000,000 (compared with profit from operations of £4,214,000). If the company can regularly generate this amount of cash, it should be able to avoid serious cash flow problems. There are no signs of problems in managing working capital; only receivables have increased in the period.

- The main reason for the net cash outflow is that there have been asset purchases of nearly £3,000,000. This means that the company should be able to continue to generate profits and cash inflows in future periods.

- Cash has also been used to repay some of the company's loan stock. Therefore cash outflows to pay interest will reduce in future periods.

- The company still has a positive cash balance; it has not overdrawn its bank account.

Conclusion: the company is probably managing its cash flow well and there appear to be no liquidity problems.

CHAPTER 6 Non-current assets

1 Cost of offices:

	£'000
Building	300
Legal fees	5
Alterations (50 – 5)	45
	350

2 The double entry to record the revaluation is:

DEBIT	Freehold property: Cost/valuation	£100,000	
DEBIT	Freehold property: Accumulated depreciation (W)	£31,250	
CREDIT	Revaluation reserve		£131,250

Working

Accumulated depreciation at 31 December 20X5:

250,000 × 5/40 = £31,250

3 Carrying amount at 1 January 20X3:

	£
Cost	20,000
Accumulated depreciation (20,000 × 2/10)	(4,000)
	16,000

Depreciation charge for the year ended 31 December 20X3 is 25% × 16,000 = £4,000.

4 Carrying amount at 1 January 20X3:

	£
Cost	20,000
Accumulated depreciation (20,000 × 2/10):	(4,000)
	16,000

Depreciation charge for the year ended 31 December 20X3 is 16,000 ÷ 5 = £3,200.

5 Gain on disposal:

	£'000	£'000
Sales proceeds		700
Less: carrying amount		
Valuation	500	
Accumulated depreciation (500 × 4/50):	(40)	
		(460)
		240

6 Assets are rights or other access to future economic benefits controlled by an entity as a result of past transactions or events. Although the staff give the company access to future economic benefits (revenue from selling the products that they develop), the company almost certainly does not control these benefits. Employees are normally free to leave the company and work elsewhere.

Therefore neither the staff, nor their skills, can be recognised as assets in the company's statement of financial position and IAS 38 specifically states that a workforce cannot be treated as an intangible asset.

7 The expenditure does not meet the IAS 38 criteria for capitalisation, as the outcome is uncertain. Therefore the expenditure must be written off to profit or loss (the income statement) in the period in which it is incurred.

8 IAS 38 prohibits the recognition of internally generated brands as assets.

9 Recoverable amount is £110,000 (the higher of fair value less costs to sell and value in use).

Therefore the impairment loss is £40,000 (150,000 – 110,000).

Because the property has been revalued, the loss is recognised in other comprehensive income. (Note that recoverable amount is higher than depreciated historic cost; therefore none of the loss needs to be recognised in profit or loss.)

CHAPTER 7 Inventories, taxation, provisions and events after the reporting period

1 Inventory valuation:

	Cost	NRV	Lower of cost and NRV
	£	£	£
A	2,880	3,420	2,880
B	5,500	5,034	5,034
C	3,310	3,185	3,185
Closing inventory is valued at			11,099

2 Journal entry:

DEBIT	Corporation tax charge (income statement)	£150,000	
CREDIT	Corporation tax payable (statement of financial position)		£150,000

Being the corporation tax charge for the year ended 31 December 20X2

3 a) Corporation tax charge for the year ended 30 June 20X5:

	£
Corporation tax based on profits for the year	50,000
Adjustment in respect of prior period (overprovision)	(2,000)
	48,000

b) The corporation tax liability at 30 June 20X5 is £50,000.

4 **Income statement for the year ended 31 December 20X4 (extract)**

	£'000
Profit before tax	X
Tax (W)	(175)
Profit for the year	X

Working

	£'000
Corporation tax based on profits for the year	150
Adjustment in respect of prior period	5
Deferred tax	20
	175

Statement of financial position at 31 December 20X4 (extract)

	£'000
Non-current liabilities:	
Deferred tax	130
Current liabilities:	
Tax payable	150

5 Is there a present obligation as the result of a past event? Yes. The company has a legal obligation under the guarantee.

Is the transfer of economic benefits in settlement probable? Yes. IAS 37 states that in this and similar situations, the individual obligations should be considered as a whole.

Can a reliable estimate be made of the amount of the obligation? Yes. The company should be able to use its past experience to predict the percentage of items that will need to be repaired or replaced.

Conclusion: Recognise a provision for the best estimate of the costs of repairing or replacing items sold before the year-end under the guarantee.

6 Sale of land and buildings: this is a non-adjusting event because it does not concern conditions that existed at the year-end. The sale should be disclosed in a note to the financial statements.

Liquidation of a major customer: this is an adjusting event; it provides evidence of conditions that existed at the year-end (a trade receivable is worthless). The £15,000 that relates to sales made before the year end should be written off as a bad debt.

CHAPTER 8 Further accounting standards

1 Examples of transactions or arrangements whose substance may be different from their legal form:

- lease contracts (where the lessee effectively owns the asset)
- sale or return agreements
- factoring of debts

2 This is a finance lease.

The following factors suggest that the risks and rewards of ownership have been transferred:

- the lease term is for the whole of the asset's useful life (five years)
- the present value of the minimum lease payments (£95,500) amounts to substantially all the fair value of the leased asset (£98,000).

3 The answer is no. Revenue does **not** include items such as profits from the sale of the entity's own property, plant and equipment. This is because this kind of income does not arise from the company's ordinary activities.

4 The advance payment is recognised as a liability, not as revenue. The goods have not yet been transferred to the buyer. Only when the goods are delivered should revenue be recognised.

CHAPTER 9 Interpreting financial statements

1 User groups:

- investors and potential investors
- lenders
- suppliers and other trade creditors
- employees
- customers
- governments and their agencies
- the public

2 a) ROCE $\dfrac{\text{Profit from operations}}{\text{Capital employed}}$ $\dfrac{300}{1{,}500} \times 100\% = 20\%$

b) Net profit margin $\dfrac{\text{Profit from operations}}{\text{Revenue}}$ $\dfrac{300}{2{,}000} \times 100\% = 15\%$

c) Asset turnover $\dfrac{\text{Revenue}}{\text{Capital employed}}$ $\dfrac{2{,}000}{1{,}500} = 1.33$ times

3 Current ratio $\dfrac{\text{Current assets}}{\text{Current liabilities}}$ $\dfrac{4{,}750+11{,}350+2{,}900}{7{,}400+2{,}100} = 2$

Quick ratio $\dfrac{\text{Current assets} - \text{inventories}}{\text{Current liabilities}}$ $\dfrac{11{,}350+2{,}900}{7{,}400+2{,}100} = 1.5$

4 Inventory turnover $\frac{\text{Cost of sales}}{\text{Closing inventory}}$ $\frac{4,200}{1,200} = 3.5$

5 The liquidation and the bad debt write off is not the reason for the increase. In fact, a large bad debt write off at the year end would decrease trade receivables and, thereby, receivables days.

Possible reasons:

- Some customers have been allowed extended credit terms (for example, because they are so significant that the business needs to maintain good relations with them).
- Sales were unusually high just before the year end or were increasing throughout the year. If this were the case, receivables at the year end would be high in relation to total sales for the year.
- Credit control procedures have not been applied during the last few months of the year.

6 Revaluation of assets normally increases asset values. This means that the depreciation charge also increases. The revaluation surplus is taken to a revaluation reserve, which increases owners' equity (shareholders' funds). Sales are not affected.

As a result:

- earnings are reduced
- capital employed is increased.

This means that:

- return on capital employed (ROCE) is lower
- asset turnover is lower
- net profit margin is lower.

However, gearing is reduced.

The company may appear to be less efficient and less profitable, but also less risky as an investment or as a loan creditor.

CHAPTER 10 Group accounts: the consolidated statement of financial position

1 The answer is yes. Although Moat Ltd only holds 20% of the total share capital, it holds 60% of the voting rights. Therefore it has the majority of the voting rights and Grange Ltd is a subsidiary according to the definition in IAS 27.

2 Goodwill:

	£'000
Cost of investment	4,000
Net assets acquired (60% × 6,000)	(3,600)
	400

3 Consolidated reserves:

	£'000
Church Ltd (1,080 + 96)	1,176
Steeple Ltd	50
	1,226

4 Trade receivables:

	£
X Ltd	20,000
Y Ltd	15,000
Less inter-company balance	(1,500)
	33,500

5 Inventories:

	£
Kilvert Ltd	100,000
Woodford Ltd	50,000
Less: provision for unrealised profit (30,000 × 25/125)	(6,000)
	144,000

CHAPTER 11 Group accounts: further aspects

1 **Consolidated income statement for the year ended 30 June 20X9 (extract):**

	£'000
Profit before tax	775
Tax	(180)
Profit for the year	595
Attributable to:	
Equity holders of the parent	580
Non-controlling interests (25% × 60)	15
	595

2 To cancel the sale:

DEBIT	Revenue	£40,000	
CREDIT	Cost of sales		£40,000

To eliminate the unrealised profit:

DEBIT	Consolidated retained earnings (80% × 5,000)	£4,000	
DEBIT	Non-controlling interest (20% × 5,000)	£1,000	
CREDIT	Closing inventory (10,000 ÷ 2)		£5,000

3 **Summarised consolidated statement of financial position at 31 March 20X9**

	£'000
Non-current assets:	
Intangible assets: goodwill (W1)	8,500
Property, plant and equipment	78,151
	86,651
Current assets	29,377
	116,028
Equity:	
Share capital	30,000
Retained earnings (W2)	19,109
	49,109
Non-controlling interest (40% × 32,690)	13,076
	62,185
Non-current liabilities	40,000
Current liabilities	13,843
	116,028

Consolidated statement of changes in equity for the year ended 31 March 20X9

	Equity holders of the parent £'000	Non-controlling interest £'000	Total equity £'000
Balance at 1 April 20X8 (Balancing figure)	41,819	12,000	53,819
Changes in equity for the year			
Profit for the year	7,290	1,076	8,366
Balance at 31 March 20X9 (from statement of financial position)	49,109	13,076	62,185

WORKINGS

1 Goodwill

	£'000	£'000
Cost of investment		28,000
Non-controlling interest		
Fair value of net assets acquired:		
Share capital	7,500	
Retained earnings	22,500	
	30,000	
NCI share (40%)		12,000
Fair value of net assets acquired		(30,000)
		10,000
Less: impairment loss (15% × 10,000)		(1,500)
		8,500

2 Consolidated retained earnings

	£'000	£'000
Chervil plc		18,995
Lovage Ltd:		
At year-end	25,190	
At acquisition	(22,500)	
	2,690	
Group share (60%)		1,614
		20,609
Less: impairment loss (15% × 10,000)		(1,500)
		19,109

4 Investment in associate

	£'000
Group share of net assets of associate (30% × 1,250)	375
Goodwill (W)	200
	575

Working

Alternative calculation (proof):

	£'000
Cost of investment	500
Add: share of associate's profit since acquisition (30% × 250)	75
	575

Goodwill	
Cost of investment	500
Less: net assets acquired (30% × 1,000)	(300)
	200

HOW MUCH HAVE YOU LEARNED? – ANSWERS

CHAPTER 1 Introduction to financial statements

1 The objective of financial statements is to provide information about an entity's financial position, financial performance and changes in financial position that is useful to a wide range of users for assessing the stewardship of the entity's management and for making economic decisions.

2 In the UK, investors and potential investors are regarded as the most important users of financial statements.

3 Information is reliable if:

- it can be depended on to represent what it purports to represent or could reasonably be expected to represent
- it is free from deliberate or systematic bias or material error
- it is complete
- if it has been prepared under conditions of uncertainty, a degree of caution has been applied when exercising judgement.

4 The standard-setting structure consists of:

- the International Accounting Standards Board (IASB)
- the International Accounting Standards Committee Foundation
- the Standards Advisory Council
- the International Financial Reporting Interpretations Committee (IFRIC).

The IASB is the body that actually develops and issues accounting standards.

5 The *Framework* sets out the important concepts and principles which the IASB believes should underlie the preparation and presentation of financial statements. It is not an accounting standard, but the IASB uses the ideas in it when it develops new accounting standards.

6 The underlying assumptions are:

- accruals; and
- going concern.

7 Elements:

- Assets
- Liabilities
- Equity
- Income
- Expenses

8 Although the contract looks like a liability it does not meet the definition in the *Framework*. The business has an obligation to transfer economic benefit but only if the managing director actually does work for the business for the next five years. Therefore there is no *past* 'obligating event' that would result in a liability.

CHAPTER 2 Introduction to limited companies

1 The answer is a), c) and d).

2 The double entry to record the share issue is:

DEBIT	Bank (200,000 × 80p)	£160,000	
CREDIT	Share capital (200,000 × 50p)		£100,000
CREDIT	Share premium (200,000 × 30p)		£60,000

3

Reserves	*Distributable*	*Non-distributable*
General reserve	✓	
Plant replacement reserve	✓	
Retained earnings	✓	
Revaluation reserve		✓
Share premium		✓

Although the directors may not intend to distribute the general reserve or the plant replacement reserve to shareholders, they are still legally distributable.

4

	£
Profit from operations	140,000
Debenture interest (150,000 × 9%)	(13,500)
Profit before tax	126,500
Tax	(74,000)
Profit for the year	52,500

5 **Hearts Ltd:**
Income statement for the year ended 31 December 20X2

	£'000	£'000
Revenue		16,100
Cost of sales (4,515 + 10,493 – 5,292)		(9,716)
Gross profit		6,384
Distribution costs	727	
Administrative expenses	3,185	
		(3,912)
Profit from operations		2,472
Finance cost		(105)
Profit before tax		2,367
Tax		(280)
Profit for the year		2,087

Statement of financial position at 31 December 20X2

	£'000	£'000
Assets		
Non-current assets: Property, plant and equipment		5,852
Current assets:		
Inventories	5,292	
Receivables	3,578	
		8,870
Total assets		14,722
Equity and liabilities		
Equity:		
Share capital		840
Revaluation reserve		1,365
Retained earnings (3,955 + 2,087)		6,042
		8,247
Non-current liabilities:		
Debentures		2,100
Current liabilities:		
Trade payables	3,675	
Tax liabilities	280	
Bank overdraft	420	
		4,375
Total liabilities		6,475
Total equity and liabilities		14,722

CHAPTER 3 Published financial statements of limited companies

1 Accounting principles:

- going concern
- accruals

2 **Income statement for the year ended**

	£'000
Revenue	X
Cost of sales	X
Gross profit	X
Distribution costs	X
Administrative expenses	X
Profit from operations	X
Finance costs	X
Profit before tax	X
Tax	X
Profit for the year from continuing operations attributable to equity holders	X

3 Current assets:

Inventories
Trade and other receivables
Cash and cash equivalents

4 Statement of financial position as at

	£'000
Assets	
Non-current assets:	
Property, plant and equipment (W1)	11,407
Current assets:	
Inventories	3,061
Trade and other receivables (W2)	4,217
	7,278
Total assets	18,685
Equity and liabilities	
Equity:	
Share capital	3,000
Share premium	1,950
Revaluation reserve	525
Retained earnings	4,503
	9,978
Non-current liabilities	
Loans	5,400
Current liabilities	
Trade and other payables (W3)	1,375
Tax liabilities	1,458
Bank overdraft	474
	3,307
Total liabilities	8,707
Total equity and liabilities	18,685

Workings

1) Property, plant and equipment

	Cost	*Acc depn*	
	£'000	£'000	£'000
Land	3,439	–	3,439
Buildings	4,285	468	3,817
Fixtures and fittings	1,867	649	1,218
Motor vehicles	3,786	1,764	2,022
Office equipment	1,308	397	911
	14,685	3,278	11,407

2) Trade and other receivables

	£'000
Trade receivables	4,294
Less allowances for doubtful debts	(171)
	4,123
Prepayments	94
	4,217

3) Trade and other payables

	£'000
Trade payables	1,206
Accruals	169
	1,375

CHAPTER 4 Reporting financial performance

1 Earnings per share

$$\text{Earnings per share} = \frac{17{,}500}{500{,}000} = 3.5\text{p}$$

2 **Accounting policies** are the specific principles, bases, conventions, rules and practices applied by an entity in **preparing** and **presenting financial statements**.

3 A company should only change an accounting policy if the change:

- is required by a standard; or
- results in the financial statements providing reliable and more relevant information.

4 False. If a change arises from a new standard, the transitional provisions may require prospective application (the effect of the change is dealt with in the current period).

5 The answer is B. Statement 1 is incorrect because only material prior period errors are corrected.

6 **Statement of comprehensive income for the year ended 31 December 20X5**

	£'000
Profit for the year	300
Other comprehensive income for the period:	
Gain on property revaluation (500 – 350)	150
Total comprehensive income for the year	450

Statement of changes in equity for the year ended 31 December 20X5:

	Share capital	*Share premium*	*Revaluation reserve*	*Retained earnings*	*Total equity*
	£'000	£'000	£'000	£'000	£'000
Balance at 1 January 20X5	1,000	300	–	700	2,000
Changes in equity for 20X5					
Total comprehensive income for the year			150	300	450
Dividends				(50)	(50)
Issue of shares (100,000 x 1.2)	100	20	–	–	120
Balance at 31 December 20X5	1,100	320	150	950	2,520

CHAPTER 5 The statement of cash flows

1 True.

2 The answer is D.

Deposits must be repayable on demand to qualify as cash. A deposit is repayable on demand if it can be withdrawn without notice. A short term deposit normally has a fixed maturity date and cannot be withdrawn earlier without incurring a penalty. However, depending on the term of the deposit, it could be part of cash equivalents.

3

Heading	*Item*
Operating activities	(d)
Investing activities	(c)
Financing activities	(b)
Increase/decrease in cash and cash equivalents	(a)

4 Cash flows from financing activities:

	£
Proceeds from issue of share capital (22,000 – 16,000)	6,000
Additional loan stock (15,000 – 10,000)	5,000
Net cash from financing activities	11,000

Bank overdrafts are normally included as part of cash, rather than treated as financing items.

5 a) The two methods are:

- list and total the actual cash flows: the direct method
- adjust profit for non-cash items: the indirect method.

b) IAS 7 allows either method.

6 Cash flows from investing activities:

	£
Payments to acquire property, plant and equipment (W)	100,000
Receipts from sale of property, plant and equipment	(5,600)
	94,400

Property, plant and equipment: cost

	£		£
Balance b/f	400,000	Disposals	20,000
Additions (bal fig)	**100,000**	Balance c/f	480,000
	500,000		500,000

7 Reconciliation of profit from operations to net cash from operating activities for the year ended 30 June 20X5

	£'000	£'000
Profit from operations (270 + 62)		332
Adjustments for:		
Depreciation		305
Operating cash flows before movements in working capital		637
Increase in inventory (1,009 – 960)		(49)
Increase in receivables (826 – 668)		(158)
Increase in trade payables (641 – 563)		78
Cash generated from operations		508
Interest paid		(62)
Tax paid		(53)
Net cash from operating activities		393

Statement of cash flows for the year ended 30 June 20X5

	£'000	£'000
Net cash from operating activities		393
Investing activities:		
Purchase of property, plant and equipment (W)		(559)
Financing activities:		
Increase in long-term loan (610 – 460)	150	
Dividends paid	(59)	
Cash from financing activities		91
Decrease in cash and cash equivalents for the year		(75)
Cash and cash equivalents at the beginning of the year		100
Cash and cash equivalents at the end of the year		25

Working

Property, plant and equipment

	£'000		£'000
Balance b/f	1,776	Depreciation	305
Additions (bal fig)	**559**	Balance c/f	2,030
	2,335		2,335

CHAPTER 6 Non-current assets

1 This is routine maintenance expenditure and must be treated as an expense in the income statement in the period in which it was incurred. It cannot be added to the cost of the building (IAS 16).

2 a) False. IAS 16 states that where an item of property, plant and equipment is revalued, all assets of the same class should be revalued.

b) False. The company must keep the valuations up to date, but IAS 16 does not require annual revaluations. Revaluations should be carried out with sufficient regularity to ensure that the value at which an item is carried in the statement of financial position is not materially different from its actual fair value at the end of the reporting period.

c) Journal entry:

DEBIT	Freehold properties: Cost/valuation (440 – 370)	£70,000	
DEBIT	Freehold property: Accumulated depreciation	£30,000	
CREDIT	Revaluation reserve		£100,000

Being the revaluation of properties.

3 IAS 16 does not prescribe a method of depreciation. The directors should select a suitable method that reflects as fairly as possible the pattern in which the asset's economic benefits are consumed by the entity.

4 Depreciation must be based on the revalued amount. Therefore the charge for the year ended 31 December 20X2 is £2,000 (60,000 ÷ 30).

5 Investment property is property held to earn **rentals** or for **capital appreciation** or for both, rather than for:

- use in the **production or supply of goods or services** or for **administrative purposes;** or
- **sale** in the ordinary course of business.

6 IAS 38 states that an intangible asset arising from development should be recognised if an entity can demonstrate all of the following:

- the technical feasibility of completing the asset;
- its intention to complete the asset and its ability to use or sell it;
- how the asset will generate probable future economic benefits;
- the availability of adequate resources to complete the development;
- its ability to measure the expenditure reliably.

Both projects appear to meet the definition of development (they involve the use of scientific knowledge in order to develop a specific new product). Both projects also appear to meet some of the IAS 38 conditions.

There is a possibility that adequate resources will not be available to complete Project A as the company still has to obtain external funding. Therefore the expenditure must be written off immediately through profit or loss (the income statement).

Project B is likely to be completed within the next few months and funding to complete the project appears to be available. On the basis of the information provided all the conditions appear to be met. Therefore the company should capitalise the expenditure as an intangible asset.

7 The answer is A and C. B is incorrect because intangible assets with an indefinite useful life are not amortised. D is incorrect, development expenditure should be recognised as an asset if the project meets certain conditions.

8 An impairment loss should be recognised in other comprehensive income if the asset has previously been revalued upwards.

The loss is also recognised in equity (set against the revaluation reserve) until the carrying value of the asset falls below depreciated historical cost; then the remainder of the loss is recognised in profit or loss.

CHAPTER 7 Inventories, taxation, provisions and events after the reporting period

1 The cost of inventories comprises all costs of **purchase**, costs of **conversion** and other costs incurred in bringing the inventories to their present **location** and **condition**.

2 Gross profit for April:

	FIFO	*AVCO*
	£	£
Sales	5,000	5,000
Cost of sales	(2,705)	(2,775)
	2,295	2,225

FIFO

Closing inventory is £625 (25 × £25).
Cost of sales is £2,705 (3,330 – 625).

AVCO

Closing inventory is £555 (25 × £22.2).
Cost of sales is £2,775 (3,330 – 555).

3 Corporation tax charge:

	£
Corporation tax on profits for the year	85,500
Adjustments relating to previous years	(11,000)
Transfer to deferred taxation	25,400
	99,900

4 IAS 12 defines temporary differences as differences between the carrying amount of an asset or liability in the statement of financial position and its valuation for tax purposes (tax base). These differences will result in additional taxable amounts in future periods when the carrying amount of the asset or liability is recovered or settled.

Another way of thinking of temporary differences is that they are differences between taxable profit and reported profit which arise because some items are charged to tax or allowed for tax in a period that is different from the one in which they are recognised in the accounts.

5 **Legal proceedings:**

Because the company will probably not be found liable, there is only a possible obligation to pay damages. Therefore the company should not recognise a provision.

However, there is a contingent liability, and information about the case should be disclosed unless the possibility that the company will have to pay damages is remote.

Staff retraining:

There does not appear to be any kind of obligation to carry out the retraining. The directors could still decide not to retrain the staff and to avoid the expense. Therefore no provision for training costs or loss of income should be made.

Because there is no obligation, there is no contingent liability.

6 **Events after the reporting period**

	Adjusting event	**Non-adjusting event**
Damage to inventory as a result of a flood		✓
Insurance claim received	✓	
Issue of shares		✓
Opening new trading activities		✓
Sale of property		✓

CHAPTER 8 Further accounting standards

1 An item that meets the definition of an element (eg, an asset or a liability) should be recognised if:

- it is probable that any future economic benefit associated with the item will flow to or from the entity; and
- the item has a cost or value that can be measured with reliability.

2 IAS 1 *Presentation of financial statements*.

3 The company has a finance lease or leases. The note shows that leased assets have been capitalised.

4 **Revenue** is the gross inflow of **economic benefits** during the period arising in the course of the **ordinary activities** of the entity.

CHAPTER 9 Interpreting financial statements

1 Net profit margin is $\frac{\text{Net profit}}{\text{Revenue}}$

Revenue is 80,000 (20,000 × 100/25)

Net profit margin is $\frac{10{,}000}{80{,}000} \times 100\% = 12.5\%$

2 ROCE = Net profit margin × asset turnover

Therefore asset turnover = $\frac{\text{ROCE}}{\text{Net profit margin}} = \frac{20\%}{10\%} = 2$

3 Lenders and potential lenders would be most interested in ratios that show short term and long term liquidity and solvency:

- Gearing (long term solvency)
- Current ratio (short term solvency)
- Quick ratio (short term solvency)

They would also be interested in the way in which an entity manages its working capital, because this influences its solvency; therefore they will pay attention to:

- Inventory turnover
- Receivables days
- Payables days

4 **Asset turnover** = $\frac{\text{Revenue}}{\text{Capital employed}}$

Current ratio = $\frac{\text{Current assets}}{\text{Current liabilities}}$

Receivables days = $\frac{\text{Receivables}}{\text{Revenue}} \times 365$

Gearing = $\frac{\text{Debt}}{\text{Capital employed}}$

5 **Gearing ratio** = $\frac{\text{Debt}}{\text{Capital employed}} = \frac{39{,}000}{26{,}000+39{,}000} = 60\%$

Alternative answer:

Debt to equity = $\frac{\text{Debt}}{\text{Share capital and reserves}} = \frac{39{,}000}{26{,}000} = 150\%$

6 Income statement for the year ended 31 December 20X3

	£	£
Revenue		100,000
Cost of sales:		
Opening inventory (7,500 ÷ 3)	2,500	
Purchases (balancing figure)	80,000	
	82,500	
Closing inventory (75,000 × 36.5/365)	(7,500)	
		(75,000)
Gross profit (100,000 × 25%)		25,000
Operating expenses		(20,000)
Profit before tax		5,000
Taxation (30%)		(1,500)
Profit for the year		3,500

Statement of financial position at 31 December 20X3

	£	£
Non-current assets (7,500 × 25/75)		2,500
Current assets:		
Inventory	7,500	
Trade receivables (100,000 × 40/365)	10,959	
Cash	1,541	
	20,000	
Current liabilities:		
Trade payables (80,000 × 30/365)	6,575	
Other payables (balancing figure)	5,925	
	12,500	
Net current assets		7,500
Capital employed (7,500 × 100/75)		10,000
Equity:		
Share capital		5,000
Reserves (balancing figure)		5,000
		10,000

CHAPTER 10 Group accounts: the consolidated statement of financial position

1 The following are subsidiaries of A plc:

- C Ltd (majority of equity shares)
- D Ltd (a member and can appoint a majority of the directors).

B Ltd and E Ltd are not subsidiaries because the investor does not have a majority of voting rights. (Neither preference shares nor loan stocks carry voting rights.)

2 Control is presumed to exist where the parent owns **more than half** the voting power of an entity, unless it can be clearly demonstrated that such ownership **does not constitute control**.

Control also exists when the parent owns half or less of the voting power of an entity when there is:

- power over **more than half** of the **voting rights** by virtue of an agreement with other investors;
- power to govern the **financial** and **operating policies** of the entity under a statute or an agreement;
- power to appoint or remove the majority of the **members of the board of directors**; or
- power to cast the **majority of votes** at meetings of the board of directors.

3 a) *Consolidated reserves*

	£'000
Left plc	28,000
Right plc (95% × 5,000 – 2,000)	2,850
	30,850

b) *Goodwill*

	£'000	£'000
Cost of investment		8,000
Plus: non-controlling interest:		
Net assets acquired		
Share capital	5,000	
Reserves	2,000	
NCI share (5%)	7,000	350
Less: net assets acquired		(7,000)
		1,350

c) *Non-controlling interest*

	£'000
Share capital	5,000
Reserves	5,000
	10,000
NCI share (5%)	500

4 Why fair value adjustments should be made

- The consolidated statement of financial position should reflect the assets and liabilities of the subsidiary at their cost to the group.
- If the subsidiary's assets and liabilities are not adjusted to fair value, goodwill will be overstated.

5 **Consolidated statement of financial position at 31 March 20X7**

	£'000
Assets	
Non-current assets:	
Intangible assets: Goodwill (W2)	1,200
Property, plant and equipment (8,000 + 6,000)	14,000
	15,200
Current assets:	
Inventories (2,400 + 1,440)	3,840
Trade and other receivables (2,640 + 2,400 – 960)	4,080
Cash and cash equivalents (480 + 360)	840
	8,760
Total assets	23,960
Equity and liabilities	
Equity attributable to owners of the parent	
Share capital	5,000
Retained earnings (W3)	10,920
	15,920
Non-controlling interest (W4)	1,440
Total equity	17,360
Non-current liabilities (1,200 + 1,080)	2,280
Current liabilities:	
Trade payables (2,500 + 1,700 – 960)	3,240
Tax liabilities (860 + 220)	1,080
	4,320
Total liabilities	6,600
Total equity and liabilities	23,960

Workings

1) Group structure

Salt Ltd owns 80% (800,000/1,000,000) of the equity share capital of Pepper Ltd.

2) Goodwill

	£'000	£'000
Cost of investment		4,000
Plus: non-controlling interest:		
Net assets acquired:		
Share capital	1,000	
Retained earnings	2,500	
	3,500	
NCI share (20%)	3,500	700
Less: net assets acquired		(3,500)
		1,200

3) Consolidated retained earnings

	£'000	£'000
Salt Ltd		7,960
Pepper Ltd	6,200	
Less: pre-acquisition reserves	(2,500)	
	3,700	
Group share (80%)		2,960
		10,920

4) Non-controlling interest

	£'000	£'000
Net assets of Pepper Ltd at year-end:		
Share capital	1,000	
Retained earnings	6,200	
		7,200
NCI share (20%)		1,440

CHAPTER 11 Group accounts: further aspects

1 The consolidated financial statements must reflect the operations of the group. If a company sells goods to another company in the same group, the group has not made a sale and no profit has been earned. Sales and profits should only be recognised when the goods are purchased by a customer external to the group.

Any purchases that are unsold at the year end will be included in inventory. The value of the inventory should be its cost to the group, not its cost to the individual group company that purchased it.

2 Non-controlling interests are £1,375,000 (25% × 5,500,000).

The parent sold goods to the subsidiary and therefore non-controlling interests are not affected by the provision for unrealised profit on inventories.

3 The answer is C.

	£
Denston Ltd	950,000
Hawkedon Ltd	500,000
	1,450,000

4 An **associate** is an entity (other than a subsidiary) in which another entity (the investor) has **significant influence**.

Significant influence is the power to participate in the **financial** and **operating policy** decisions of the investee.

5 **Consolidated income statement for the year ended 31 December 20X3**

	£000
Continuing operations	
Revenue (2,280 + 1,200 – 600)	2,880
Cost of sales (1,320 + 660 – 600 (W2))	(1,380)
Gross profit	1,500
Operating expenses (360 + 180)	(540)
Profit before tax	960
Tax (240 + 120)	(360)
Profit for the year	600
Attributable to:	
Equity holders of the parent	564
Non-controlling interest (240 × 15%)	36
	600

Workings

1) Group structure

Thames Ltd owns 85% of the equity share capital of Stour Ltd.

2) Intra-group sales

To cancel the sale:

DEBIT	Revenue	£600,000
CREDIT	Cost of sales	£600,000

6 **Consolidated income statement for the year ended 31 December 20X9**

	£'000
Continuing operations	
Revenue (39,500 + 13,250 – 2,500)	50,250
Cost of sales (21,200 + 5,250 – 2,500)	(23,950)
Gross profit	26,300
Distribution costs	(10,470)
Administrative expenses	(6,190)
Profit from operations	9,640
Finance costs	(640)
Profit before tax	9,000
Tax	(2,640)
Profit for the year from continuing operations	6,360
Attributable to:	
Equity holders of the parent	5,968
Non-controlling interest (40% × 980)	392
	6,360

Consolidated statement of changes in equity for the year ended 31 December 20X9

	Equity holders of the parent £'000	Non-controlling interest £'000	Total equity £'000
Balance at 1 January 20X9 (W1, W2)	23,000	4,800	27,800
Changes in equity for the year			
Profit for the year (from consolidated income statement)	5,968	392	6,360
Balance at 31 December 20X9	28,968	5,192	34,160

WORKINGS:

1 Opening balance: Equity holders of the parent

As the acquisition was on the last day of the previous year, there are no post acquisition retained earnings in Percy Ltd at the beginning of the year. Therefore the equity of the group at the beginning of the year is the opening equity of the parent only. (The share capital and share premium of Percy Ltd are not part of the equity attributable to the owners of the parent; they are cancelled out on consolidation.)

2 Opening balance: Non-controlling interest

	£'000
Net assets at year-end	12,000
NCI share (40%)	4,800

INDEX

Notes

Notes

Notes

Notes

Notes

Notes

Notes

Notes